THE ROMAN RE
BRITTANY, NORMANDY AND
THE LOIRE VALLEY
A Guide Book

James Bromwich

LUCINA BOOKS

An environmentally friendly book printed and bound in England by
www.printondemand-worldwide.com

This book is made entirely of chain-of-custody materials

THE ROMAN REMAINS OF BRITTANY,
NORMANDY AND THE LOIRE VALLEY

Copyright © James Bromwich 2014

A catalogue record for this book is available from the British Library

ISBN 978-178035-662-4

First published 2014 by
LUCINA BOOKS
An imprint of Upfront Publishing of Peterborough, England.

CONTENTS

Figures

Plates

Unless otherwise stated, the photos
have been taken by James Bromwich

ACKNOWLEDGEMENTS

I wish to thank the many French curators and archaeologists who have helped me; the British archaeologists and classicists I have consulted, particularly Professor Barry Cunliffe and Mark Hassell; the librarians of the Institute of Archaeology (UCL) and the Institute of Classical Studies, both in London, with especial thanks to Sue Willets; and once again Edward Oliver for producing so many fine maps. The calm assurance of my editor Katy Carter who removed so many errors, the mistakes and infelicities that remain are of course my own. Thanks too for the cover designed by Lucy Woolier, and Kate Bellairs for drawing people and explaining bytes. Above all, this book could not have been written without my wife Anne and her careful reading of my many attempts to get it right, her gentle advice, but of most significance her tolerance and unwavering support during the many visits to France, the long hours doing background research and the even longer hours of writing.

INTRODUCTION

My purpose in writing is the same as it was when I began my first guidebook to Roman remains in France: 'only destruction, insensitive modern building, and sometimes reconstruction can destroy our intuitive sense of the past; greater knowledge cannot.' I hope this book once again reflects some of my passion for understanding the past.

The book is based on a large number of archaeological and historical studies both French and English covering the west of France, only some of which are listed in the bibliography. I want to stimulate readers' interest where I can and enhance their experience when visiting places: this is a guidebook not an academic study. The bibliography is for the very inquisitive to help them continue exploring the region; the publications listed there range from original sources and general works on the Roman world or Roman France, to further studies illustrating an aspect of regional development.

The west of France

The areas covered are Brittany, Normandy, Pays de la Loire and the four Loire departments of the Centre region. The regional and departmental boundaries that define the selection of sites may appear to be unrelated to the Roman world, but this is not as arbitrary as it might seem. The region's north and west are defined by the coast and though sea levels have changed since Roman times, the general shape has not. The southern limit is the lower and middle Loire, not the river itself, but the land on both sides that has traditionally been drawn towards it. All the territory here was included in the Roman province of Lugdunensis, in fact the southern boundary with Aquitania is not too dissimilar to that of the departmental boundaries used here. The picture is essentially the same for the north-eastern limits. Like the Loire, the Seine itself was never a frontier. The rolling Caux chalk hills end at the deep valley of the Bresle, a boundary marker for both Normandy and Lugdunensis with the Roman province of Belgica. The eastern limit for this book is the Beauce tablelands, before they give way to the varied landscape and mixed soils around Paris. The rest of Lugdunensis, including its capital *Lugdunum* (Lyon) – and much more – is covered in my book on northern and eastern France.

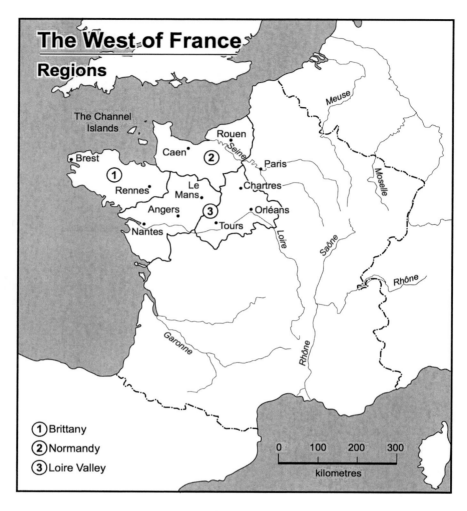

Map 1

The selection of material

My selection of sites and museum collections has been driven by three criteria: what is visible; what research over the centuries has revealed; and, inevitably, having visited them, my own judgement. To give some context, the historical introduction concentrates on the Gallo-Roman period, but it also provides an overview of the Iron Age and late Antiquity. As my investigations progressed for this book, my choice of two topics for special treatment emerged both with a particular regional resonance. The first highlights the far west where people had traditionally looked to the sea for their livelihood. Here it is the great vats at Douarnenez which reveal how

2

Armorica became a major source for that quintessential Roman food product: *garum* sauce. The background and the particular significance fish and salt had for this Roman region gave it prime importance. The second topic provides depth to a perhaps surprising feature of the west, the widely found remains of defensive ramparts, most spectacularly the walls at Le Mans and the fortress at Jublains. I hope that this description of how they were built and the context they sprang from will be helpful.

The changing pattern of archaeological study in the west of France

Archaeological research in the west has evolved in stages. Initially, it was the antiquarians who provided the stimulus; they had the ability to recognise Roman building and a passion for collecting antique objects. From the end of the seventeenth century they carried out the first excavations, they formed learned societies and their collections provided the foundations for the first public museums after the Revolution. The nineteenth century saw the emergence of more specialised archaeologists, rarely paid for the task, rather they were people filled with a love for their 'pays' and a sense of what might be hidden from view beneath the soil. They gradually developed the professional skills to interpret what they found. Men such as Abbé Cochet in the Seine-Maritime and J B Jollois in the Loiret led the way; many others followed. Their publications provided the foundations for outlining pottery sequences or jewellery distribution patterns; their finds filled the provincial museums. State involvement was relatively small, but the first steps were taken to protect standing remains – one early example being Jublains fortress – when the historic monuments commission was created in 1834 and appointed Prosper Mérimée as its Inspector-General.

Although regional archaeological investigation had been widespread, no single archaeologist of national stature emerged in the nineteenth century. Nor, in the first half of the twentieth century, were there the outstanding figures who dominated the field in other regions such as Jules Formigé and Joseph Sautel in Provence. Progress was at best intermittent until the 1960s. The main stimulants for renewed activity were the revival of the French economy and population growth. The transformation of farming threatened the countryside and the boom in moribund cities like Tours and Orléans led to massive new building projects that destroyed swathes of archaeological material. But the new prosperity also led to expanding university studies, the design of professional training courses and a recognition that new scientific techniques could be applied to archaeology. This coincided with new government support for archaeology both with funds and full-time career opportunities (though resources for both are being cut back at the time of writing).

Today each region has a DRAC (Direction Régionale des Affaires Culturelles) which answers to the Minister of Culture in Paris. DRACs are responsible for the 'patrimoine' or heritage of the region and are divided in to two main sections, one responsible for museums and one for archaeology – the Service Régionale d'Archéologie (SRA). This means that there are professional archaeologists permanently available to undertake research and publication. Some cities, such as Chartres, also have their own archaeological services as do some departments, such as Mayenne, with its team based in Jublains. The SRAs work closely with universities which will often undertake longer-term excavations such as the joint Brest and Oxford universities' study of Le Yaudet. In addition, there are still independent archaeologists, for example Alain Provost, but their work is largely paid for by the state.

Probably the most important innovation has been the creation of INRAP (l'Institut National des Recherches Archéologiques Préventives) in 2002. Since 1941 the state has claimed the right to approve all archaeological excavation and through the CNRS (Centre Nationale de la Recherche Scientifique) has a body of national experts with a wide range of scientific and professional skills. The need for numerous rescue digs in the 1970s brought into existence AFAN (l'Association pour les Fouilles Archéologiques Nationales), a state body of specialist archaeologists whose task was to examine a site before it was destroyed: however, INRAP represents a big step forward. All development plans now have to be reported and subsequent action varies from a brief survey to a full-scale excavation, the costs being shared by the state and the developing organisations; it can even mean preservation. INRAP is by far the largest single body in France employing archaeologists – more than 2000 compared with around 300 in the universities. Ninety-five per cent of archaeological investigations start with an INRAP role; it played a major part in bringing to light Carhaix's Roman past.

The speed of response and the quality of research have improved dramatically over the last 20 years or so, and not only is there now significantly more for the interested visitor to see in western France, but the quality of presentation has improved markedly. Some of the best sites are in small places, such as Corseul, Jublains and Vieux. Here conflicts of interest have been minimal. In large cities commercial pressures are far greater. I find it depressing that Rouen's one preserved Gallo-Roman structure is in fact a fountain moved from its find site and displayed in a shop window. Choosing between preservation and progress will never be easy, but the balance still seems to lean too far towards blotting out the past.

Museums in the region vary considerably. Amongst the finest are those put together by archaeologists: Vieux is outstanding. There are also those created with an obvious local belief in their intrinsic value, such as the communal museum at Thésée or the salt marsh museum at Batz-sur-Mer. Then there are the major public museums. The Musée Dobrée in Nantes has updated its galleries, not simply with better presentation, but also to introduce recent work and finds. Sadly too few others have been able to do this. Rouen museum has a superb nineteenth century Gallo-Roman collection but it is confined in tiny rooms with no space for recent archaeological finds, whereas room after room is filled with third-rate art. As Rennes museum demonstrates, contemporary communication techniques without a proper respect for archaeology do not deliver either. One suspects that in some DRACs high fences still guard sectional interests preventing combined action to improve matters.

Entry charges and opening times

Prices change too often to make them worth inclusion. Times are given in the text, but these cannot be relied upon: I have been to places where the premises were declared open, but were locked and others where the hours change annually, but no one seems to know this beforehand. Tuesday is a common closing day for state and municipal museums, but where a town has a number of galleries and museums, other days may be chosen for closure (generally Monday).

Finding sites: maps, plans and GPS

My maps and plans should help you find the sites and museums described here. If you are coming by car and have sat-nav it will get you to many places but not all. A road atlas will not only show places on the map but also list them in the index. I find a general road map, such as Michelin's standard red 989 or 916, valuable; used with 1:200,000 maps it will do the job for most sites. For the rest, IGN's 1:25,000 maps, the equivalent of the UK's Ordnance Survey series, are excellent and should enable you to find even the most obscure rural site.

Most tourist offices will provide free summary town maps, though these tend to cover no more than the town centre and some do not even mark all the street names. Assistants are usually helpful, but sometimes simply do not know about what to them are obscure Gallo-Roman remains. Blay-

Foldex and IGN town plans are comprehensive and have street indexes. In villages, the local Mairie will frequently respond enthusiastically to helping visitors find their site or museum – even so, avoid lunchtime.

Global Positioning System. GPS provides the most accurate form of location possible today. Using my receiver, I have recorded grid reference numbers for the vast majority of sites and these appear under the IGN map number at the beginning of a site description or in the text when a number of locations are identified, for example along the Carhaix aqueduct. The grid reference numbers used here are not latitude/longitude but the Universal Transverse Mercator (UTM) which divides the world into 1km squares. France uses UTM 30 (the number defining the time zone): there are two sets of seven numbers each, one set denoting north/south the other east/west. You can use these GPS grid references in two ways:

1. All modern IGN 1:25,000 maps are GPS-compatible and the GPS grid is marked in blue on the outer edges of the map. Along the top are three numbers marking the vertical north–south lines. The first number in western France is a zero and this is conventionally left out; I include the zero in all my references. Down the sides of the maps four numbers mark the horizontal east–west lines. The extra three numbers on each set specify metres from the grid lines; with them you can work out a precise location on the map. An example: Valognes baths are positioned at 0611+865 and 5484+995, meaning that the baths are in the north-eastern corner of the 1km square. In this case the site is marked on the map, but where sites are not, you should be able to locate the visible remains.

2. If you have a GPS receiver, you can mark a point at a distance from the site, then input the grid numbers to pinpoint the location (the method will vary according to the age of the machine and manufacturer); it should then indicate direction, a distance as the crow flies and a time estimate for getting there. If your receiver is equipped with detailed map software of the region, then you will be able to identify the location and work out out a route to reach it. Some sat-nav systems will allow the input of grid coordinates but many of these are limited to latitude and longitude and do not include UTM.

Using the Web

Maps. Google and www.mappy.fr provide useful though limited maps. Roads and streets are indicated, but without any geographical features. Archaeological sites are certainly not marked. The aerial photographs available with these Web maps can help, but trees and buildings can obscure sites and you will need to know where they are to find them. Even then, aerial coverage is not complete.

Information on sites and museums. As with other sources of knowledge on the Web there is often a frustrating mix of the useful and interesting along with the desperately limited or fanciful. The website www.faton.fr takes you to the journal *Archéologia* where brief summaries of articles can be consulted and the journal ordered. There are useful websites on places covered in this book, such as www.reze.fr for the excavations in Rezé suburb of Nantes or www.pagesperso-orange.fr/*Vorgium* for a summary of the excavations in Carhaix-Plougeur. The latter can also be found through one of the better general websites for archaeological discoveries in France as a whole, www.archeophile.com. This site allows you to input department names and get a list of websites dealing with archaeological sites, providing maps (including places like Mané Véchen in Morbihan), and even an article on the Roman roads in the Ille-et-Vilaine. For museums, www.culture.gouv.fr/documentation/museo provides summaries on most of the museums in the region, but it is more difficult to get any details on museum collections and particularly their Gallo-Roman material. One of the most useful websites for reports on current work is of course www.inrap.fr. The easiest way to find where INRAP has been working in the west is simply to key in department names. You can then go through the list and choose entries that seem interesting; each entry is a mini-article with description and analysis.

For academic follow-up, websites like www.intute.ac.uk provide access via 'Humanities', 'France' or 'Archaeology' to relevant websites that in some cases reproduce full texts from journals and project reports. If you are able to use a specialist university library, then ask them about Project Dyabalo, which has created a massive online bibliographic resource.

CHRONOLOGY

Date	Roman Government	Gaul
510BC	*Republic* established	Tribal states and coins *Oppida* and widespread farms
100–27BC	Late Republic dominated by great men	Gallic Wars 58–52BC
44BC	Julius Caesar murdered Civil War across Roman world	
40BC	Octavian takes control of Gaul	Lyon founded. Agrippa starts roadbuilding
31BC	Octavian defeats Anthony	
27BC	Octavian proclaimed Augustus	

27BC–AD284 EARLY EMPIRE

27–68 *Julio-Claudian family*

27BC–AD14	Augustan period	Roman towns laid out and first villas
14–37	Tiberius	21 Last Gallic rebellion
41–54	Claudius	43 Army leaves to invade Britain Spurt in city building
54–68	Nero	
68–69	Civil war	

69–96 *Flavian family*

69–79	Vespasian	Stone public buildings in many towns
79–81	Titus	
81–96	Domitian	

96–180 *Emperors by adoption*

96–98	Nerva	
98–117	Trajan	
117–38	Hadrian	
138–61	Antoninus Pius	160s Empire-wide plague
161–80	Marcus Aurelius	

193–235 *Severans*

193–211	Septimus Severus	193-7 Civil war, Gaul supports defeated claimant Albinus
211–17	Caracalla	
217–35	Later Severans	

Urban building stops
'Gallic Empire' 260–73
Barbarian raids begin

284–476 LATE EMPIRE

284–305 *Diocletian*
Restructures Empire
Trier made capital of Galliae

286–96 Carausius' British based
Empire controls north Gaul

306–337 *Constantine*

Christianity accepted and gets state support
At death: Roman Empire divided into West and East

378   Adrianople: terrible Roman defeat by Visigoths

379–95 *Theodosius* last effective Emperor
392   Laws against paganism

395–423 *Honorius*

Lives in Ravenna

Arles replaces Trier as Galliae
capital
406 Mass crossing of Rhine by
barbarians

410   Visigoths sack Rome

412 Visigoths settled in Aquitaine

420s–50s Aëtius last successful western Roman
general

451 Huns defeated in Gaul by
Visigoths, Franks and Aëtius

460s

Roman warlords in west of Gaul

Franks control NE Gaul

476 *Romulus* Western Emperor replaced by barbarian king

Fifth and sixth centuries: LATE ANTIQUITY

486–511 **Clovis** king of the Franks

Adopts Roman Christianity and Roman administrative forms

Franks take over Normandy and Loire. British-Armorica resists
Franks

Breton kingdoms begin to emerge

Gradual and partial adoption of Christianity in the region

HISTORICAL DEVELOPMENT OF WESTERN FRANCE

The West of France: environment

The Armorican massif

The term 'Aremorica' was used by Julius Caesar to describe some of the tribes he met in the west, though the list varies through his *Gallic Wars* (*BG*), it always includes a core group in Brittany. The word itself was Celtic, meaning 'Land of the Sea'. The coasts of Brittany are rugged, stark rocks lining long inlets sometimes fed by short rivers. The inner upland, traditionally known as the Argoat or 'Land of the Trees', has a thin, acidic soil now largely supporting poor pasture and moorland. The narrow coastal plain of Brittany is richer, encouraging more agriculture and settlement. The Atlantic climate has ensured plentiful rain, but though the summers are not hot, winters are warm.

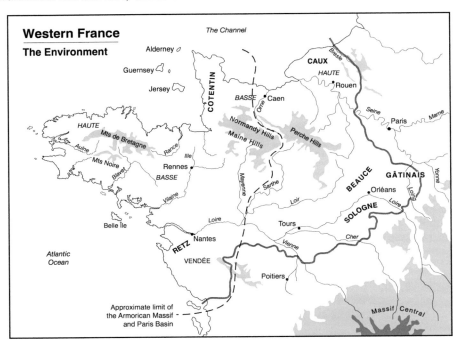

Tidal flows are massive, currents swirl offshore, gales are dangerous, but the inlets provide protected harbours. The seas have been rich in fish. Knowledgeable seamen, facing the vast unknown to their west, learnt the currents, winds and stars, so connected Armorica not simply with the contrasting coastal regions nearby down to the Garonne or along the Channel, but with the remarkably similar regions of south-western Britain, Wales, Ireland, Scotland and even north-western Iberia: the Atlantic zone. Their inhabitants were linked not so much by trade, but by environments that created similar lifestyles and beliefs: small-scale self-sufficiency based on a broad spectrum of resources maintained beside the awe-inspiring ocean vista.

The eastern half of the massif is generally flatter but drains badly. Low ridges and narrow valleys, with sluggish streams but numerous springs, have encouraged isolated farms and hamlets, where farmers have created small fields and tracks marked by hedging and trees, often enhanced with baulks of earth. This type of countryside known as bocage, is found in upper Brittany, western Normandy and the Vendée.

The western Paris basin

During the final Ice Age the seas shrank and the major rivers cut their final routes to the sea: the Seine went north, whilst the Loire turned west cutting through a break in the Armorican massif. Soils were varied, but everywhere richer than on the Armorican massif, helped too by a temperate climate: colder in the winter but hotter in the summer and lacking the harsh Atlantic storms. As forests were cleared the potential for agriculture was realised. Movement was easier both along the valleys and across the tablelands; nothing prevented people and ideas travelling easily. For the core of Armorica the ocean may have provided the easiest external links, but the long beaches of Normandy provided few natural harbours; the Seine clearly offered these and the narrowest point on the Channel lay not far to the north. Undoubtedly the most important linkages lay to the east and south-east where there were no significant limitations. To reach the valley of the Marne, the Champagne plains and central Europe beyond simply meant crossing the Seine. Similarly western France was linked to the Mediterranean via either the Loire valley itself or the Gâtinais down to the Sâone and Rhône.

The pre–Roman conquest inhabitants

'The Celtic world'

The name 'Celts' was first used by the Greeks for a people who lived in central Europe. Modern scholars took these literary allusions to mean the distinctive artistic flowering associated with the archaeological La Tène culture. Tracing this art suggested core sites in central Europe from which the people spread out taking their art with them. Later migrations transformed most of the Celtic world but left a 'Celtic fringe' including Ireland, Scotland, Wales and Brittany relatively untouched; historians of the Celts used the particularly rich myths and stories from there to help interpret the archaeological record, creating a picture of a Celtic world reaching across from Hungary to Ireland. This picture has been challenged.

Archaeologists in the 1960s and 1970s increasingly rejected the concept that cultural change automatically came through migration and conquest: altered tastes need not mean the movement of people. Recent studies of both Brittany and Normandy have seen little more than gradual regional evolution from at least the late Bronze Age. Some writers have gone further, pointing out that the self-identification of the Celtic fringe as Celtic is a recent phenomenon, closely connected with burgeoning nationalism. By the 1990s, maps of the ancient Celtic world could omit the British Isles: a strange paradox when the one part of Europe that claimed a continuous Celtic heritage was excluded.

The problem is to resolve the lack of evidence for dramatic breaks with the similarities found so widely north of the Mediterranean civilisations. I am convinced by those who argue that this communality emerged in the Bronze Age, something Gordon Childe argued in the 1920s, and that this is expressed in assemblages and find sites. The bronze swords and axeheads may differ in detail but not in the kinds of warrior value societies they reflect; even evidence for their religious beliefs – such as depositing swords in water – suggests common behaviour. Historical linguists, like J T Koch, are equally persuasive: language forms across northern Europe in the late Bronze Age were 'Proto-Celtic'. He has even proposed a mechanism for the development of Celtic. Groups speaking localised indigenous variants needed a means enabling them to interact. This was a world before commercial transactions, when gift exchange involved warriors and retinues of poets, musicians and artisans. Both petty conflict and convivial peace-making needed 'a common high-register language': Celtic. The exchange of goods would in turn spread values, styles and techniques.

The subsequent transition from Bronze to Iron Age did not entail a sudden transformation, but rather a loosening of the ties between, on the one hand, a northern Atlantic zone embracing Scotland, Ireland, Wales, south-western Britain and the Armorican peninsula (Brittany); and on the other, west central Europe, which included the bulk of France. In Brittany, an isolating environment, extended family settlements and a variety of potential foodstuffs helped keep communities conservative and small-scale. In west central Europe, things were more dynamic but less stable. Here, agriculture had far greater potential for a surplus and combined with the development of iron-making skills enabled the emergence of an elite warrior class who could build (and destroy) much larger social groupings.

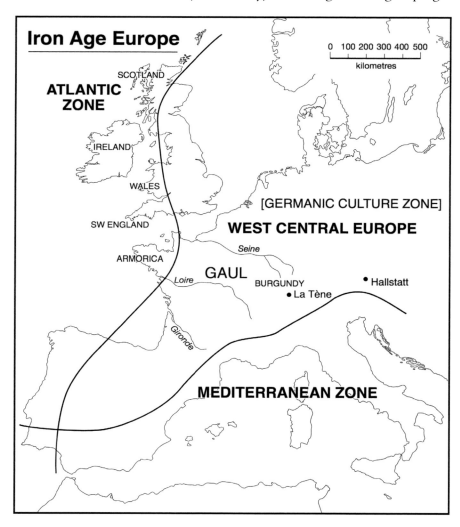

Table: European Late Bronze and Iron Age

Period	Dates from	West-Central Europe	Western France	People and change
Late Bronze Age	1200/1150BC	Urnfields Hallstatt A Hallstatt B	Final Bronze Age	Warrior societies Proto-Celtic language
Early Iron Age	800/700BC 625/600BC	Hallstatt C or I Hallstatt D or II	Early Iron Age or Hallstatt	'Princedoms'
Middle Iron Age	500/475BC c400BC	La Tène A or I La Tène B	Early La Tène	
	c250BC	La Tène C or II	Middle La Tène	Gallic tribal states emerging
Late Iron Age	c120BC 80BC	La Tène D or III	Late La Tène Final La Tène	Romans conquer southern Gaul

The Iron Age

There was no sudden adoption of iron to denote the beginning of a new metallurgical era; smelted since 1100BC in the eastern Mediterranean, iron was taken up piecemeal across temperate Europe. Most archaeologists use the term 'Iron Age' and its constituent phases as a shorthand with rough chronological and socio-economic implications. Others are happy to accept sequences such as 'Hallstatt' and 'La Tène', based on sites in Austria and Switzerland respectively, as models from which they can work to identify what may be marked differences in comparison with the original typesites. I have used both in this book.

Early Iron Age or Hallstatt. In western France, iron remained a rarity; bronze and pottery continue to be made following local traditions. Late on, Hallstatt design (angular geometric forms and simple stiff figures) appears, but largely in ceramics, not metalwork. Isolated examples of Etruscan and Greek metalwork have been found in Brittany and the Loire valley. Maybe gift exchange with no meaning beyond scarcity value, perhaps markers of a trade route to obtain raw materials like tin?

Middle and Late Iron Age or La Tène. During the fifth century BC a homogeneous culture emerged stretching from France to Hungary. Its characteristics were first described by the great French prehistorian Déchelette in 1908. Most striking are torcs: open-ended necklaces, typically made of bronze, but the finest of gold. They are found widely in La Tène regions, but are totally alien in the Mediterranean. Other metalwork was distinguished by characteristic flowing geometric-based designs, often drawn from foliage or very stylised animal and human forms. It is found on weapons including graceful swords, lances, helmets and shield fittings, ornamental jewellery and fine bronze tableware, and even on coinage when this began to appear in the late second century. A goblet or coin design might be traced back to a Mediterranean source but rapidly dropped the realism of the original decoration. La Tène society was imaginative, energetic and aggressive. New more widely spread wealth encouraged population growth followed by migrations southwards as warrior leaders attracted groups to head towards Italy and Greece in the hope of booty and land.

Development was continuous during the La Tène period peaking during the second and first centuries BC. Rome exerted a growing influence: its wealth led to a massive rise in demand, whilst its producers could export sought after wine, pottery and metalwork; the new opportunities these brought helped families and clans draw together into tribes often led by elected kings. Yet it is clear from Caesar's account of the Gallic wars that political power in all tribes still reflected the traditional social structure: a mass of dependent farming families and artisans underpinned an elite who were frequently in conflict amongst themselves and with other tribes. Successful warfare brought new supporters, won slaves and increased wealth; power was being concentrated in the hands of fewer noble families. Gift exchange within and between tribes remained crucial involving locally produced gold or silver coins, craft products, beer and imported wine.

The settlement archaeology of the late La Tène supports this evolving picture. Agriculture was increasingly productive as iron tools were adopted; much previously ignored land was being exploited and field systems were being established; ditch and fence enclosures surrounded hamlets and farms. Communications were enhanced, utilising river networks and tracks strong enough to support carts. Populations grew rapidly. Research has made it abundantly clear that the open-ended Roman term used by Caesar for a settlement, an *oppidum*, sometimes meant no more than a rampart and huts, but at the other extreme could refer to a real town with streets, public buildings, workshops, distinct religious and domestic quarters, and areas set aside for meetings, all enclosed by imposing and extensive ramparts made of earth, timber and stone. Modern archaeologists have adopted the term, using it equally loosely. In the countryside major sanctuaries were created, where the mass slaughter of animals took place, followed by the complex separation of bones and their burial in ditches around a central temple.

Late Iron Age trends in western France. Though Armorica retained distinctive traits, linking it still to the Atlantic zone, the west had by the first century BC come to share in a common Gallic culture. Though characteristic decorated metalwork is rare in the region, examples are being unearthed. The finest have been discovered in Normandy, such as that from the warrior burial at La Mailleraye (see ROUEN), or the superb Amfreville helmet (see ÉVREUX). More common is pottery using La Tène patterns and copying metallic forms, although local traditions in ceramics are persistent. Whilst cremation helps define core La Tène culture, inhumation declined gradually here.

What modern archaeology has shown is that, even if the pace of change differed, by the end of the Iron Age there is undoubted evidence that the inhabitants of western France shared in the growing prosperity of temperate Europe. *Amphorae* from Italy reached the region, either via Burgundy and the Loire corridor or via the Carcassonne gap, the Gironde valley and the sea carriers of southern Brittany. Trade may have helped provoke change, but natural resources in the region were being exploited far more effectively than in the past. Aerial photography and rescue archaeology, associated particularly with motorway construction, has shown a countryside filling with field networks, enclosures, granaries, storage facilities and farms or hamlets with rectangular timber and thatch houses.

Certainly classic hillforts, a typical form of iron Age settlement, continued to be used: ramparts, often massive, but with limited settlement inside suggesting emergency, seasonal and ritual usages. Excavations in the Loire valley, such as those at Amboise and Chênehutte, have revealed more intensive occupation, but Moulay, near Mayenne, has transformed the picture of *oppida* in the region. INRAP, since 2004, has shown that this vast hillfort contained a real town extending over at least 80ha. This strongly supports the likelihood that there are a significant number of other such towns, *oppida* largely hidden under cities like Nantes, Le Mans, Évreux and Rouen, which is supported by the numerous Gallic houses revealed at Orléans and most recently at Angers.

There is little to suggest that the west differed markedly in belief and religious practice from the rest of Gaul. Caesar indirectly confirms this when he explains that the Druids, the revered Gallic holy men, held their annual inter-tribal assembly (*BG* VI.13) in Carnutes territory. Many Gallo-Roman temples have evidence in the form of ritually bent La Tène swords and other characteristic La Tène material indicating they were preceded by Iron Age sanctuaries. At Fesques (Seine-Maritime), human skulls and weapons were buried alongside selected animal bones whilst at Thaon (Calvados) horse bones were buried on reddened stones. Both sites suggest a ritual recalling the massed bones at Gournay and Ribemont (for a description of these amazing sites see JL Brunaux's *The Celtic Gauls*).

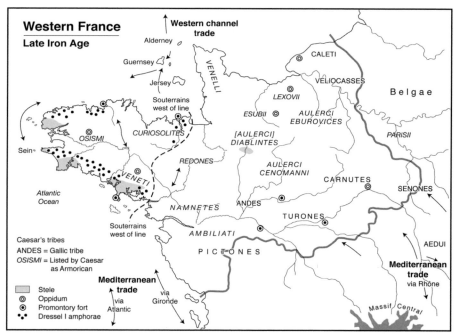

Continuity with the past is more apparent in Armorica. Upright slabs – stele – scattered across the landscape, believed to have once marked burials, recall the famous Neolithic megaliths. Stone was also still used in building (as elsewhere in the Atlantic zone), and accounts for the survival of Plouvigner, a rare example of a middle La Tène hamlet. Other occupation sites are distinguished by their souterrains, extended cave-like cellars dug beside farmsteads for storage and probably ritual. In France, they are only found in Breton coastal districts; they are familiar as fogous in south-west Britain. However it is now apparent that Armorica had many features in common with the rest of western France.

A large hillfort like Huelgoat was probably a meeting place, whilst a coastal promontory fort like Quiberon is more likely to have been a spiritual centre with a rampart dug to isolate and emphasise the mystical wonder of the ocean. Yet Alet (St Malo) and Le Yaudet on the northern coast must be considered *oppida* and there were certainly others on the south coast (eg Vannes and the still unidentified Corbilo mentioned by Strabo; IV. 2.1). Mediterranean *amphorae* have been found in significant numbers. Trade from Armorica may well have included food. Agriculture was being intensively practised: thousands of farmsteads have been revealed in aerial surveys and motorway rescue digs. Around the coast from Retz into Normandy there were hundreds of saltworks, indicating the development of a major late Iron Age industry extracting salt to preserve fish and meat. Excavations at Paule (see RENNES) suggest a late Iron Age aristocracy of landowners in the countryside living not in *oppida* but castle-like dwellings, controlling the distribution of imported and locally produced goods. Here too, a more complex political shape was evolving. A late Iron Age innovation in the region was coinage: distribution maps based on coin designs and Caesar's writings help identify different peoples coalescing into more structured groups during the first century BC.

The Gallic Wars

We know that western France had some familiarity not only with Roman products but also with Roman merchants. Indeed, Caesar mentions that merchants were quartered in *Cenabum* (Orléans) and would have visited various other trading centres in the west. Yet when Caesar's soldiers came they brought a form of warfare like nothing before: it must have been a shattering experience. For more than eight years, Julius Caesar and his generals used an army, never fewer than 10 legions, to slaughter, terrorise, ravage, crush and murder its way through Gaul. Brilliant, risk-taking and cool in action, Caesar even had the literary skills to produce in his Gallic Wars a masterpiece of war reporting.

Much of western France played a relatively minor role. On the basis of prior intelligence, it is likely Caesar considered the Veneti the most dangerous of the Armorican tribes and so concentrated on destroying their power in 56BC. Interestingly, Caesar must have considered the Breton tribes so devastated by this action that no troops were quartered in this area and they played no part in resisting conquest again until 52BC. The tribes of the western Parisian basin were even less prominent, though in 52BC the Aulerci were roused to help the Parisii, and then had their old chief killed in the defeat. Control of the central Loire was always important to Caesar as it gave access to all parts of the west and a major route to the north; Carnutes territory was equally significant as the religious and judicial centre of Gaul associated with the Druids. Caesar regularly quartered troops in the territory of the Senones, near enough to deal with the main enemy of the early years, the Belgae, or to intervene quickly amongst the Carnutes. The region's response to the crisis in 52BC when Caesar laid seige to the main Gallic forces at Alesia, led by the dynamic Vercingetorix, was not lacking enthusiasm: 86,000 soldiers for the Alesia relief force, a third of the total and almost as large as Caesar's entire Roman army. The Gauls' defeat was followed by two Roman campaigns ending resistance in the region. Caesar's Gallic Wars make quite clear all tribes were split between those leaders wishing to resist Roman imperialism and those who considered this futile and wished to make the best of the inevitable.

After effects and steps to a new world

At first, Gallia Comata – 'longhaired Gaul', the territory of Gaul outside the Mediterranean zone – was simply conquered territory. It embodied two things: Roman troops and the payment of tribute, and little effort was made to change it. The road building, initiated by Agrippa in 39BC, that turned *Lugdunum*/Lyon into a virtual capital city, was, in the first instance, undertaken to speed up the movement of Roman armies. Even the 27BC census was primarily intended to give a rational basis to tax collection. For the Gauls themselves, defeat was followed by a long period of desolation and occasional disaffection. Environmental studies suggest that agriculture suffered substantially and there is evidence of land reverting to forest and pasture. It may be that the wars had a major impact on population levels. Some historians see this phase as lasting until the later years of Augustus, others consider that recovery only occurred in the middle of the first century. In the West, archaeological evidence is accumulating, but is not conclusive.

The administrative framework was created by Augustus. Gaul's capital at *Lugdunum* was formalised with the foundation of the *Condate* altar, dedicated to proclaiming the greatness of Rome in 12BC. At their annual meeting priests drawn from the leading families in Gaul could demonstrate their loyalty. They learnt the Roman approach to religious ritual in which political and social power were also expressed through religious leadership. This enhanced their status and made it easier for them to accept Rome's determination to destroy the Druids.

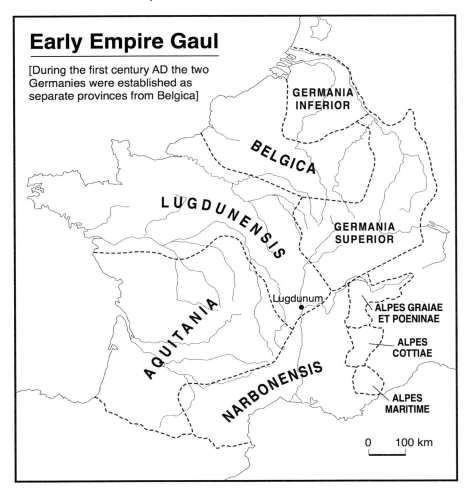

Early Empire Gaul

[During the first century AD the two Germanies were established as separate provinces from Belgica]

GERMANIA INFERIOR

BELGICA

LUGDUNENSIS

GERMANIA SUPERIOR

Lugdunum

ALPES GRAIAE ET POENINAE

ALPES COTTIAE

ALPES MARITIME

AQUITANIA

NARBONENSIS

0   100 km

Three new Gallic provinces were established: Lugdunensis, Aquitania and Belgica, each with its own imperial governor responsible for maintaining order with a procurator in charge of imperial taxation. All of western France lay within Lugdunensis. Day-to-day administration would be carried out by individual tribes, each re-fashioned as a Roman *civitas*. Some tribes were swallowed up by others, some like the Viducasses were small sub-tribes raised in status. *Civitates* were distinguished by having a town as a capital and centre of communal life, the model being Rome and its supporting countryside.

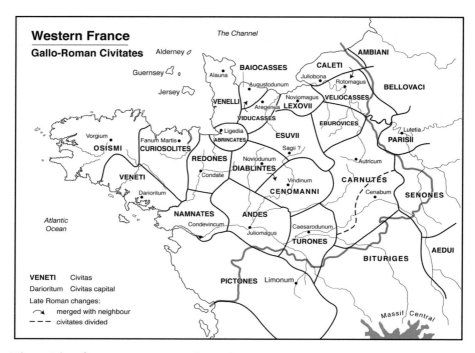

Western France

Gallo-Roman Civitates

The Channel

Alderney

Guernsey

Jersey

AMBIANI

CALETI

BAIOCASSES
Alauna
Augustodunum
Juliobona
Rotomagus

BELLOVACI

VELIOCASSES
Noviomagus
Aregenua LEXOVII

VENELLI

VIDUCASSES

EBUROVICES
Lutetia

PARISII

Ligedia
ABRINCATES

ESUVII

Sagii ?

Vorgium
OSISMI

Fanum Martis
CURIOSOLITES

REDONES
Noviodunum
DIABLINTES

Autricum

VENETI
Darioritum
Condate

Vindinum
CENOMANNI

CARNUTES
Cenabum

SENONES

NAMNATES
Condevincum

ANDES

Caesarodunum

Atlantic
Ocean

Juliomagus
TURONES

BITURIGES

AEDUI

VENETI   Civitas
Darioritum   Civitas capital
Late Roman changes:
⌒⌐ merged with neighbour
- - - civitates divided

PICTONES Limonum

Massif Central

The grids of most *civitas* capitals in the western region were laid out under Augustus (31BC–AD14) or Tiberius (14–37), but buildings were insubstantial and widely spread with little obvious public building. Only the Loire valley towns of Angers, Tours and Orléans seem to have experienced more concerted construction work, most other places only moving to well-built wood and plaster housing and their first stone public building from the mid-first century. Yet we are far from the Mediterranean heartland of Roman civilisation. It would take time to attract architects and masons from southern France where so much work was being done in many cities at the turn of the millennium; time to develop the appropriate local skills necessary to construct buildings in the Roman way; time to absorb the culture that made sense of both city and villa living.

The Early Roman Empire

First century events and second century peace

Gaul was largely untouched by either rebellion or warfare from the 20s until the 190s and took on the distinctive appearance called Gallo-Roman. The pace of change was rapid in the later first century. Though the main towns were laid out under Augustus and the first villas appeared during his reign, Claudius (41–54) provided incentives for more dynamic growth.

The invasion of Britain (43) with the need to supply army and navy would have stimulated demand for many products encouraging investment near and far. In a more general way, Claudius' birth in Lyon and his speech allowing Aeduan nobility to enter Roman careers that could lead to the Senate, with its implicit pledge to the aristocracy of all Gallic *civitates*, may have encouraged a more intensive commitment to Romanisation. The civil wars (68–9) that marked the death of Nero did little to stop Gaul's increasing prosperity and the Flavian period (69–96) was widely one of construction; renewal was to continue into the early third century.

Yvan Maligorne (2006) has argued that the elite of western France – for him Armorica, but the case is broadly the same for the rest of the region as well – never became especially wealthy. It took many years for monumental buildings to be completed, and some never were. The few inscriptions that have survived show that private donations for building were rare and small scale when they occurred; public building was therefore funded from the public purse. *Civitas* income came from local taxes; rents, primarily agricultural but also urban; and liturgies or fees paid by magistrates as a charge to their position. Maligorne thinks the major stimulant encouraging town officials to undertake building programmes would have been the grant of new charters from the Emperor. These would have enhanced their power within their communities, enabled them to become Roman citizens and gain the advantages of Roman law. The only written evidence of charters that has survived is from the Spanish provinces, but the rare regional memorial inscriptions involving public officials (see RENNES) do not conflict with this idea, whether in the titles or rituals they describe.

The Civitas Capitals

Estimating the size of these urban centres in the west of France is difficult. Most capitals were new foundations, Orléans and Angers being the main exceptions. They involved laying out a grid forming rectangular blocks of land or *insulae*. Archaeological work can painstakingly build up a picture indicating which *insulae* were eventually occupied and which were not giving an approximate living area for the town. What is indisputable is that they were always small, ranging in size from 20ha to 120ha, but averaging only 40–60ha.

The tribal elite now ruled through a council (*ordo*) as *decuriones*, appointing magistrates, not only for taxation and justice, but also with responsibilty for public building. Followers, or 'clients', could plead for help in avoiding taxes, gain judicial favour and win building contracts for the public baths, theatres, temples and fine houses needed in adopting the Roman way. The new towns that emerged are immediately recognisable from hundreds of other examples found in the Empire. None in the west equalled Provence in size or grandeur and whilst many of the cities that later covered their Gallo-Roman predecessors left few visible remains of their Roman past (though in most cases rich museum collections), others stagnated or declined. Undoubtedly those that failed have benefited archaeologists and visitors: Lillebonne has one of the finest amphitheatre-theatres in the north; Corseul and Carhaix whole quarters; Jublains a sanctuary, baths and theatre; Vieux a *domus* exposed and open fields to explore.

Romananised Religion

The numerous local gods remained significant and are best experienced through spring sites like Plougastel-Daoulas or a *fanum* like Oisseau-le-Petit. However, recent work has made clear that Gallo-Roman religion meant more than the adoption of Roman names for local gods and the distinctive *fanum* temple design. Great sanctuary sites were constructed across the region, some in the countryside – for example Aubigne-Racan – but many close to the capitals. Some were even multi-temple complexes, such as the huge, enigmatic Le Vieil Évreux and the newly discovered sanctuary at Neuville-sur-Sarthe. A key element was an elaborate enclosure enabling the elite to present ceremonies and feasts dedicated to the tribe and Emperor, enhancing social cohesion and demonstrating their power to the community. Haut Bécherel is a particularly well restored example; Allones is less impressive, but its modern excavation has heightened awareness of both construction methods and how a sanctuary was used. Collections at Vienne-en-Val and Yzeures-sur-Creuse allow the sculpture and reliefs that decorated such sanctuaries to be examined closely whilst the magnificent animals and figures found at Neuvy-en-Sullias [see ORLÉANS] give a rare glimpse of sanctuary treasures.

The Countryside

Aerial photography and field walking have transformed our knowledge of the landscape. Traditional Gallic farmsteads continued for many years, but a significant number of rectangular enclosures indicate the adoption of Roman farm design. Centuriation, the name used for the Roman division of land into surveyed rectangles divided by roads to facilitate farmwork, has been proposed for both the Caen and Beauce plains. In many areas the numbers of known villas has doubled since the 1970s: they range from small two- to three- room examples, distinguished by their use of tiles, painted plaster and Roman artefacts, to the farm-buildings (villa rustica) and homes (villa urbana) of the wealthiest landowners. The fine mosaics of Ouzouer-sur-Trézée and the villa at Quiou (see CORSEUL), at last give an idea of a grand villa urbana in this region. Detached baths at Plestin-les-

Grèves, a dramatic tower mausoleum overlooking the Loire at Cinq-Mars and a private aqueduct at neighbouring Luynes show other forms of conspicuous spending by the Romanised wealthy.

Small towns dotted the countryside. Often lacking monumental stone building few of them present visible remains: the Entrammes baths and the massive stone warehouse-like building at Thésée-Pouillé are exceptional. They would have functioned as district markets and centres of craft production. Whilst agriculture must always have been the largest industry in the whole region, archaeology has shown that the biggest export was focused on the coast: the processing of fish. Calculations based on the well preserved factory complex at Douarnenez show Brittany to have been the most important producer of salted fish and *garum* – an essential ingredient of Roman cooking – for the northern imperial markets. Another recently excavated site (Mané Véchen at Plouhinec), also conserved, has been interpreted not as the classic luxury coastal villa it first seemed, but as a much less common guildhouse-villa for landowners and merchants whose wealth derived as much from exploiting the sea as the land.

The Third Century Crisis

The Empire experienced numerous challenges during the third century. The seriousness and extent of some of these problems has been questioned and the appropriateness of the term 'crisis' debated, but undoubtedly when we compare the position in the early third with the early fourth century, the west of Gaul had changed fundamentally.

External threats to the Roman state were greater than ever before. Most frontiers were threatened, whether from the revitalised Persians in the east or the Germanic peoples and others along the Danube-Rhine line. Warfare became endemic. Inevitably the Roman military came to play a central role in the Empire. Pay was increased steeply and 'donatives', or gifts of money to reward 'loyalty', became a regular feature. Three quarters of imperial revenue was spent on the army. In the third century the men who became Emperors were almost all generals, who had often been born in the least Romanised border provinces and had made their way simply through an army career. Winning the imperial purple was often by brutal army takeovers and civil wars were frequent. Between 235 and 284, an emperor lasted on average 2¼ years, compared with 10 years during the previous two centuries.

How far did these problems affect the region? There is no convincing evidence for barbarian raids reaching this far before the 250s, and after a serious incursion in 259/260, a breakaway 'Gallic Roman Empire', led by the Rhine commander Postumus, provided security in the 260s. Struggles for imperial power left western Gaul largely untouched before Aurelian's victorious campaign to reclaim Gaul in 274. The following year, sources describe a major barbarian assault that spread terror throughout Gaul. At sea Roman control was also increasingly being challenged and coastal settlements became vulnerable to pirates. Carausius, the commander responsible for fighting them, chose to challenge for joint Emperor status in 287 with support from Britain and northern Gaul and he succeeded in bringing Diocletian's co-Emperor Maximian (286-305) to Gaul: it took six years to defeat Carausius and his successor. Instability in the region is obvious too in the appearance of *Bagaudae* 'country folk and bandits' (Aurelius Victor Caesar, 39.17), in the 290s, who destroyed estates and even for a time controlled cities north of the Loire.

Compared with the woes of many other provinces in the Empire northern Lugdunensis suffered rather less and later. Yet this conclusion focuses too much on events. The crudity of the struggles between the generals can only have undermined belief in a god-like Emperor. Increased spending on the army was in part funded by heavier taxation, in part by debasing the silver coinage. The pressure on magistrates to ensure taxes were collected – and for the payment of liturgies – made them increasingly unwilling to take on the responsibility, especially as the decline in silver in the 'silver' coinage, from around 75 per cent in 194 to one per cent in 270, undermined their income as well. It is known a plague hit Egypt then Rome (165–190) with a second major outbreak in the 250s. Probably smallpox, an incurable disease, it decimated communities; such epidemics were unlikely to have missed Lugdunensis. Their deeper economic impact may be uncertain, but undoubtedly they would have brought widespread and indiscriminate suffering.

The extent of urban contraction and the level of dilapidation in specific towns in the west of Gaul can be debated; however, what is certain is that growth stopped. Indeed it is virtually impossible to find any examples of new public building in towns after 235. The picture is the same for sanctuaries great and small. Villas show more vitality, but many of these were experiencing difficulties by the end of the century. It has been argued that this was a pre-industrial society entering a period of diminishing returns and so declining population. What we are definitely witnessing is a fundamental social change taking place: the elite withdrew from what, for 150–200 years, had been their way of demonstrating support for the Empire. Few memorial inscriptions survive from before 235, but none in the rest of the century; many milestones are no longer made from freshly cut stone, but from recycled columns. Most instructive of all, material from public buildings and tombstones is used wholesale in the new city walls, not in a moment of panic after the barbarian raid of 275–6, but in careful work carried out over the next 30–40 years. The old Gallo-Roman world had ceased to be.

The Late Roman Empire and western France

That the Empire did not disintegrate was the result of the measures taken by two determined and competent leaders, Diocletian (284–305) and Constantine (306–37). Maybe their least conscious decision concerned Rome itself. Emperors were frequently on the move to deal with the many problems that confronted them. During the fourth century the capital ceased to be the imperial residence and therefore politically significant, though it remained the cultural and emotional heart of the Empire. The preservation of Gaul and the German provinces – and with them much of the western half of the Empire – focused on Trier, which developed all the features of an imperial capital. In the south, Vienne provided similar facilities and great warehouses for supplies, linked in turn with the Italian capital at Milan.

Diocletian attempted to handle imperial control by formalising shared responsibilities. His 'tetrarchy', or four man rule, entailed two full Emperors (Augusti) and a supporter for each (Caesars). Inherently unstable, the experiment did not last. After Diocletian's retirement strife led back to one-man rule with periodic upheavals: usurpers did not disappear. Yet the underlying logic of the tetrarch was sound: the Empire was too much for one person to handle and in the second half of the fourth century it became the norm for Emperors to appoint fellow Emperors and divide responsibilities, often with assistant Caesars; an east – west split became increasingly common and from 395 it was automatic.

An enlarged bureaucracy
The creation of courts for two Augusti and two Caesars quadrupled the number of high officials and absolute power also encouraged the proliferation of courtiers. To increase imperial control and to prevent the development of local power bases, a new administrative level called the diocese was inserted; all of central and northern Gaul together with Rome's German provinces were combined in one diocese, within which Lugdunensis was divided into four smaller provinces, each with its own governor, deprived of soldiers, but of course with his own officials and courtiers.

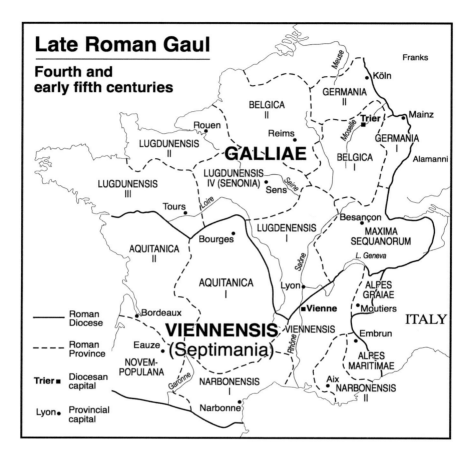

Late Roman Gaul

Fourth and early fifth centuries

Franks

GERMANIA II

Köln

BELGICA II

Trier

Mainz

Rouen

Reims

GERMANIA I

LUGDUNENSIS II

GALLIAE

BELGICA I

Alamanni

LUGDUNENSIS III

LUGDUNENSIS IV (SENONIA)

Sens

Tours

Bourges

LUGDENENSIS I

Besançon

MAXIMA SEQUANORUM

L. Geneva

AQUITANICA II

AQUITANICA I

Lyon

ALPES GRAIAE

Moutiers

Vienne

ITALY

——— Roman Diocese

Bordeaux

VIENNENSIS (Septimania)

VIENNENSIS

Embrun

– – – Roman Province

Eauze

Trier ■ Diocesan capital

NOVEM-POPULANA

ALPES MARITIMAE

Lyon● Provincial capital

NARBONENSIS I

Aix

NARBONENSIS II

Narbonne

Meuse, Moselle, Seine, Loire, Saône, Rhône, Garonne

Military reform

The army, it is now recognised, was not suddenly changed, but had evolved into a new force. The need for greater mobility had led to field armies. One of these, a *comitatus*, was commanded by a *magister militum*, or 'master of the soldiers', directly responsible to an Emperor or Caesar. The old legions multiplied in number frequently becoming part of the static frontier forces or *limitanei*. These legions were much smaller, typically 1000 men instead of about 5000 as before. It was not perhaps a major change because they had long fought in smaller units or vexillations, but it did reduce the difference between them and auxiliary units. Recruits, too, were different, drawn increasingly from less Romanised sources: Danubians had dominated in the third century and in the fourth Germans, especially Franks, became the major source for the western armies and could be found at all levels including commanding armies. There were also more men in the army. The total during the second century is generally thought to have numbered 250,000–300,000, but now there were perhaps as many as 400,000.

Changes in taxation

The third century crisis had made it clear that to ensure stable government and an effective army a better taxation system was needed. Diocletian introduced a standard unit to be used by census officials in calculating the tax load. In principle it was much fairer, taking into account variations in real income. It may have produced higher revenues, though never enough to fund imperial needs. The *civitates* were still the mechanism for collection, but now imperial curators came to check that towns delivered. Whilst gathering taxes had never been popular, and making up shortfalls even less so, for those with municipal authority the compensation had been the enhancement of local prestige by acts of public patronage. The third century had broken this link; despite laws passed to make service on town councils compulsory, rich men in the fourth century avoided local responsibility and taxes. Some sought the increased number of positions available at court or entered the church as bishops, both roles providing tax exemption; some concentrated on their estates, avoiding obligations through simple corruption.

The towns

Undoubtedly urban life suffered. Where ramparts had been constructed, they enclosed only a fraction of the inhabited areas and clearly much of the land outside fell into ruin. Perhaps the situation was slightly less stark for some centres: urban renewal in Tours and Rennes has revealed districts with fourth century extra-mural construction of roads, drainage and buildings. Outside some towns suburban villas continued to function and *domus* in Carhaix and Vieux, both without walls, were either newly built or renovated in the fourth century. Little is known about what kind of building lay inside the walled towns but the obvious inference is that civilian and military adminstration could continue in relative security and for the same reason some of the elite would have abandoned their country villas. Equally important to the survival of many cities into the Middle Ages was the appearance of Christianity.

The Church

It is likely that there were Christians in western Gaul before Christianity was legalised by Constantine in 313, but there is no reliable literary or archaeological evidence for them. The Church's organisational structure was modelled on the Empire with bishops at the level of governors and archbishops at diocesan level, naturally they based themselves in towns. In the west, a scatter of bishops appear during the fourth century, most famously the missionary ascetic St Martin of Tours. More bishops are known in the fifth century, but evidence for church building is very rare until the sixth. When imperial rule began to crumble the Church was able to offer converts the certainty of one god, the communal experience that had been lost with the ruin of the sanctuaries, and even a new social philanthropy. Progress was undoubtedly more limited amongst the *pagani*, the country-dwellers.

The countryside

Pollen analysis suggests that significant sections of the rural environment in the region reverted to forest and waste land. In Brittany virtually no small town existed after 300. In the Loire valley and Normandy some small towns were abandoned, others shrank to become villages or hamlets. The disappearance of villas is no less dramatic. It has been claimed there were 70% fewer in Brittany in the fourth century than the third, and the figures for the rest of the region are not markedly dissimilar. A few fourth century elite residences with new reception rooms and rich décor have been identified; none can be compared with those in Aquitaine. Most villa structures that survived were redesigned for small-scale domestic occupation, used for industrial purposes, or even as military posts.

Such evidence, when combined with the reduction in imported materials (especially pottery) and the equally marked fall in coin finds after 360, has helped paint a dark picture of contraction and depopulation, only partially compensated for by the settlement of barbarian soldier-farmers and their families. Most current interpretations adopt a different perspective. More sensitive excavation suggests that some supposed abandoned sites continued in use: coins were reused, and locally produced pottery, which can now be more accurately dated, suggests longer time scales. The domains or estates continue. The rich landowners who survived the third century shocks would have had the opportunity to buy up more properties; in the fourth and even fifth centuries, nobles often owned lands across many provinces and countries so reducing the overall need for villas. The Roman villa like the monumental city is unlikely to have had the same automatic prestige it held in the early Empire: this was a less secure, more self-sufficient and more isolated world. Lesser owners would have chosen the cheaper options of cob, timber, wattle and daub, rather than brick and stone. Prestige could be as easily maintained with clothing, jewellery and, as the Roman grip weakened into the fifth century, weaponry – an echo of the ancestral culture of the Gauls and the new barbarian settlers.

The loosening grip

Under Constantine and his sons the barbarian threat to the Rhineland borders was largely contained. Then in 350 supporters of Magnentius, a field army commander born of British–Frank parents, murdered the

western Emperor, Constans. Magnentius recruited a large arm
but suffered total defeat at Mursa Major (353) losing thousand·
For western Gaul this meant new exactions, reduced manning]
arbitrary military behaviour and more barbarian recruitment to fill the gaps.

Campaigns against German inroads conducted by Julian (356–9, at that
time Caesar), and Valentinian I (Emperor 364–75) fought off a series of
attacks and culminated in the last great phase of frontier fort building.
Most of the fighting still appears to have taken place outside western Gaul,
though unrecorded raids along the Channel must have occurred. The
Gallic elite enjoyed the continued vitality of Trier as western capital, but for
the people of western Gaul, there is no evidence for any improvement in
conditions. The passive acceptance in 383 of another usurper Magnus
Maximus, raised by the army in Britain, is not surprising; he remained in
control of Gaul for five years.

Imperial power in Gaul might have been more effective but for two
decisive battles. The shattering defeat at Adrianople in 378, when the
Visigoths killed the eastern Emperor Valens and two thirds of his field
army, shocked the entire Roman world. It inspired Arbogast (a Frank), the
western Master of the Soldiers, to manipulate his Emperor into
challenging the eastern ruler Theodosius. The battle at Frigidus (394) was
extremely bloody and most of the western mobile army was destroyed. But
Theodosius and his eastern successors were unable to find a solution to the
Visigoths, who wished to be accepted within the Empire; nothing proved
long-lasting. Their wanderings eventually took them to Italy where the
western Augustus, Honorius, had neither the energy nor the resources to
meet the challenge. In 410 the Visigoths, led by Alaric, entered Rome, the
first barbarians to do so since the Gauls, 800 years before.

Western Gaul by the end of the fourth century was extremely vulnerable.
Trier had become too insecure and the imperial court withdrew first to
Milan and then Ravenna. Many of the regular frontier troops had departed
either to meet their deaths at Frigidus or to provide some sort of army in
Italy. When Vandals, Suebi, Alans and others crossed the frozen Rhine in
405, it was the intervention of yet another usurper, Constantine III, which,
with the last available troops drawn from Britain, initially restricted the
invaders to north-eastern Gaul. His incompetent attempts to establish
himself in the south only induced the invaders to spread across the rest of
Gaul, to be eventually defeated by the Visigoths – who then established
themselves in south-western Gaul. Jerome, the great Christian
controversialist, despaired: 'Innumerable and most ferocious nations
occupy all Gaul' (*Epistulae*,123.5). With Rome finally abandoning Britain in
410, western Gaul faced a very uncertain future.

Late Antiquity and western Gaul: the fifth and sixth Centuries

Reconstructing the history of this period presents considerable difficulties, since neither written nor archaeological sources are sufficient for a detailed narrative or coherent picture. Official documents of limited focus and reliability, rare comments made by Greek historians far from events, letters by writers more concerned with their literary status than describing their environment and religious documents summarising Church councils or making moral points combine to produce a murky outline.

The End of Roman imperial power

For a time, despite the odds, it still appeared as if Roman imperial order could be restored, just as it had been after the third century crisis. In the 420s and 430s Aëtius, western Master of the Soldiers, who had been brought up by the Huns, was able to enforce recognition of Roman authority with Hunnish support; his field army was small but effective. The decisive change came in 451. When the Huns and their tribal coalition decided to act on their own, crossed Germany and invaded Gaul, Aëtius led the force that defeated them, but this army was almost entirely drawn from barbarian settler groups in Gaul; failure to control his former friends led to his assassination in 454. The last gasps of Roman authority quickly followed. The Visigoths hardened their control in the south and the Burgundians moved down into the Saône and Rhône valleys. In the west, Armorica was becoming isolated and looking more and more to its traditional Atlantic links. During the 460s and 470s, much of Normandy and the Loire valley was ruled by the shadowy figure of Aegidius and his successor Syagrius in the name of the Empire; they seem to have been little more than local warlords. Their authority crumbled and ended with Syagrius' defeat by the Franks at the battle of Soissons (486).

The authority of the Western Roman Emperors declined so rapidly after 451 that the child Emperor Romulus (475–6) was retired without replacement – and allowed to live. The only chance of any meaningful revival now depended on the eastern Roman Empire; could the West be re-conquered? Until the 530s the eastern Emperors had too many problems of their own, but Justinian (537–65) made the re-conquest of 'remaining countries which the ancient Romans possessed to the limits of both Oceans' (Novel 30) a real imperial project. However, though north Africa was regained easily the project petered out after many years of fighting in Italy; no Byzantine troops came to revive imperial Roman Gaul.

Newcomers –barbarians and others

While distinctions between raiders, invaders, migrants, allies and Romans could rapidly blur, the names used by contemporary Roman (and Greek) writers for groups of barbarians are rarely explained. Typically, the most that can be said is that federations such as the Suebi or Vandals emerged in north-eastern Europe, whilst nomadic horsemen, like the Alans and Huns, came from the vast steppes. How groups saw themselves is even more obscure – or derived from sources produced centuries later.

Laeti **and** *foederati.* It was a long established Roman practice to minimise the need to destroy barbarians, by turning enemies into friends. Caesar, in his conquest of Gaul, had regularly demanded the provision of fighting men from tribes who submitted; many became auxiliary units in the Roman army. Equally, with barbarians outside the Empire, Rome recruited men and provided subsidies to tribal leaders to reduce the threat they presented. Practice in the later fourth and fifth centuries was a pale reflection of the past. *Laeti* were captured barbarians under the command of a Roman officer. *Foederati* were barbarian groups accepted as mercenaries, rewarded with land within the Empire and/or a share of imperial taxes wherever they were settled, but the group retained not only their right to fight under their own leadership but also their own laws. Whilst small groups of *foederati* might be absorbed into the community, a large or determined group could, given the opportunity, carve out a virtually independent state.

The Franks. From the third century onwards the Romans divided German barbarians into two broad groups: the Alemanni, who caused most of the problems for central and southern Gaul, and the Franks, whose impact on western Gaul was the most enduring. The term 'Frank' seems to have derived from the German for 'fierce', but came to mean 'the free'. Many Franks were recruited to the Roman army to become its foot soldiers and its generals. As imperial control in the German frontier regions weakened, sources began to distinguish two groups: the Saliens, the most Romanised Franks, spread across north-eastern Gaul and the more barbarian Rhineland Franks concentrated around Köln. The Merovingians, a warrior family, established themselves as leaders of the Salians in the middle of the fifth century, initially operating as *foederati* for the Empire.

The Visigoths. *Foederati* since the 380s, but without secure status or land, they had arrived in southern Gaul (414), moved on to Spain (416) where supplied by the Romans they defeated the Vandals and Suebi, then returned to settle in Aquitaine (418). Though the Visigoths were to claim origins on the borders of Scandinavia, their travels through eastern and southern Europe, over the 40 years since their victory at Adrianople, must have made them a very mixed group of migrants. They were to expand their influence to the southern banks of the Loire.

The Burgundians. The third of the major barbarian collectives to settle in Gaul, they had no direct impact on western Gaul. Their importance lay in establishing themselves around Geneva (436), and then in taking the old Gallo-Roman capital Lyon (469), creating a self-governing protectorate straddling central France. With their arrival western Gaul had lost its seamless imperial provincial links to the Mediterranean world.

The Saxons. First mentioned by the Romans in the third century, they seem to have been a new confederation of tribes, clustered in the north of Germany between the Elbe and Weser. Like 'Franks', the term 'Saxons' was used very loosely by contemporaries, until the later fifth century referring to little more than pirates or raiders from the sea. The groups who came to the shores of the Channel and down the Atlantic coast, no doubt attracted seamen from all along the North Sea coast. In the 460s, sources describe one group using island bases to penetrate far up the Loire.

The Britons. After the conquest (AD43) the lowlands of Britain had largely accepted Romanisation, but the highland region remained far less affected. In Wales and the south-west villas and towns were rare and forts common, whilst beyond them lay free Ireland. The Romans had always recruited from inhabitants who clung to traditional warrior virtues though the numbers of those drawn from here is debated. It has been argued that a body of Britons was recruited for the defence of Armorica as early as the reign of Constantine and that more recruits followed in the late fourth century. Undoubtedly significant numbers of British migrants left the British Isles for Armorica in the fifth century.

The *Bagaudae*. During the late third century troubles, Maximian had crushed the *Bagaudae*, rebellious locals particularly associated with Armorica. Though the name does not recur in the fourth century, Ammianus, writing at the time, certainly suggests that there were peasant disorders in Gaul that had to be put down militarily, but were too ignoble to describe. The fifth century brought intensified efforts to raise the taxes needed to pay troops and the *Bagaudae* reappear at this time. They were active in 407–17, 435–7 and 442, though whether their resistance can be classed a social rebellion led by peasants or local landowners remains obscure.

As Salvian, a contemporary living in Marseille, lamented, 'they [the people of Gaul] migrate either to the Goths, or to the *Bagaudae* or to other conquering barbarians' (*De Gub. Dei*, V.21–22).

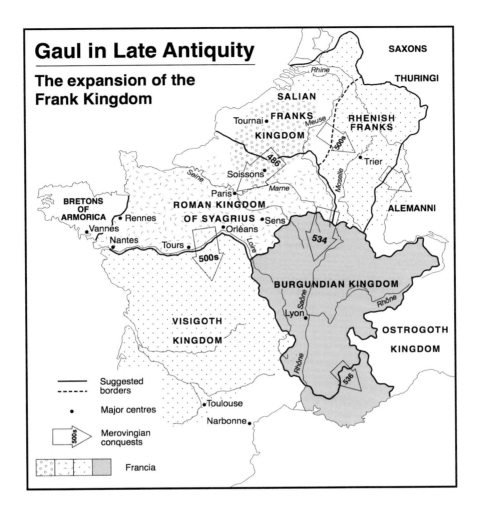

Gaul in Late Antiquity

The expansion of the Frank Kingdom

SAXONS

THURINGI

SALIAN FRANKS KINGDOM

Tournai

RHENISH FRANKS

Trier

Soissons

Paris

Marne

BRETONS OF ARMORICA

Rennes

ROMAN KINGDOM OF SYAGRIUS

Sens

ALEMANNI

Vannes

Orléans

Nantes

Tours

500s

BURGUNDIAN KINGDOM

Lyon

Rhône

OSTROGOTH KINGDOM

VISIGOTH KINGDOM

534

536

OSTROGOTH KINGDOM

Toulouse

Narbonne

Rhine

Meuse

Moselle

Seine

Loire

Saône

Rhône

486

Suggested borders

Major centres

500s Merovingian conquests

Francia

The archaeology of newcomer settlement

The difficulties in identifying newcomers are manifest and firm conclusions are rare. Salian Frank settlement in north-east Gaul can be traced most easily because of the widespread appearance of wood built settlements with one or more larger end-on post buildings surrounded by much smaller hovels or outbuildings; sunken floors are frequently present, a distinctively German feature. Their cemeteries involve clothed burials, whereas late Roman practice was simply to wrap a body. Higher status men are marked by their distinctive belts, *fibulae* (brooches) and sometimes weapons; women by bracelets, bead necklaces and *fibulae*. Ouen-du-Breuil (Seine-Maritime) has a fourth century settlement of this type while two burials there include cross-bow *fibulae*, suggesting Roman military status,

35

and a hoard of gold and silver coins could be mercenary pay rather than hidden treasure.

Finds elsewhere are rarely as clear-cut. At Cortrat, in the Beauce on the fringes of the Paris basin, a cemetery of 38 burials was excavated. Two males had cross-bow brooches and Germanic belt buckles and three women had German bell design *fibulae*. These burials probably involved two German warriors with their families (but who were the others buried here without grave goods?) Could they be *laeti* or were they *foederati*? The evidence for a group of Alans (a steppe tribe associated with the Huns) settled by Aëtius in the area during the fifth century is otherwise limited to place-names that include 'allain' and a style of beads. Suggestive perhaps, in a ghostly way.

The most interesting material comes from the Normandy plain. A late third century panegyric mentions a force of *laeti* settled in the area and according to the *Notitia Dignitatum*, Bayeux was made a *laeti* headquarters. At St Vigor-le-Grand seven burials were found including German style belt fittings and bell *fibulae*, whilst outside Caen, at St Martin-de-Mondeville, a 1980s excavation revealed a typical German settlement, replacing a Roman *vicus* in the early fourth century. On the coast at Le Bessin, north German finds suggest Saxon settlement. Were they mercenary defenders of the Channel coast – or invaders?

The most startling finds in this area were those made at Moult in 1876 ('the Airan treasure') and in St-Martin-de-Fontenay cemetery in the 1980s. Both produced large, extraordinary, cross-bow *fibulae* with semicircular plates and tapering feet, the Moult examples with gold and jewel decorations. They are typical of the western steppe and Danubian plain in the fifth century when the Huns dominated that region. The discovery of a significant number of burials showing skulls that had been bound in childhood, a very distinctive feature of the steppes, reinforces the belief that these were a group of Huns or Alans settled here by Aëtius. St-Martin-de-Fontenay revealed more: whilst extended skulls were found in 10–20 per cent of burials of fifth century date, they fell to 5–10 per cent in the sixth and disappeared in the seventh century: the gradual change argues absorption into the local community.

How Roman were the new states in western France?

The *Regnum Francorum*

The brutal and effective Merovingian king Clovis (480–511) murdered most of his relatives and then turned on his neighbours, defeating fellow

Franks to take the northern Rhineland and the Alemanni to take the southern Rhineland, pushing the Visigoths out of most of Aquitania and conquering the Burgundians. The state was divided into four parts when he died and after 566 settled into a pattern of three mini-kingdoms that were periodically re-united. This pattern was to mirror the late Roman Empire in both the frequency of family slaughter and the constant belief that 'Francia' should be one super state. Clovis was made consul by Emperor Anastasius (491–518) and the Merovingian kings dreamed of winning recognition as the new western Roman Emperors. Until 576, Frankish gold coins bore the head of the Emperor, not their kings.

Most of western France was within **Neustria**, the 'New West Lands', with an occasional royal residence at Orléans. Both the archaeological and historical record suggest that the Franks were thinly spread. Their legal position was defined by the early sixth century *Pactus Legis Salicae*, in large part based on Roman practice. Its application would have been limited anyway. Much of it dealt with farming practice, but it contains little evidence for an influx of German peasants. Another major aspect of the *Pactus*, violent family feud, would only have real significance for those who formed the military and (less frequently) civilian power structure of the state or the limited numbers of new landowners.

For most of the Gallo-Roman population, the world must have seemed little changed. Warfare was frequent and new settlers a constant for many years: the difference between Roman and Frankish rule must have seemed minimal. The taxes collected were the same as those of the fourth century, the laws that ran were late Roman, modified by royal decree, just as they had been by imperial Edict, and the practice of petitioning to mollify the oppressiveness of the regime hardly differed. Even if the villas fell into ruin and some landowning families were replaced by Germans the estates had not disappeared; household slaves and tied labourers were still present, though increasingly they lived in hamlets and villages. The move away from a market economy, with reduced long-distance trade and the gradual disappearance of low value coins, had been continuous since the later third century. Latin was the written language of all educated people and forms of Gallo-Latin were still spoken by the vast majority.

How then did Gallo-Romans perceive themselves in this world? Social class was one deep-seated division between people. The distinction between the *honestiores* (the honourable elite) and *humiliores* (the humble masses) remained. Whilst Roman law was gradually modified it did not change the fundamental position of the wealthy, who could still avoid torture and receive lesser forms of punishment. Given that the power of landlords and military men had not changed, even if the holders of that power had, for the mass of 'Roman' inhabitants the strongest feelings will have been for family and locality. As Christianity slowly spread, so some came to feel that this too formed part in their identity.

The Gallo-Roman elite of late Roman Gaul had been gradually adjusting to new realities throughout the fourth, fifth and sixth centuries. Of course some were killed and others fled, but to survive as a group and retain as much wealth as possible – primarily their estates – the elite had to accept a change of role. During the fourth century they lost any realistic stake in military matters and during the fifth century they gradually learnt there was no future in a traditional Roman administrative or political career. South of the Loire grandiose villas survived into the fifth century; these are conspicuously absent in western France, but income from estates here would have helped maintain this style of Roman luxurious living.

The key to the retention of any power now lay in their Roman cultural heritage. Rhetoric, literature and legal expertise were needed by the barbarian states and elite families could supply advisers, courtiers and lawyers, just as they had to governors and Emperors. More crucial, because it gave them a status less dependent on the whims and immediate needs of kings, was to adapt their control of communities by becoming bishops in the Christian Church. Whilst the fourth century bishops are shadowy figures or militants often from a low status background, in the fifth century the great landowners moved in: episcopal sanctity enhanced them as patrons and brokers between the people and the state. Many aristocratic families competed fiercely for episcopal sees. The sixth century historian, Gregory of Tours (c539–594), was typical of these families. From the Auvergne, his family had secured bishoprics in Langres, Geneva and Lyon, as well as Tours. Gregory boasted that out of 18 bishops since the foundation of the see, 13 had been from his family.

The Bretons

The development of the Armorican peninsula in the fifth and sixth centuries is veiled in uncertainty. It was not conquered by barbarians and because of this could claim to be unconquered Roman territory; yet archaeological evidence suggests it had lost much of its Roman gloss. Land had been abandoned and it is likely that the population had fallen noticeably in the fourth century; woodland and peat-bogs expanded at the expense of agriculture, though this, at least in part, must have been due to climatic change in the period. What is certain is that west of the arc formed by Nantes, Vannes and Rennes, town life had disappeared and very few villas survived into the fifth and sixth centuries; those that did were reduced to farming essentials. As elsewhere, much new construction used degradable materials, at the same time small settlements with stone enclosures and houses roofed in thatch were also being built. Like the re-use of earlier Iron Age sites and the appearance of south-west British pottery types, this points to a revival of the northern Atlantic zone.

Zosimus, a Greek historian writing at the end of the fifth century, reports events here in the early fifth century: 'The whole of Armorica and other Gallic provinces, in imitation of the Britons, freed themselves by expelling the Roman magistrates and establishing the government they wanted.' (*Historia Nova*, VI.5.2–3). This is clearly a reference to the *Bagaudae*, but makes a link with Britain, where people also saw the destruction of their society both through failed imperial rule and the coming of barbarians. The mid-sixth century British cleric Gildas adds more: whilst many Britons had been killed or butchered by barbarians 'others made for lands beyond the sea' (*De Exidio Britanniae*, C.25.1); he himself came to Armorica and this was clearly the emigrants' landfall. The scale of the migration was great enough to bring fundamental change: peninsular Armorica became 'Britannia', used first by Gildas' contemporary the Greek historian Procopius [*De Bello Gallico*, 8.20].

The pattern of migration from Britain is debatable. It is possible British troops and their families came in the fourth century, certainly there was a wave of migrants in the fifth century and probably another in the sixth. Britons who lived along the western seaways knew the peninsula, how close it was and how similar attitudes were and would have been drawn to settle here. Whether Riothamus – 'high king' – and his 12,000 Brittoni, who claimed to fight in the Roman Emperor Anthemius' name, and were defeated by the Visigoths in the Loire valley in the 460s, came from Brittany or from Britain is unknown, but the impact of migrants can be seen in a number of ways. Many place-names are common to Brittany, Devon, Cornwall and Wales and the 'Brittoni' language is most convincingly explained by linguists as the product of Celtic British rather a revival of Celtic Gaulish (though it is likely this had an impact in the region around Vannes). A large number of Breton saints can be traced back to Welsh or even Irish backgrounds, helping make a common and distinctive form of Celtic Christianity across the Atlantic zone, characterised by the hermit-preacher, making converts through simple lives and missionary zeal rather than status and power.

We know nothing about how quickly the populations integrated: Gregory of Tours sees them as a single alien group, but as an outsider unable to appoint any bishops in Brittany this may mean nothing. A new society evolved here, but how rapidly? Gregory wrote that the clothes people wore here differed from those in the Frankish kingdom, but not how. Celtic practices were introduced to the Roman legal code at some point between the sixth and eighth century. Political structure too remains hazy. It is probable that Brittany was dominated by warrior groups, sustained by raiding and booty. In the eastern border zone, Gregory of Tours mentions one. Led by Waroc, they carved out a territory around Vannes called Broërec. Gregory knew nothing of groups further west, but princedoms emerged along the north coast and in Finistère, respectively called Dumnonia – the Celtic name for the Roman *civitas* in south-west Britain – and Cornovia or Cornouaille, equally linked to south-west Britain. Nor were these Bretons cowed by the Franks, pushing the borders eastwards, absorbing Vannes and much of the territory of Nantes and Rennes. The world of the Middle Ages had begun.

THE SITES OF BRITTANY

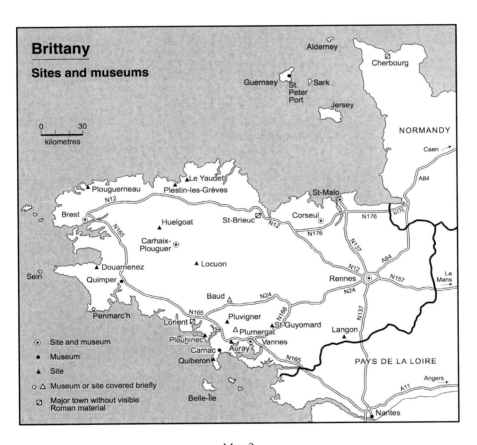

Map 2

BREST, Finistère
IGN 0417 ET

Fort and museum.

The magnificent wide Brest bay with only a narrow passage leading out to the Atlantic is virtually a vast, deep, inland lake; this is a natural naval base for any power controlling the mainland. The Penfeld river estuary lay nearest to the narrowest stretch and gives protection from the prevailing westerly gales and therefore a safe harbour. However there is little evidence of Roman occupation anywhere near the river mouth before the late third or early fourth century. Possibly there was settlement 3km to the north, but the evidence is slender, although there are perhaps early Roman remains still hidden; the continuous military presence over the centuries has made archaeological exploration difficult. Like Le Conquet, close to the Pointe de St-Mathieu, or Landéda at the mouth of the Aber Wrac'h, Brest could be *Gesocribate*, shown as the last stop on the Peutinger Table's Breton itinerary. As yet there is no convincing evidence.

Undoubtedly, a late Roman *castellum* was constructed here, guarding the river harbour. This may have been the base for the prefect in charge of the Osismi Moroccan (*Mauri*) troops, detailed in the late fourth century *Notitia Dignitatum* as being under the command of the *dux tractus Armoricani*. It is possible too that as other major troop concentrations are associated with defended sites and as the Osismi *civitas* capital at CARHAIX shrank dramatically in the fourth century, then this became the late Roman administrative centre. However, there are only hints in the later written evidence, no inscriptions and a settlement by the Penfeld estuary below the château is assumed rather than known.

Château de Brest
29200 Brest

The château is still a military establishment. Much of it is closed to the public and it has a formal and rather intimidating atmosphere. However, René Sanquer was allowed to carry out limited research in the 1960s and early 1970s, when he confirmed what local archaeologists had asserted since the 1900s: this was originally a Roman fortress. Essentially a rampart cut off the promontory. Various modern military buildings covered the interior, but Sanquer was able to confirm by identifying the odd fragment of rampart and circular tower that the *castellum* had followed the topography producing a trapezoidal shape. The ramparts were at least 8m high and just over 4m thick, built with a rubble core and facings of *petit appareil* stone courses separated by brickwork. Towers were circular and hollow with c.6.7m diameters, and projecting three quarters in front of the walls; ten defended the main rampart and there were at least ten more around the fort.

The main rampart

Despite later enlargement of the château and the massive medieval gateway covering what must have been the Roman entrance, there is considerable evidence of Roman construction between each of the corner towers, le donjon/Duchesse Anne (north) and la Madeleine (south and the modern entrance to the museum). The **exterior north of the gateway** faces a reserved car park, but pedestrians can walk here. The Roman stone and bricks are most obvious lower down; sections filled with much poorer uneven stonework indicate where Roman towers once stood. The **exterior south of the gateway** towards the entrance has similar but larger and more obvious Roman facing. The towers here are once again only indicated by rough stonework outlines; Sanquer was able to confirm this by finding the foundations of one tower. A postern gate is recognisable by Roman herringbone pattern stonework and later fill.

Musée de la Marine

Château de Brest

Hours: April – mid-Sept. 10am-6.30pm daily
Mid-Sept. – March 10am-noon, 2-6pm closed Tuesdays

Only fragmentary courses of Roman stonework are visible in the cellars of the Madeleine and Duchesse Anne towers. In the latter, a reconstruction drawing and plan illustrate a good historical panel on the *castellum*.

Plougastel-Daoulas

7km SE of Brest across the Elorn.

The town museum contains a Gallo-Roman statue 1.3m high. It is considered a naïve but vigorous representation of 'a god of fecundity'. It was found at the Notre-Dame de la Fontaine (GPS 30 U 0402253/5327265), a charming site used for pardons, c.1.5kms towards Diffrout. A large number of first and second century coins found here suggest the continuity linking springs and religious belief.

Locmaria-Plouzané

11km W of Brest by D789.

The Léon region, that is the whole of the peninsula to the north, west and east of Brest, contains more than three hundred Iron Age stele, the largest concentration in Brittany. Most of these are tall, well-made uprights, though there are also dome types.

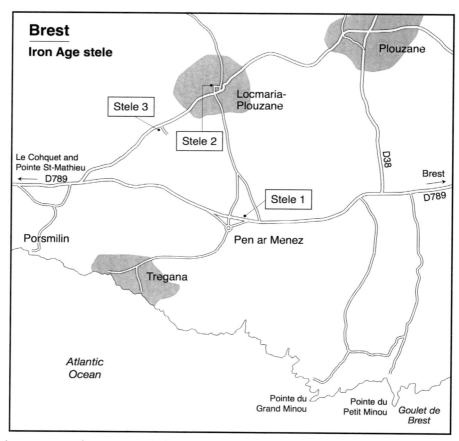

Brest

Iron Age stele

Plouzane

Locmaria-Plouzane

Stele 3

Stele 2

Le Cohquet and Pointe St-Mathieu

← D789

D38

Brest →

D789

Stele 1

Porsmilin

Pen ar Menez

Tregana

Atlantic Ocean

Pointe du Grand Minou

Pointe du Petit Minou

Goulet de Brest

A recent study suggested they were raised with declining frequency from the early La Tène until the Roman arrival. Many have been moved – including all those found here – but seem, from the find sites of a few others, to have been burial markers. Those at Locmaria-Plouzané are simply a sample within easy reach of Brest. Many, like those listed below, have been Christianised by adding crosses on top. For other sites in the district ask at the mairie.

1. **D789 roadside.** GPS 30 U 0378957/5357464. The Pen-ar-Menez upright quadrangular stele 1.25m high. By the north side of the Brest–Le Conquet road, 150m before Locmaria-Plouzané turning, in the lay-by beside a mobile phone tower.

2. **Town centre.** GPS 30 U 0378292/5359233. Two upright stele, one octagonal 1.95m high, one quadrangular 1.65m high. In front of the mairie.

3. **Porsmilin road.** GPS 30 U 0376968/5358434. The massive 3.70m high

'Croas Teo' quadrangular stele, with a diminutive cross on top, was brought here as recently as 1980. By the rue des Genêts, on the south of the main road 1.5km from the town centre.

CARHAIX-PLOUGUER, Finistère
IGN 0717 O
GPS 30 U 0457181/5346977

City sites and aqueduct.

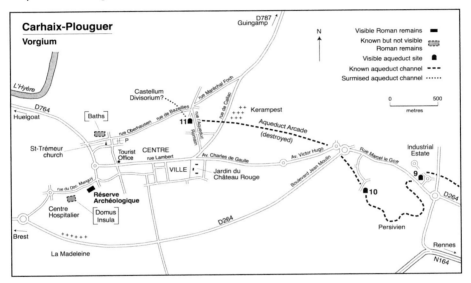

It is at first a surprise to realise that this small inland town, which has only in the last few years gained in confidence and dynamism, is located where the Roman authorities created a tribal capital, *Vorgium*. The reason they selected this site lies perhaps in the nature of the Osismi tribe and the geography of the region. The Osismi occupied virtually all the western half of the Breton peninsula, but the most densely populated areas were along the coasts rather than in the bleaker and more arid granite Armorican plateau. Yet the deep indentations of both the Atlantic and Channel shores produced clusters of settlements and thus more localised identities; these people naturally formed pagi. Whilst the Camp d'Arthus at HUELGOAT had been chosen to give security to a central place of assembly for the Osismi, *Vorgium* was sited to provide easy communications from the rest of the province and yet ensure all the *pagi* were within easy reach.

The city was laid out in the depression between the Arrée hills and the Monts Noires near the meeting of major prehistoric routes coming west from Vannes and St Michel. These were replaced by surveyed Roman roads and a new road was built along the plateau ridge linking the town to

Rennes, while a string of roads radiated out to the lesser centres of the Osismi. Signs of previous Iron Age occupation are minimal (a souterrain on the hospital site). It is possible that Caesar's army camped here, but there is no evidence for this. The decision to build the city is likely to have been Augustan with the grid's central crossroads at the tourist office; traces of Roman drains and newly discovered Roman road surfaces broadly confirm this. Development came slowly in the first century and like other Breton *civitas* capitals, *Vorgium* experienced its maximum extent in the second and early third centuries, when it spread over 120–30ha.

Carhaix's recognition of the value of its Roman heritage is recent. Though eighteenth century scholars had remarked on how extensive the remains were, only isolated and limited excavations took place until the late nineteenth century. Work remained intermittent until the 1970s when Louis Pape's work of synthesis (1978) showed how haphazard research had been. An exhibition on Roman Carhaix (1987) finally produced the breakthrough: the 1990s saw large-scale rescue excavations, a modern scientific study of the aqueduct and an important site (La Réserve Archéologique) conserved.

No inscriptions have ever been recorded in Carhaix. Traditionally this has been taken to imply a far-away backwardness, yet the inhabitants were not averse to other kinds of Romanisation. Graffiti shows Latin was known to some inhabitants and an inscription in Rennes records that *Vorgium* had the usual town council of elite citizens (an *ordo*). Architectural elements found here, such as column drums, capitals and entablature, are evidence for a typical Roman urban centre. Certainly no *forum* or major temple has been identified so far (just a small *fanum* on the edge of town), but the 27km aqueduct – the only one associated with a *civitas* capital in Brittany – indicates that *ordo* had money and the ambition to give its city a reliable water supply, fountains and baths. Traces of a large bath complex, probably public, have been identified NW of St-Trémeur. Several discoveries point to the existence of fine housing: a well-made domestic bath system (1987–91, rue l'Aqueduc Romain); painted plaster décor using costly red and blue pigments (from Spain and Egypt); real shells added to the plaster in a *frigidarium*; and schist floor pavings, though only one simple mosaic fragment has been found. The discovery of villa remains at Persivien demonstrates that *Vorgium* had prosperous suburban farms supplying the market.

The rescue dig on the site of the Centre Hospitalier (1995–6) identified for the first time a whole block with typical first century lightly built housing, and second and early third century commercial buildings. More surprising was the fourth century *domus* that succeeded them, covering the whole *insula*. A garden courtyard was surrounded by rooms. On the north there was a double rank, split in the middle by an enormous cruciform reception room. The walls of this side of the house were thick enough to have supported another floor and even a loft storey above that. This discovery conclusively demonstrated that the town did not simply collapse in the later third century, but was seen as viable enough for the very wealthy to want to live here until the 350s, when rudimentary repairs were soon followed by ruin. This suggests that the final transfer of Osismi administration to Brest took place in the second half of the fourth century. Nothing has so far been found to show that Carhaix's subsequent insignificance did not continue throughout the early Middle Ages; 'Carofes', its name then, simply meant crossroads.

Office du Tourisme
Rue Brizeux

A good town plan, maps, publications and advice are available here and upstairs there is a small museum of archaeological material. The tourist office also has information on special exhibitions of recent discoveries and on guided tours, including La Réserve Archéologique and the aqueduct.

Jardins du Château Rouge
Rue des Martyrs

Fragments of Roman monumental architecture, drainage system and stone coffins decorate these gardens.

La Réserve Archéologique
Le Manec'h,
5, rue du Docteur Menguy

Open to the public during summer excavations.

Sondages carried out in 1996 demonstrated Le Manec'h's importance and the temporary stay on new building became full-scale excavation and conservation when the State bought the land in 2000 making this the first such site in Carhaix.

The road. This east–west *decumanus* saw six relayings over two centuries, suggesting constant use. Impressions of wooden guttering were found on each side.

The fountain. Grand appareil foundation stones survive of the base and are grooved to take the four uprights of a trough, waterproofed with a sand mortar lining. Piping from the *castellum divisorium* would have supplied fresh running water for the inhabitants of the area. This is a rare find (for a working version go to Lyon).

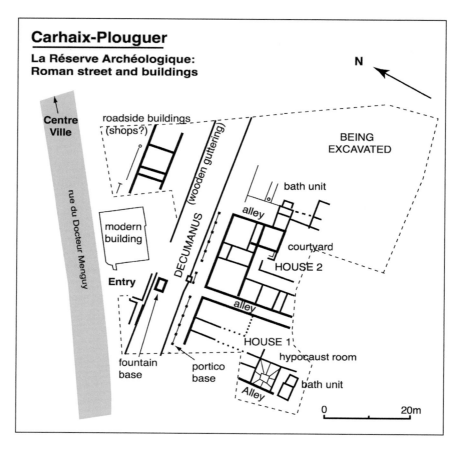

Northside buildings. These are poorly preserved and their use is unknown.

Southside buildings. Two premises face onto the main road and have porticos that probably supported a second floor over the sidewalk. An alley separates them. They both have large front rooms – for commercial use? – and many of the rear domestic rooms are paved in schist. **House 1** had a very large hypocausted room and a smaller one attached. **House 2** had a gallery round an inner courtyard and a small bath system. These could have been the residences of prosperous merchants. Underneath them were earlier structures.

The Aqueduct

Carhaix in fact had two aqueducts, both bringing water from springs to the east of the town. The earlier aqueduct is considered to have been constructed at the end of the first century, taking water from springs around Kerhon, 11km away. However, the small channel, a mere 0.45m wide and 0.60m high, was only capable of delivering a low volume of water: the town's second century expansion created a demand for much more.

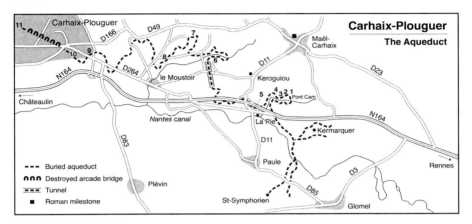

The later (main) aqueduct drew water from springs on the Montagnes Noires between St-Symphorien and Kermarquer east-south-east of Carhaix. From just beyond Kerangall to the *castellum divisorium* in the north of Carhaix, the fall was 153 down to 146m above ground level, but across uneven ground. The longer the route, the more marginal the slope became, yet tunnels and arcades added enormously to cost. The compromise was to have one long tunnel (900m) and one kilometre-long arcade, up to 14m high, crossing the final valley of Kérampest into Carhaix, whilst the rest hugged the contours and was buried in a trench: a total distance of 27km with an average slope of 0.32m per kilometre. Unfortunately neither the main surveying instrument – the *chorobates* – nor engineering technique could ensure an even fall over the whole distance; some lengths sloped more steeply whilst others had no slope at all, or even uphill. As debris certainly clogged up sections of the aqueduct, as indicated by the attempts made to improve the flow with extra layers of waterproof cement on the channel floor, it was perhaps cost cutting that led to the decision to build the channel with a typical 60cm width, but only 90cm height, when normally it would have been high enough for cleaners and repairers to walk rather than crawl through. A team of overseers must have been hired with the surveyor, though local contractors, labourers and miners from nearby lead mines would have been available. Yet the whole project must still have been hugely expensive: perhaps some Osismi leading citizens had contacts in Rome and got an imperial subsidy, but it would be very unusual for the town not to have paid a significant proportion. This great enterprise was carried out in the Severan era and fell out of use during the fourth century.

Sondages have now demonstrated the existence of the masonry supports that carried the arcades 14m above Kérampest. The pity is more did not survive: this would have provided not only a classic Roman monument for us to see, but perhaps more information on how the engineers integrated the two aqueducts.

All references below are to the main aqueduct except in the middle section where the two aqueducts ran close together. The first three sites are in Carhaix. For the remainder, directions are from the D264. The numbering refers to the brown and blue signposts and site panels; present at the time of writing. They correspond to the numbering on the map.

Rue de l'Aqueduc Romain (11 brown)
GPS 30 U 0457831/5347552. This tiny section was constructed with floor, walls and vault made of concrete. On the channel walls is the waterproof layer, a mix of sand, cement and crushed brick. The constructors chose concrete walling and vaults for the few hundred metres from the *castellum divisorium* to the Kérampest depression and for the bridge channel itself, as a few fragmentary remains found there have shown.

Rue le Guyader (10 brown)
GPS 30 U 0459127/5347104. An equally small section – not signposted – on the eastern side of this housing estate road. The masonry channel has been cut exposing a short section.

Rue Bollardière (9 brown)
GPS 30 U 0459989/5347115. A heavily restored section in the Villeneuve industrial estate above the major eastern Carhaix roundabout. This 20m stretch gives the clearest picture of the aqueduct's standard channel design. The trench was given a foundation of broken schist for drainage then a concrete floor. The channel itself had masonry walls and vaulting of rough cut stone, while floor and walls were again lined with coats of waterproof cement.

Porz an Plas (8 blue)
GPS 30 U 0463258/5346936. From Carhaix roundabout 2.5km by the D264 to le Moustier where a panel opposite the church tells the story of the first Aqueduct. Turn north to Crec'h ar Venglé (1km) then east towards le Hélesser; passing the turning for Porz an Plas by c50m. The road cuts through both aqueducts, running parallel here, leaving channels exposed on both sides of the road.

Le Hélesser (7 blue)
GPS 30 U 0464554/5347023. Continue to le Hélesser, turn south (towards

embodied a spiritual aspect. A more functional approach points to marking burials or land ownership. Unfortunately, there are few that have not been moved – like the examples here – which makes conclusive argument difficult. Another panel examines the souterrain question. These underground tunnels, frequently found associated with Iron Age settlement, are for us enigmatic: were they for food storage, or were they cellars for worship, perhaps the severed head cult? Places to hide from enemies? A case can be made for all these explanations. In the Gallo-Roman period evidence has certainly been found elsewhere in France for cellars having both a storage and a religious role. Also displayed is material representing the many excavations along the Breton foreshore that have revealed the widespread Iron Age manufacture of salt from seawater (see SALT, FISH AND ROMAN COOKING).

The Gallo-Roman and post-Roman sections

Three grand villas, all excavated in the nineteenth century, provide much of the material here. Le Lodo (see VANNES); Legenès, now totally eroded by the sea (mosaic fragments); and Bosseno, Miln's 1875 excavation. (For the major modern excavation of a luxury coastal villa, see PLOUHINEC). Painted plaster fragments from a *frigidarium* indicate the Armorican taste for adding real shells for decorative effect – flickering Roman lamps would have made them glint. Small finds include a solid metal bull, largely lead, a white earthenware mother-goddess and a unique carved handle in the form of Eros, probably made from tortoise-shell; the last was found in one of the third century hoards displayed. Nearby was Roman **Locmariquer**, here represented by a plan of the theatre. This is still 'visible' in the shape of the cemetery situated below the great passage grave of the Table des Marchands. A grandiose but unfinished aqueduct crossing the Auray must have been designed to supply a small town or large sanctuary, perhaps even dedicated to Caesar's victory over the Veneti in 56BC. Pictures illustrate the revival of sub-rectangular houses during the fourth to sixth centuries and link them to the influx of British and Irish migrants.

CORSEUL, Côte d'Armor

IGN1016ET
GPS U 0561580/5370121

Major site.

11km W of Dinan on the N176, then NW by D734. Parking: the most convenient place is 100m behind the mairie, taking D44 to Languenon.

Fanum Martis is listed in the Peutinger Table as a stop on the road west from Rennes. The name could apply simply to the commanding sanctuary at Haut-Bécherel 1.7km east of Corseul, but it is generally taken to refer to the Roman town as well. In 1840, Prosper Mérimée, in his role as Inspector-General for Historic Monuments, had been impressed enough to list the temple as in need of immediate protection. Chance finds had been made in and around Corseul itself since the eighteenth century, but it was the local teacher Roland Ricordel who, from 1942 onwards, using his pupils as assistants, inspired the community to value and support research into their heritage. That this was the main urban centre created for the Curiosolites tribe was confirmed in the 1960s and 1970s: the excavation of the Champ Mulon site combined with the earlier work, then aerial surveys by Loic Langouët, suggested a formal grid of roads reaching up to 110ha with extensive building in central areas. This knowledge stimulated the decision to excavate the Monterfil site, led first by Fichet de Clairfontaine, then Hervé Kérebel (1986–99). Since then, diagnostic trenching has identified the *forum* north-west of Monterfil.

Based on the Monterfil excavations, Kérebel identified five archaeological periods. The first embraces the earliest material found. The new settlement with its timber framed housing with clay fill is most easily explained as the result of Augustus' visit to Gaul in 16BC, when the Emperor set about transforming the tribes into the *civitas* that would underpin the provincial administrative framework. The Curiosolites would have been pressed to create a capital on the Roman model – one in which their aristocracy could live and increasingly follow a Romanized lifestyle. The outline of the grid was probably decided then but serious development began only in the second period, broadly covering AD14-68AD (Tiberius – Nero). Proper roads were constructed and the central *insulae* began to fill with substantial buildings, including the first *domus*.

The third period, during the later first century, is marked by the emergence of full urbanisation with the construction of a number of public or semi-public structures along with the Haut-Bécherel sanctuary. Development then tailed off until in the fourth period there was a new spurt under the Severans (193–235), when a number of buildings were modernised. The fifth period, dated to the later third century, is marked by hoards and serious destruction, followed by the rapid rundown of the town. The evidence was inconclusive as to whether decline was everywhere and continuous. There are no signs of late Roman recovery at Monterfil, but at Champ Mulon, it was claimed, a fourth century bath complex was constructed, perhaps for Constantinian troops on leave from their work dealing with Channel pirates. But the baths were poorly dated and current opinion favours a Severan date for them. It seems likely that the town was abandoned in the early fourth century with its remaining inhabitants moving to the more secure Alet (see St-MALO).

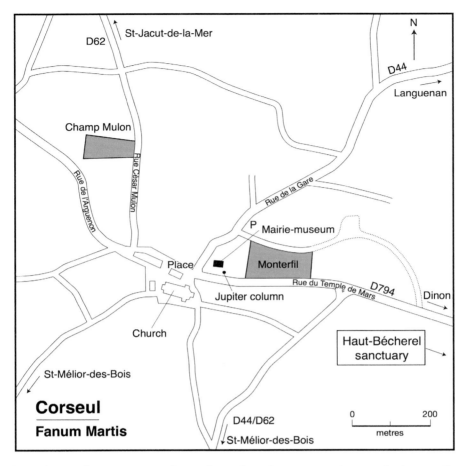

Outside craftsmen must have introduced construction techniques for housing, mosaics and wall painting and Kérebel has suggested that a military presence might explain the technical expertise displayed in the early construction work. This is possible, but when military equipment finds are minimal and no evidence of a fort has been found, the presence of early sigillata and coins seem a thin basis for this proposal. The maximum size of the town is now thought to have been a more typical 50-60ha. Development took place in a series of spurts, so changes occurred in *insulae* sizes; density of occupation also varied widely and some parts of the grid were left unfinished and unoccupied. Gallo-Roman cemeteries must eventually be found and the *forum* firmly identified; a theatre is a strong possibility. A number of good springs and wells made a costly aqueduct unnecessary.

Monterfil
Rue du Temple de Mars (D794)

The site is on a slope next to the post office. Flowers and plantings bear testimony both to civic pride and awareness (some even being shaped to suggest staircases and columns). Excellent panels in French and English describe the site.

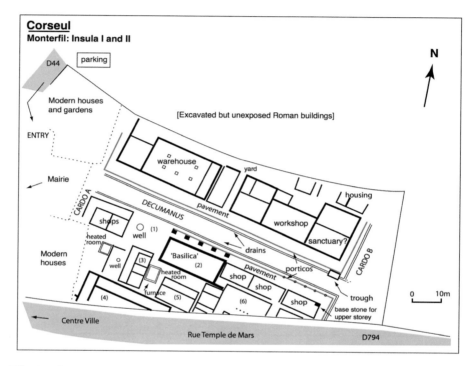

The roads
The *decumanus* dividing the site into northern and southern *insulae* was the main axis for the town and linked the road from Carhaix to Corseul's port settlement at Taden on the Rance; it is likely that the *forum* stood beside it on another *insula* to the west. As the town grew during the early first century, the first gravel road was given a schist block surface and provided with new drainage ditches and pavements: this narrowed it from 10 to 7m, still twice the width of either *cardo*. Rainwater from the drains filled the animal drinking trough. The street is lined with reconstructed portico columns which used the Tuscan order: a square base capped with a round cushion and a plain shaft, apart from a decorative moulding near the simple capital. This type was equally prevalent in domestic house porticos.

Insula I (north of the road)
One building, 280 Roman feet long, originally ran the length of the *insula*.

This 'réserve archéologique' preserves the restored walling of a large mid-first century (Claudian) *domus*. It took up half an *insula* and followed the Mediterranean style with a porticoed gallery or peristyle looking out on a central garden. The largest rooms are likely to have been reception rooms where important guests could be entertained, dependants could be greeted and discussion could take place between owner and estate manager. Fragments of an inscription were found here, first in the 1860s and again in the 1960s, recording a leading *decurion* of the Curiosolites who became a *sacerdos* or the chief priest at the assembly of the Three Gauls in Lyon, the top provincial position to which a Gaul could aspire.

A new phase began with the construction of a large bath complex. To the west of the exposed area a variety of bath rooms were constructed, while a massive *palaestra* or exercise area with its own suite of rooms was erected over the *domus* foundations; according to the excavators, this was done at the beginning of the fourth century. Given the dramatic decline at Monterfil, Kérebel asserted a Severan date would be more convincing, a view now widely accepted. He has even suggested the '*palaestra*' might be a *macellum* or enclosed market. Unfortunately, with most of the remains from this phase removed or of low quality and all the records of the excavation destroyed, it is difficult to review the evidence.

Musée de la Société Archéologique de Corseul
Mairie de Corseul
22130 Plancoët

Hours: (when town hall open):10am–noon, 2 –6.30pm

Nineteenth century finds were taken to Dinan or to Rennes (where you can see a fine classical *lares* god found here). The Société Archéologique de Corseul, inspired by and drawing on the work of Roland Ricordel, created this museum in 1977; one of the three rooms is dedicated to him. Most of the material on display was found prior to the work at Monterfil, though there is a model of this site and the Haut-Bécherel temple. Amongst the small finds are good examples of Iron Age coins – Curiosolites and Redones – and decorated firedogs; an interesting Gallo-Roman bronze of a dancing figure holding rings perched on a lion; and white moulded pipeclay ware, signed '*Rextugenos*' (see RENNES). Schist slates with geometric and shield designs were found in various *domus* sites; the best fragments of plaster, which come from the Champ Mulon baths, are decorated with swathes and seashells and some even imitate mosaics. One case has real seashells, once used to help soil drainage.

Corseul. Pipeclay Venus with solar wheels symbolising fertility and regeneration.
Musée de la Societé Archéologique. Crédit A. Gautier

The 'Jupiter' column

Outside the mairie are architectural fragments and a 2.07m granite column with an unusually elaborate capital. It is assumed that the weathered corners were once faces and that the rings carved between them represent wheels or sun symbols sacred to Jupiter. A square hollow on top implies a fixing for a statue that should have been either a small version of the god as a horseman riding over an agonised giant or a lone figure of Jupiter, upright or seated.

could dedicate itself to the Emperor before a gathering of the Curiosolites people. Secondly, though traces of other *fana* have been found in Corseul, few doubt that this was the sanctuary that gave the town its name and that therefore Mars would have been worshipped here.

The sanctuary was built in the latter half of the first century (Flavian) and was never modified. The measurements and design suggest a specialist using the Roman foot (11.6 in/0.296m) and a multiple of the width of the *cella* for the length of the sacred area (6x40 Roman feet). No evidence has been found of any preceding Iron Age temple here, but the relationship with the spring at nearby St-Uriac needs further investigation. The latest coin finds are from the second-half of the third century when the sanctuary was destroyed by fire. For me, the northern and western wings have been over-restored.

St-Méloir-des-Bois
GPS 30 U 0555448/5367437. 8km WSW of Corseul by the parish church.

The four columns are not in situ. Two are without decoration, but a third was converted into a milestone that stood by the Vannes road two leagues from Corseul as part of a propaganda effort to promote the Gallic Roman Emperor, Victorinus. It mattered little: he was murdered by his troops in 271, within two years of taking power. The fourth is similar to the 'Jupiter' column at Corseul, but this time with poorly finished volutes and projecting heads replacing the rings. This format reflects, however badly, the capitals on Jupiter columns in eastern Gaul. Alternatively, the column may have been a pagan altar hollowed to hold offerings. More convincingly, the hollow was a later conversion into a Christian font.

Le Quiou
30km SE of Corseul by D794 and D766. Left by D64 to St Juvat and Tréfumel, then D39 to Le Quiou.

This large villa site is being opened to the public. The INRAP excavators began work in 2001 and revealed the earliest known villa in Armorica. From the Augustan period onwards it functioned both as a working farm and as a source for building materials used in the construction of Corseul, including both stone and lime. It developed into a noble home with fine living quarters whilst retaining a farm section. There were baths, barns and a separate building, possibly for a farm manager or *vilicus*.

DOUARNENEZ, Finistère
IGN 0518 OT or IGN 0419 ET

Roman fish processing and promontory forts.

25km NW of Quimper by the D765.

Douarnenez bay is the embodiment of western Brittany. The granite rocks of the south-western shoreline, stretching out to the Pointe du Raz, form cliffs, broken and battered by Atlantic storms. Behind them is a bleak and open landscape. To the east the coast softens slightly. Strands of sand and low hills, divided by streams and small rivers, form the heart of the bay. Here, the sea and its fish, not the land, have provided key elements in the inhabitants' livelihood.

At Douarnenez itself there was late Iron Age settlement on the Île Tristan, and by the Rhu ford (now the bridge), the protected inlet made a natural small haven. Land communications to other Osismi centres and south into Veneti territory were good. Occupation of the island and in the port area continued in the Gallo-Roman period, with a few modest villas added on the Tréboul side of the inlet. The isolated hamlets nearby did not coalesce into a town, yet a surprisingly large temple built at the turn of the first century AD has been found at Trégouzel (the excavated remains are now covered with loose soil and gorse). Then came the fish processing factories. Whilst the growing wealth of the owners perhaps led to the temple's construction, the smell of rotting fish must have made the neighbourhood less than desirable! For a time, these factories were to make Brittany one of the most important salted fish suppliers in the Roman Empire.

Most valuable would have been the huge shoals of sardines that visited the bay during the summer months. To benefit from this plenty, the catches had to be preserved and salting was the most widely used conservation method in the ancient world. Three products could be made: salted fish (*salsamentum*), fish sauce (*garum*) and fish paste (*allec*). The fish were gutted and laid in large vats interlaced with salt where the mix was pressed down by weights – generally flat roof tiles. Over some weeks the fish would lose water and absorb salt, leading to fermentation and a significant slowing of decomposition; the salt fish would then be packaged in jars (or perhaps barrels) and exported inland. The fish sauce was also made in vats with offal and/or smaller fish, herbs or spices, and salt; then stirred and sometimes heated to speed up fermentation and to break down the contents. The marinated mix was then filtered, separating the liquid from the more solid residue which could be used as paste. Both sauce and paste would be stored in jars. The liquid, most widely known as *garum* but also under other names, was perhaps the most distinctively Roman feature in

These three sites are not just linked by proximity. Small statues (c60cms high) of Hercules, resting on his club, were found at all of them; whilst the Ris example has been lost, the other two are in QUIMPER and RENNES museums. Careful analysis suggests that their presence was not accidental: statues of Hercules, wearing a laurel crown and in this upright pose are typical representations of this god as protector of Roman salt dealers. The Italian connection is emphasized further by the use of Carrara marble for the Plomarc'h Hercules and the discovery at Ris of an inscription to Neptunus Hippius – a lone Gallic example of a Graeco-Roman manifestation of Neptune – dedicated by a Caius Varenius Varus, curator of the *conventus*, a court limited to dealing with Roman citizens. Certainly a strong case can be made for the Douarnenez factories representing a Roman-owned concern likely to have personal links with merchants based in Rome, so raising awareness of distant markets and of how to exploit the necessary technology.

The remains

The site has been explored since 1905, with the major excavations being those undertaken by R Sanquer 1976–8 and J-P Bardel in the 1990s when the decision was taken to restore and leave exposed the best-known and largest building, number 4. Building 1 was clearly associated with Goret creek where the sardine catch was landed and raised up the bluff. A hypocaust was identified here, though its role remains uncertain: was it for making *garum* quickly or an oven of some kind for making salt from brine? Buildings 2 and 3 contained lines of processing vats.

Building 4. The builders dug down in to the granite bedrock creating a flat area for the 3.6m deep vats and yard. The rear wall supported a massive sloping roof to protect the vats from sun and rain. Timber uprights stood in cavities along the side walls and on top of the vat junctions using granite bases. Extra buttressing on the shore side resists the pressure of the downhill slope. Ten of the vats had waterproof plaster linings, their rosy pink colour deriving from crushed tiles; five were unlined.

During excavation floor deposits in vat 13 were examined in detail. They had formed a dark, caramel coloured substance, consisting of a thick mass of fragmented bones and scales from a huge number of sardines: this was the residue of *garum* making – even in 1977, it still had a strong fish smell! This vat also produced a stone fragment of a man's leg, tentatively identified with Neptune, and part of a millstone, believed to have been used to grind up sardines. The deeper unlined vat 1 contained fragments of two ovoid jars. Deposits on them showed that they contained fish-scales and tiny fish bones, probably *allec*; perhaps this double vat (along with the other unlined vats?), was used to store the finished product before dispatch.

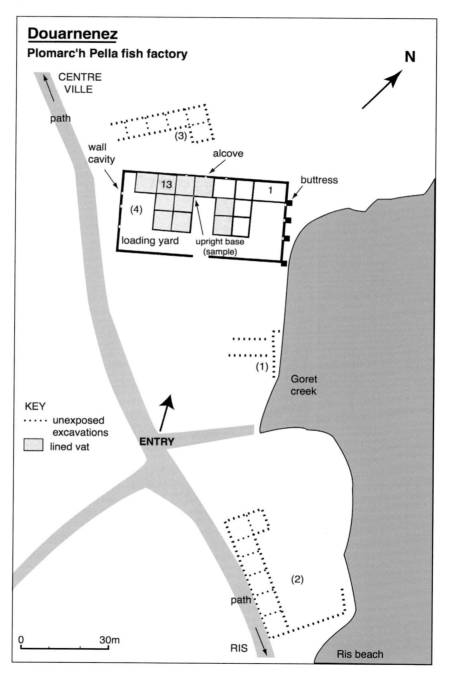

Douarnenez
Plomarc'h Pella fish factory

N

CENTRE VILLE

path

(3)

wall cavity

alcove

buttress

13

1

(4)

loading yard

upright base (sample)

(1)

Goret creek

KEY

····· unexposed excavations

☐ lined vat

ENTRY

(2)

path

0   30m

RIS

Ris beach

The rear wall alcoves would have been perfect for small statues: Hercules (a copy of the find stands in one alcove), probably Neptune, and perhaps Jupiter in the middle. They would once have overseen what must have been backbreaking work carried out in a constant stench.

By 270-80 the factory was abandoned, marked by a thick sterile level in the vats, though in the fourth century the vats were used once again, this time as crude habitations.

Other fish processing sites

There are two further excavated sites, but these have no visible remains. Their value lies in showing the context and environment in which Roman fish processing took place. *Le Ris*. In the cove at the eastern end of the beach, where the Douarnenez–Châteaulin road (D7) crosses the Névet stream. On both banks by the shoreline, there were remains of buildings and vats. A bath complex, hypocaust and mosaic also suggested housing. The Neptunus Hippius inscription was found here. *Kerlaz*. At the western end of the great sweep of Trezmalaouen beach some 50m before the cliffs, a four-vat site was revealed after violent storms. Traces of building stone are still just visible on the shoreline. Approach via the hamlet of Lanévry, then take the road and track to the beach.

Promontory forts

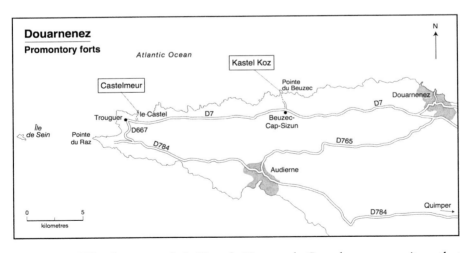

Mortimer Wheeler regarded Kastel Koz and Castelmeur as sites that typified Iron Age Veneti 'cliff castles', though few Veneti promontory forts – the more prosaic term used widely today – equal these two forts in Osismi territory (see QUIBERON for one that does). He felt their stark drama: 'These cliff castles are essentially of the Atlantic, the eyries of deep-sea sailors, places where families could be stowed away whilst the younger menfolk were at sea. For the most part their sullen crags, *d'un effet grandiose et impressionant*, are suspended in an enduring sea-mist between the mournful screaming of the sea-birds and the relentless crashing of the breakers.' (*The Hillforts of Northern France*, 1957, pp5-6)

No further research has been carried out to demonstrate that the ramparts were Iron Age (widely accepted though) or what role these '*oppida*' had: perhaps they were refuges for families, secure places of final resort in troubled times. Yet the harsh power of the ocean and the immensity of the sea and sky have an inescapable impact on the visitor: perhaps the ramparts never really had a defensive purpose, serving rather as spiritual markers; their primary purpose then, would have been as sacred spaces by the ocean.

Kastel Koz
GPS 30 U 0386798/5327246

Pointe de Beuzec. W 14.5kms of Douarnenez by D7; N by D507 from Beuzec-Cap-Sizun.

A narrow triangle of 1.2ha. was isolated from the downward slope of the landmass by three ramparts and ditches; these are poorly defined today, but once the inner rampart was faced with cut stone and the outer was topped with a stone wall. Huts were found by Le Men during his 1869-74 diggings, running along the length of the promontory; some would have been Iron Age. Unfortunately, Wheeler was unable to conduct new excavations instead examining old collections that mixed material from the Neolithic to medieval, with a significant later Iron Age element.

Castelmeur
GPS 30 U 0374181/5324611

Pointe de Castelmeur. 28kms W of Douarnenez by D7; N by track to Le Castel hamlet and parking place.

At the narrowest point of the promontory, sharply defined triple ramparts cut off the fort (2ha) from the mainland, with steep drops onto the rocks only metres away to east and west. About 300m long the fort is at the most 50m wide, but 60m above the sea below. A path follows the central ridge and the hollows of huts excavated by Du Chatellier in 1889 are still clearly visible. Again the pottery finds indicated Neolithic, Iron Age and medieval occupation.

Île-de-Sein

Viewed from the Pointe du Van and the Pointe du Raz, 7.5–10km out to sea, is the low-lying island of Sein. Boats available from Audierne.

Sein has been identified as Sena (Pape, 1995), described by Pomponius Mela as the home of a Celtic oracle tended by virgin priestesses who could cure disease, control the elements and predict the future. Traces of Gallo-Roman occupation have been found, but no sanctuary. Though the identification seems good, Mela also considered the island to be part of the Cassiterides, generally thought to have been the Isles of Scilly. Strabo too mentions an isle of priestesses: his version gives them a Greek gloss, with annual ecstatic trances; he places his island in the mouth of the Loire.

HUELGOAT, Finistère
IGN 0617 E

Iron Age hillfort

Camp d'Artus
GPS 30 U 0444919/5358275

From modern Huelgoat by D14 2km north towards Barrien, opposite milestone. On the right a small wooden signpost by a track indicates Camp d'Artus. 300m to parking area. The main footpath (of four) is signposted to the motte (150m). Here a panel outlines the site's history; there are other occasional panels.

The local reputation of 'Camp d'Artus' was known to Prosper Mérimée in the 1830s, but it was Mortimer Wheeler's expedition here in 1938 that resulted in the first serious study of the site: since then it has not been thought necessary to undertake either a new excavation or to revise significantly his conclusions. Wheeler (1890–1976) was one of the twentieth century's great archaeologists; his appetite for work and pleasure was voracious. In 1938 he was also directing the two most important digs in Britain, at *Verulamium* (St Albans) and Maiden Castle; he was in charge of the newly created Institute of Archaeology in London and was Keeper of the London Museum; he was pursuing a love affair with a mistress of the artist Augustus John, whom he wanted to marry (and did – disastrously), whilst in his team of assistants was at least one young woman resisting his passionate approaches, one of the many he propositioned in his lifetime. Yet he had had time to plan meticulously what 'many colleagues judged was the most brilliantly executed action of his career' (J Hawkes, *Mortimer Wheeler*, 1982), a survey of hillforts throughout northern France. He brought an ability to delegate tasks and then draw from his team leaders the essence of what they had found; his writings and drawings display a wonderful precision and clarity. The work at Camp d'Artus involved a survey of the whole site, three rampart cuttings, excavations at two of the entrances and eleven sondages across the site.

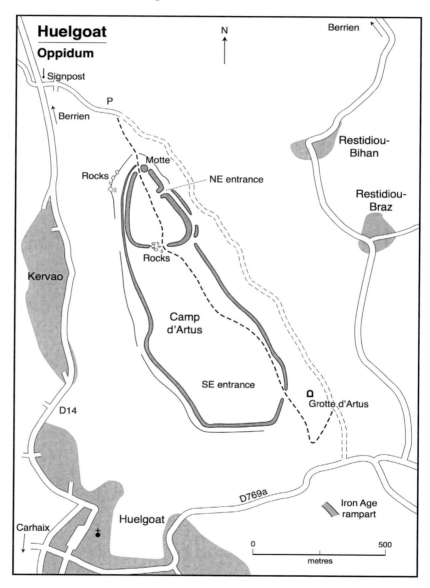

The main rampart surrounds an area of c.30ha, with a smaller pear-shaped enclosure at the northern end. It sits high along a ridge on the western

Armorican plateau. By far the biggest hill or promontory fort in Osismi territory, it was near a major north-south route across the Finistère peninsula, yet it is some distance from the natural crossroads at Carhaix. Bleak in the winter, but much more open then as the forest cover is modern; it is likely to have supported some poor farming and more pasture; this suggests a tribal assembly place rather than an incipient urban development or *oppidum*. Wheeler has been criticised for focusing too much on site defences and military campaigns. He saw the main enclosure as a defensive measure against Caesar's 56BC campaign, with the smaller enclosure being a reduced response before the final capitulation of the Armoricans in 51BC. He found no evidence to suggest economic significance, for example nothing connects the site with nearby ancient lead mining, and the single *amphora* found hardly supports commercial significance. A stronger case can be made for possible political or religious importance, though no kind of sanctuary was noted. At Le YAUDET following very detailed recent work, the excavators concluded that it was unrealistic to think its rampart could have been easily defended; the rather longer main rampart at Camp d'Artus raises the possibility that it too was constructed for tribal status and prestige. The small enclosure could still have been a response to Caesar's campaigns.

Walking the site

Trees cover much of the site, particularly on the slopes around the ridge. Despite this the ramparts are obvious and the interior is much less densely covered.

The motte. The medieval motte or mound would have been crowned with a wooden castle keep.

The interior. No more than a scatter of occupation was found in either enclosure; all the sherds and the one coin were of the first century BC. The small enclosure rampart was constructed with an external ditch and a mound rampart with an outer facing of stones. Where the path reaches it and cuts through (not an entrance), massive fissured weatherworn rocks form part of the rampart; they provide the best view across the site.

The Western ramparts. Wheeler's rampart sections demonstrated that the main enclosure was built 4m high using the *murus gallicus* method: a timber frame nailed together, filled with earth (and sand here), faced with rough-cut stones and given a sloping earth backing on the inside. Subsequent excavations elsewhere have confirmed that this rampart type was a late La Tène development (there is a reconstructed version at Mt Beuvray in Burgundy). Outside, a flat space, a low mound and a shallow ditch preceded the wall. The ridge slopes, particularly that to the north-west, are less dramatic than those on the east and outer defences were added up to 30m beyond the main rampart. In the dank wood can be seen an earth bank still 1.5m high with its own external ditch, much of it interspersed with giant granite rocks.

The south-east entrance. Facing a steep gradient outside, this was small-scale, though Wheeler found six post holes in the passage suggesting gate posts and support for a tower above. Burnt material, Wheeler claimed, marked the final collapse in 51BC.

The north-east entrance. Wooden stands make viewing from the rampart easier. This was the main gateway for the hillfort and had a classic inturned passageway formed by the facing wall, before it reached a gate with a tower or bridge over the entrance. The road in and the outer bank defending the gateway area are clear despite dense tree cover on the sharp incline.

LANGON, Ille-et-Vilaine
IGN 1121 E
GPS 30 T 0586327/5285870

Roman building and road.

From Rennes 30km S by N137, then 10km E by D772 to Messac and 12km S by D127/D65.

Chapelle Sainte-Agathe
By Hôtel de Ville

Access: see notice by gate.

This small chapel stands in the centre of Langon village. Its distinctive Roman appearance was recognised early in the nineteenth century, and in 1841 Charles Langlois daringly stripped away two later frescoes (one Romanesque) and found a Roman painting of Venus underneath.

The thick walls are faced with finely cut *petit appareil* and are divided by double brick courses up to about 2m above ground level. Above, the *petit appareil* is mixed with longer schist stonework that may represent a late Roman modification. Venus is shown emerging from the sea, indicated by the plentiful fish and dolphins. The painting is poorly preserved, but a Severan date (193-235) has been proposed.

The chapel fits into a known pattern of converting suitable Roman buildings into churches amongst early medieval Christians. But what kind

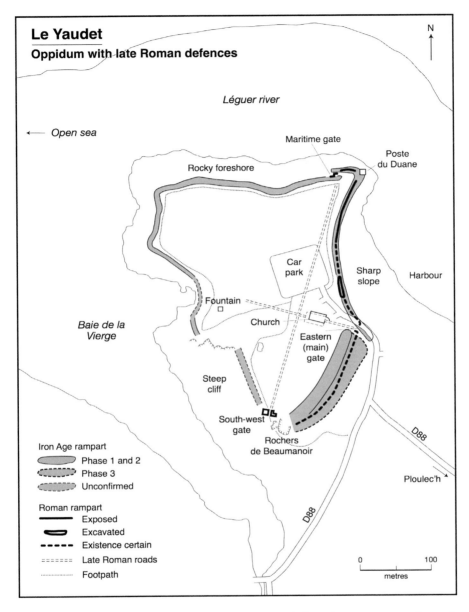

Le Yaudet

Oppidum with late Roman defences

N

Léguer river

← *Open sea*

Maritime gate

Poste du Duane

Rocky foreshore

Car park

Sharp slope

Harbour

Fountain

Baie de la Vierge

Church

Eastern (main) gate

Steep cliff

South-west gate

Rochers de Beaumanoir

D88

Ploulec'h

Iron Age rampart
- Phase 1 and 2
- Phase 3
- Unconfirmed

Roman rampart
- Exposed
- Excavated
- Existence certain
- Late Roman roads
- Footpath

D88

0   100
metres

Coin finds in the eighteenth century suggested that this was an ancient site and by the end of the 1930s traces of rampart had been correctly identified as both Iron Age and Roman. Fleuriot's excavation (1952–4) was confined to the north-east corner but demonstrated that a late Roman gate stood here. The absence of any previous large-scale work, the lack of housing and the obvious potential of the site, inspired a series of campaigns by

Franco-British teams under Patrick Gaillou and Barry Cunliffe (from 1991 into the 2000s). The archaeologists concentrated on gradually expanding zones round the Rochers de Beaumanoir, the church, the north-east and the centre-west of the headland.

Recent work has revealed a significant defended late Bronze Age occupation, which the excavators describe as a 'fortress', but peak occupation came during the late Iron Age, in the hundred years before the end of the last millennium BC. Coin finds suggest the *oppidum* lay within Osismi territory. Pottery and amphorae found here confirm external links: Glastonbury and other south-west British ware show this was a haven for cross-Channel trade, whilst the Léguer river would have enabled trans-shipment from Veneti territory and the Mediterranean. It has recently been proposed that this was *Portus Saliocenus* (a northern Gaul port-of-call mentioned by Ptolemy), a name linking it with salt: if so, it could have been one of the distribution centres for the north-western coastal salterns (see SALT, FISH AND ROMAN COOKING). A rampart, about a kilometre long, following the contours with at least two known gates, proclaimed the *oppidum*'s prosperity. Though using *murus gallicus* technique (as at HUELGOAT), the rampart was not particularly strong and was subsequently reinforced by increasing the height and thickening in vulnerable areas (Phase 2); dating evidence suggests that this was in response to Caesar's assault on the Breton tribes. A massive sloping earth mound, added to the southern wall (Phase 3), is likely to have been associated with one of the later failed risings (50s-20s BC).

During the early Roman period, Le Yaudet appears to have shrunk to little more than a village and minor anchorage. However, the growing insecurity of the mid-third century made exposed places vulnerable. Whilst coastal villas were abandoned, Le Yaudet must have seemed much more attractive both to frightened locals and military planners, equally threatened by pirates, land-based barbarian raiders and rural brigands. The concentration of coins suggests that the move took place in the 260s inspired by regional Gallic emperors. The old defences were used as foundations for a 2m thick stone rampart and new gates. Gaillou and Cunliffe's recent work revealed evidence of both a simple road grid and a cleared rectangular area. Traces of a large building under the church could have been the headquarters (*principia*) of a troop of soldiers; they also identified a series of regular houses by the new roads – the homes of the men? A *phalera*, the metal linkage disc used in a cavalryman's harness, and a military belt buckle hint at the presence of soldiers, though nothing yet to confirm their identity. It is no more than an interesting guess (Pape, 1995) that these could have been British soldier settlers (*limitanei*), brought in to fill both a security need and to make up for a depleted population in Armorica. Whilst the military interpretation of these buildings is the more likely (see ST-MALO), they could represent a civilian remodelling, the rectangular area really being a *forum* with a *basilica*. If that was the case, this may even have been a new *civitas* capital for a three part division of the Osismi; the name Le Yaudet has been intepreted as derived from '*Vetus Civitatem*'.

During the fourth century Le Yaudet did not prosper and when imperial defence collapsed in the fifth century, scrub and woodland began to reappear. By the sixth century, a small number of sub-Roman houses, farmed plots, a cemetery and traces of a cloister point to Le Yaudet becoming a monastic settlement (with a chapel hidden below the current church). It is tempting to see this as part of a wave of British immigrants led, as so often, by a religious leader.

On-site remains are minimal, yet Le Yaudet gives a strong sense of the past. The shape of the ground makes it easy to imagine how it evolved, particularly when the sky is grey, the wind is blowing, and there are few other visitors.

Car park entrance. Between here and the church were both the *oppidum* and the Roman eastern gate, considered the main gate as it led down to the harbour and the road south.

North-east corner. On the slope from the car park on the eastern side, dense gorse covers a long stretch of known Iron Age and Roman rampart remains. Beside the nineteenth century Poste de Duane are visible traces of the Roman maritime gate, a dog-leg design, which gave access to the northern shore.

Western cliffs. In the early 1990s traces of rampart were found here below the fountain. As a spring in Antiquity the latter would have supplied fresh water in the *oppidum*.

Southern corner. Dominated by the Rochers de Beaumanoir, this outcrop formed a bulwark first for the 8m wide Iron Age entrance and then for the new Roman gateway. The slope of the outer side of the rampart was increased artificially by the Phase 3 Iron Age addition, and an inner side slope was levelled for early Roman occupation. In the sub-Roman period this inner area was turned into agricultural plots, though still orientated along the rampart line. The many low stone walls here are post-Roman.

LOCUON, Morbihan
IGN 0718 E
GPS 30 T 0477446/5333249

Gallo-Roman quarry.

From Carhaix-Plouguer, 30km E by N164 to Rostrenen; D790/D23 S to Mellionnec; D76 W and then the turning S for Locuon. On the left at the beginning of the village is a path signposted to Notre Dame de la Fosse (250m) that falls sharply down into the overgrown quarry below the village church (there is also access from here by steep steps).

Locuon. Christianised Roman quarry

This is a romantic place with its canopy of trees, hidden chapel and enclosed spring, but the workings are clearly visible in the steep gullies around the hollow. Roman quarrying is most obvious on either side of the late fifteenth century chapel. On these faces of the rock are the skilful curved v-shaped grooves made by the workers picks. Blocks were removed by creating vertical cuts on either side; a groove was then cut horizontally below, socket holes were dug and wedges driven in, so splitting the block away from the face. The stone is a 'soft' granite, but the use of picks is more usual for genuinely soft limestone. Yvan Maligorne and his colleagues, who investigated the site in 2002, think this suggests that outside quarrymen brought in from elsewhere in the province when Carhaix was replacing its timber brick and clay buildings with stone at the end of the first century. Excavation on the quarry floor produced late first and second century sherds and a workmen's hut. Although 40 Roman miles from Carhaix (perhaps a three day journey for carts using the Carhaix–Vannes road), this quarry, along with others in the vicinity, provided the nearest good quality building stone.

As in other Roman quarries, masons did much of the work on site: it saved on weight for transport. Whilst there was no evidence *petit appareil* was produced here – local sandstone from around Carhaix itself was better for this size – Maligorne found plenty of *grand appareil* including rectangular blocks, column drums, capital bases and coping stones; there were even millstones and some altar rough cuts. Unfinished, unsatisfactory stonework is still scattered around the hollow.

PLESTIN-LES-GRÈVES, Côtes-d'Armor
IGN 0615 ET
GPS 30 U 0453075/5391767

Baths.

Plestin-les-Grèves is halfway between Lannion and Morlaix on the D786. The baths are on the eastern bank of Locquirec bay, 3km N by the D42 and 600m along the Corniche de l'Armorique.

The Hogolo baths

For hundreds of years the impact of erosion in Locquirec bay was benign as sand dunes covered and protected the ruins. Chance helped as well. After the remains were exposed in 1892, only desultory treasure hunting followed; war prevented any follow-up to two short excavations in 1938 and 1940 and then a squatter moved in until 1973. Renewed fears of sea-erosion and the recognition that the site was one of considerable potential led to J.-P. Bardel's work here, at first as a rescue dig in the 1980s, but culminating in full-scale conservation.

Dating evidence indicates the baths began operating in the Augustan era. The structure of the baths and the way they functioned are easily recognised. The proprietor and his guests entered by a door on the west side into the *apodyterium* where they could undress and leave their clothes; once it must have had wooden fittings along the plaster walls. In the *frigidarium* (1) they would first wash their feet, then enter the **cold bath** (2) and sit on the bench under the window. No doubt in the winter months they did not spend long admiring the bath's chessboard floor design in green and black schist – local and imported – or the shell-filled plaster mosaic on the walls. The semi-circular frame of the window, found broken in the bath itself (together with fragments of bluish glass), permitted the modern reconstruction of the upper walling. Water was supplied by an exterior pipe, represented by three iron clamps found in line pointing up hill towards a large spring near the top.

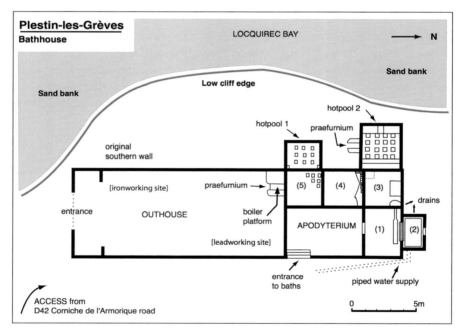

The hot rooms begin with a **vestibule** (3). Once again black schist was used extensively: on the floor alternating with bricks, on the lower walls with limestone plaques and covering a platform against the northern wall. No trace of what stood here has survived, but there would perhaps have been a statue, demonstrating the family's adherence to Roman culture, and of the believable – but with minimal supporting context, such as dates – and the mythical. He describes how the saint came from Wales to Brittany during the early sixth century, landing first on Ouessant, then moved to the mainland and eventually became the first bishop of Léon. He is portrayed always as the Celtic holy man leaving the administration of his diocese (based in St-Pol-de-Léon) to others, then spending his last years once again as the hermit monk on the Île de Batz.

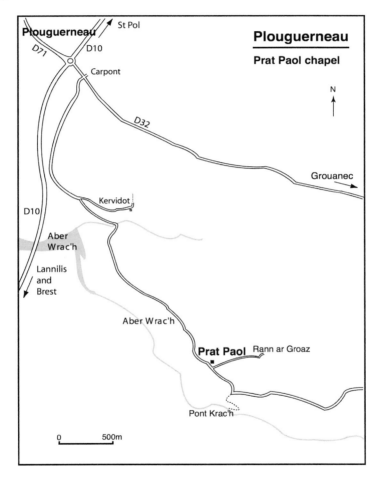

Scraps of evidence suggest that he may have been related to Ambrosius Aurelianus, the Roman-British leader who fought the Anglo-Saxons at Mt Badon and that he is the same Paulinus who came from Wales and lived in Cornwall (where his prestige made him its patron saint) before coming to Brittany. In Wrmonoc's biography, Prat Paol is where St-Pol miraculously severed the head of a dragon, whose body bounced three times before reaching the river and there formed the Krac'h bridge foundations.

Springs rise on the site and would have made this a sacred place in both the Iron Age and Roman periods. Continuity of belief and superstition is embodied in the placing of stele by the main spring, whilst association with the saint would have given Christian approval for continued worship in the sixteenth century chapel.

PLOUHINEC, Morbihan
IGN 0821 T
GPS 30 T 0483798/5279486

Mané Véchen villa

From D781, S to Le Magouër and Barre d'Etel. 400m after the turning for Vieux Passage, and 50m before the church in Le Magouër, take rue de l'École, signposted for Mané Véchen. 250m to parking. Approach site taking right hand coastal path to Le Gueldo Marrec; 100m round headland.

'You may wonder why my Laurentine place is such a joy to me, but once you realise the attractions of the house itself, the amenities of the situation, and its extensive seafront, you will have your answer.' (Pliny the Younger, *Letters*, Book II, 17). Writing at the end of the first century, Pliny expressed the Roman aristocrat's pleasure in having a luxurious 'villa maritima'. He went on to proclaim its modesty, whilst demonstrating just how grand it was. He took considerable pride in the splendid views from his dining room, right on the edge of the shore. Even if Mané Véchen was not quite as palatial as a villa belonging to a consul of the Empire, its owner(s), like other rich people with villas hidden in the twisting estuaries along this Atlantic coast, must have taken equal pleasure in the lapping waves below the windows, the summer peace, the delicate sunlight dancing on the waters of the Etel and the sunsets, whilst *Darioritum* (Vannes), the *civitas* capital, was only two days away using the nearby ferry at Vieux Passage. Surely they were members of the noble elite or people made rich through entrepreneurial activity and able to own both town and country houses. No evidence has so far emerged to identify them.

First noted in 1929, small-scale excavations took place in 1966 and 1970–74 which confirmed that this was a villa with a bathhouse set apart from the main building (see PLESTIN-LES-GRÈVES). When a private developer destroyed the bathhouse remains and unofficial digging produced two jars filled with coins, the State stepped in, bought the promontory and finally funded Alain Provost's major excavation of 2000–10. When the results are fully published undoubtedly they will reveal just how important this villa is to our knowledge of the Breton coast, but its exceptional character is already apparent.

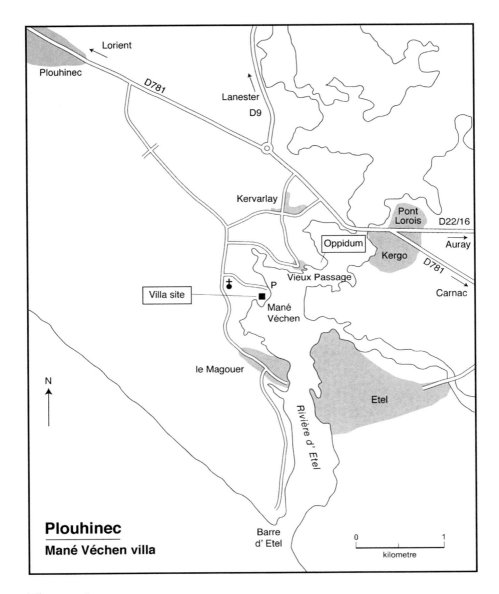

Plouhinec
Mané Véchen villa

The remains

Provost's work has demonstrated that the main house was a Severan villa with three wings around a courtyard. Each wing forms a separate unit not linked by a common portico, making it doubtful there was ever a fourth, eastern wing, even though erosion and quarrying have bitten significantly into both the northern and southern wings.

The western wing has two rooms (AB and R), which must have been grand reception rooms divided by a vestibule, each with *exedras* decorated with painted plaster and stucco; behind them was a secret garden, unique in western Gaul, surrounded by walls estimated at 7–8m high with beds of flowers and shrubs at one end and the imprint of a circular structure at the other. Provost decided the latter enclosed some kind of brazier or perfume-pan, so enhancing the guests' sensual experience. Later additions were the large undecorated storage rooms and square tower (AH) with its air-circulating passage that could have been a silo.

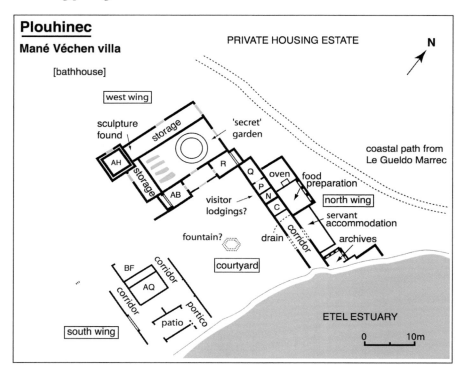

The northern wing has a series of plastered and painted rooms (Q,P,N and C) facing the court followed by a corridor which was originally decorated with more than 20 guinea fowl on the vaulted ceiling. It leads into a group of rooms of which only parts survive. One was recognised as a tablinum (estate archives) or even a library, on the basis of the recessed sections in all the surviving walls where the rolls could have stood. Behind them are three undecorated rooms with earth floors, clearly where the servants/slaves worked and lived.

The southern wing was once believed to have been the family living space, but the most recent work has raised doubts. There is a strangely public building air to it: large rooms, wide corridors, no signs of an upper storey, and an overall symmetry. Room BF, where only the southern and eastern walls survived, has produced superb fragments of painted and stuccoed décor.

Perhaps work in the courtyard and especially in the south-west zone beyond the main buildings may help resolve Provost's uncertainty over what kind of complex this was: simply a rich family's pleasure villa or something else? The warehouse-like storage space remains an enigma, but could the large public rooms, lack of obvious living accommodation (though these rooms could have been beyond the library), small 'guest' rooms and an archive/library be evidence for a *schola*, the meeting place of a guild (*collegium*) – in this case an especially grand and multi-purpose centre for rich, high status, merchants and fish processing factory owners? Whatever the conclusion it is clear that the third century owners saw themselves as part of an Empire-wide elite, able to afford not just expensive décor but also a magnificent limestone relief depicting Ariadne, Dionysus, Eros and two other figures, presented in such pure classical form that it has been called Graeco-Roman not Gallo-Roman.

Plouhinec. Mané Véchen villa: the Ariadne relief in situ. Crédit Megali Thomas

The southern wing was ravaged by fire in the 280s. The owners clearly abandoned the whole house, presumably in terror as the carefully buried coin jars stayed hidden. The buildings were re-used: fires were lit in the middle of rooms, bones and smashed pottery scattered without regard. This was occupation at a level little more than squatting – the discovery of lance points and other military artefacts points to soldiers billeting here. This phase did not last long into the fourth century: Mané-Véchen was quickly to become a forgotten ruin.

Vieux Passage promontory fort
GPS 30 T 0404411/5279876

East of the harbour.

Mortimer Wheeler noted this 1ha enclosure in 1939. A single low rampart and internal ditch, barely recognisable now, cut off the headland. A trial trench on the interior produced first century BC sherds, beads and slingshots.

PLUVIGNER, Morbihan
IGN 0820 E
GPS 30 T 0498634/5289315

Prehistoric farmstead.

Iron Age Talhouët

From Pluvigner, take D768 S for Auray 1.5km to roundabout. Turn E for Kerneur (not Talhouët). The first track northwards after c.350m reaches the signposted site. Parking by a copse of trees and near a grain factory. There are good panels in English as well as French.

Excavated in the 1980s by M. D. Tanguy, the site is well-preserved and consolidated, limiting the impact of the encroaching undergrowth. This homestead consisted of two buildings: the first was rectangular of the third century BC and the second was circular, its enclosure wall resting on that of the earlier homestead; it is unlikely to have been added later than the early second century BC, as all pottery sherds found on the site were middle La Tène. The buildings were protected by a circular wall – probably for keeping farm animals in and wild animals out – which is broken in the south-east by two sixth century burial mounds; the copse contains some smaller ones. The site was abandoned throughout the late Iron Age and the Roman period, but the discovery of a hearth here shows it was re-used for a time in the sixth century AD.

There may have been an earlier settlement nearby or perhaps this site was deliberately chosen next to the burial place of respected ancestors, though nothing is known about them. Only phosphate traces show the shallow graves cut in the bedrock once contained bodies; there were no burial goods. The mounds built over them were carefully marked out and then each was covered with a mass of stones and compacted earth.

St Pierre-Quiberon: Beg en Aud fort

At Kerhostin, take the 'Côte Sauvage' road for Portivy. Through Portivy the road becomes the route du Fozo. There is car parking some 300m short of the fort which is clearly visible in the bare landscape.

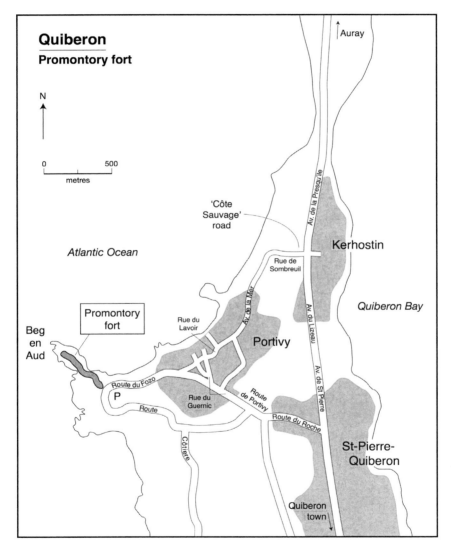

The fort is a classic Breton Iron Age 'cliff castle'. A massive ditch cuts off the end of the Pointe du Perche. It stretches c45m from rocky cliff to cliff, high above the shoreline. The bank behind rises some 5m though, with the slope and deep ditch, this seems much higher; during the Iron Age it must have been a much sharper and an even more daunting barrier. The rampart was dug in 1867 when nails, wood and pottery helped to date it, later finds across the site provided confirmation. The central entrance is modern and Mortimer Wheeler argued (1957) that access must have been along the cliff edges, but we can never know which (or both?) as the steep cliffs are constantly crumbling. They remain dangerous: some fencing and warning signs prevent walking in parts of the site.

What seems clear is that this could not have been a place defended by the Veneti until Roman pressure made them escape in their boats, (Caesar, *BG* III, 12). The rocks, the swell of the Atlantic and the uncertain currents, let alone the crashing waves, would have made it extremely hazardous except on the very mildest of days, something no one being besieged could rely on. Some scholars have even questioned whether the Veneti were using 'cliff castles' at all in this period as forts: was Caesar simply including them in his account to give it greater drama and heighten the impact of his victory?

QUIMPER, Finistère
IGN 0519 ET

Museum and site.

Quimper lies at one of Brittany's natural junction sites. An extended inlet formed by rising sea levels has created the sunken valley of the Odet. Low-lying hills surround the site, 16km from the coast, where the fords (and later bridges) of the coastal road crossed the river and meet a route, used since prehistoric times, linking the northern St-Brieuc region to southern Armorica. A scatter of Iron Age settlements has been identified on these slopes. In the Roman period, this became a significant centre but never a true town, always a place of distinct concentrations of occupation separated by uninhabited areas. Sadly, despite the considerable extent of archaeological work in Quimper since the 1980s, particularly that organised by J.-P. Le Bihan, there are no visible remains. Although the museum has one of the most attractive displays in Brittany, no attempt is made to portray this recent work or explain the Roman heritage.

Musée Départmental Breton
1 rue du Roi Gradlon
29000 Quimper

Hours: June–Sept. 9am–6pm daily
        Oct.–May 9am–noon, 2–5pm closed Mondays and Sunday mornings

In the courtyard there are examples of a domed Iron Age stele and two grooved upright stele found associated with La Tène burials. Inside the museum there are two renovated rooms, dramatically lit, housing Finistère's Roman collection, but there are no recent finds.

Quimper. Probannalec granite stele.
Cliché Musée départmental breton/Padrig Siccard

Plobannalec stele. This 3m high cone 'megalith' is the most striking and unusual exhibit. Found in Plobannalec commune in 1870, it was removed to the local château park and quickly became the 'Menhir de Kernuz' before being transferred here. Its Roman credentials are clear despite the wear on the granite's surface. There are four relief scenes illustrating various Roman gods; one is easily identified. Mercury is depicted with his winged hat, purse and wand or *caduceus*, accompanied by a child, perhaps suggesting his protector role, escorting a soul to the underworld. A **milestone**, its script badly worn, is agreed to be Claudian and is the earliest known in Brittany. It was found 15km away on the NW coast by a Roman road linking Carhaix to Landéda at Kerscao-en-Kernilis, a claimant to be Peutinger's port of *Gesocribate*. The **Jupiter-giant statue**, an 'anguipède', would show the triumph of Jupiter on horseback over a giant if it had not deteriorated so badly that it is only recognisable to experts. It once stood on top of a column. The village of Plouaret has a slightly better example in which the giant is replaced by a siren.

Quimper. The Hercules statue from Douarnenez.
Cliché Musée départmental breton/Padrig Siccard

The statue base with an inscription dedicated to **Neptunus Hippius** and one of the **Hercules** statues from DOUARNENEZ are on display here. Small finds are largely unexceptional and desperately lacking in context; certainly more could be made of the religious artefacts. The miniaturised pottery, representing a libation service, and the white earthenware Venus rising and mother-goddess – made regionally – demonstrate Breton Gallic traditions, whilst the three Egyptian figurines show how the exotic could spread across the Empire, though what meaning they held for anyone is difficult to tell: were they a merchant's charms picked up in Narbonensis?

More interesting is the small **bronze *lar***, found in the 1890s north-west of Carhaix by the Aber Wrac'h road. It must have belonged to a wealthy *paterfamilias*: this represents the guardian spirit of his household and is of course the epitome of Romanisation. Each Roman family would have had its own guardian spirits – *lares* – and a home sanctuary for them, often simply a niche or cupboard, a *lararium*. The *lar* appears to dance with joy, carrying a *patera* for offerings; he would have held a decorative drinking horn or rython in the other hand and stood with a cockerel and bearded snake, all symbols of prosperity and protection for the family. A similar *lar* bronze was found in Corseul and is in the Musée de Bretagne (see RENNES photo).

Perennou baths, near Plomelin

12km S starting by D785 to Ludugris roundabout, then the D20. Pass through Kervilien and bi-pass Plomelin. At Le Lauré turn to Le Perennou.

The baths have been excavated since 2008; the remains survive so well that the site is scheduled for public display. Like PLESTIN-LES-GRÈVES this bath system overlooks an inlet. It has been linked to a nearby villa which is also being excavated.

RENNES, Ille-et-Vilaine
IGN 0218 O

Museum and sites.

The main east–west route from Le Mans to Brest meets the north–south valleys linking the Breton coasts that divide upper and lower Armorica at the Rennes basin. Along with these routes, used since prehistoric times, the Vilaine was navigable in Antiquity southwards from its union with the Ille here. At the actual confluence the rivers crossed marshy ground, but between them rose a low hill, St-Mélaine, which became Roman *Condate*, capital of the Redones tribe. It is likely that this had previously been the

Gallic tribal centre, but Caesar's *Gallic Wars* gives no help and the archaeological evidence is extremely thin.

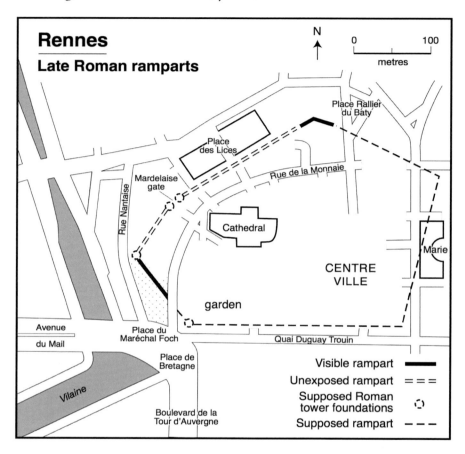

The 1840s marked a critical step forward in local awareness of Rennes' archaeological past. Discoveries made in the newly canalised rivers and in the old ramparts, then being pulled down, stimulated the creation of an archaeological society, and, in particular the work of A. Toulmouche, who researched the exposed river beds, removed and preserved the monumental remains and then wrote the first serious study of Gallo-Roman Rennes (1847). Yet this strong beginning has not resulted in the discovery or preservation of any major sites, apart from some meagre late Roman defences. In part this is due to a great fire in 1722 which destroyed more than a thousand houses and left a thick layer of debris, making the Roman levels especially deep in Rennes. Probably more important has been a determination to preserve both the remaining pre-fire buildings and the attractive eighteenth century city that grew from the ruins. This has restricted archaeological excavation, though with the dramatic modern investment in Brittany's growth, redevelopment in Rennes' centre has brought with it some large-scale rescue digs.

Altars found in the ramparts demonstrated that *Condate* had the standard urban adminstration run by the elite of the *civitas* with both magistrates (*duumvirs*) and priests (*flamen*) of the Imperial Cult. No temples, no theatre and no *forum* have as yet been found in Rennes, though there must have been a temple to Mars Mullo as he is known from inscriptions. Traces of workshops have been identified. One produced white pipeclay Venus statuettes, found widely in Brittany, embossed with a maker's name *Rextugenos*; these were clearly copied, as he was a central Gaul producer. Nineteen milestones found in one part of the rampart, some unfinished, suggest a workshop nearby. Recently, traces have been found of fine houses (*domus*) and a large public baths; there have been hints of an aqueduct.

Four cemeteries have been identified outside Roman *Condate*, suggesting the town spread over 90ha. The late Roman rampart enclosed a mere tenth of that but a major rescue dig in 2004 revealed large-scale late public building using monumental stone, new piping for water supply and freshly made roads *outside* the rampart. This then was not just a strong point or *castrum*, though there was a prefect based here responsible for a troop of *laeti* Franks recorded in the *Notitia Dignitatum*. It is likely that a cathedral was built in the fifth or sixth century, perhaps under St Pierre, as there was an unnamed bishop in the 450s and Bishop Melanus attended a council called by Clovis in 511. This equally confirms that Rennes was under Frank rather than Breton control and remained so during the Merovingian period, despite serious conflict with the emerging Bretons at regular intervals that turned the Rennes basin into a frontier zone or *limes*.

The rampart

The 1200m long rampart has been identified over most of its course. It was constructed by creating a bed of stones and brick fragments compacted in clay; a foundation layer of two courses of massive blocks or re-used monumental pieces (including milestones); and a wall, 3.5–4.0m thick, originally rising at least 6m, with stone facings and an inner core of rubble set in yellow mortar. The exterior facing was *opus mixtum*, first bricks held by a thick pink cement, then a double course of *petit appareil* followed by three courses of bricks, repeated upwards. Fragments found show it had an external geometric decoration made with pale limestone (see Le MANS). Similarities of style suggest it was constructed by a team working their way through the late Roman province of Lugdunensis III fortifying its cities. A milestone of Tetricus (Gallic Emperor 271-3) used in the construction means it must have been later than this. It may have been ordered by Probus (276-282) but the careful workmanship involved supports construction under Diocletian (284-305) or even Constantine (306-327). Two posterns are known, but only medieval main gates have been recognised; these probably stood on Roman predecessors. No late Roman towers have been documented.

Between rue Nantaise and rue de la Monnaie: at the junction of these two streets, in the garden behind the Place Foch. This stretch of rampart at the Roman town's south-west corner is marked by large foundation blocks set on a thick bedding of brick and stone fragments. Above are a few courses of facing bricks.

Passage linking place des Lices and place Rallier du Baty: the rampart survives here up to 3m high and include a small postern gate with lintel and frame made from earlier monumental blocks.

Musée de Bretagne
Les Champs Libres
10, cours des Alliés
35011 Rennes

Hours: Tuesday noon–9pm
Wednesday–Friday noon to 7pm
Saturday–Sunday 2–7pm
Closed Mondays

Since 2006 the museum has been part of a cultural centre 'for all': a striking contemporary building and a multi-media resource, with exhibitions, presentations, debates, films... Unfortunately, the designer's hand is paramount and, for Roman archaeology at least, the new museum marks a step back. Whether consciously or through lack of interest, artefacts are mistakenly presumed to be able to speak for themselves: explanatory panels and labels are frequently placed at some distance from the objects, making identification both difficult and time-consuming, the ultimate example of this being the honorary statue inscriptions and milestones. Here, labels are fixed in the floor, only readable by kneeling. Slick cases are often awkward to look into and one case, where modern and ancient materials are mixed, serves only to make the simplistic point that the use of materials changes over time. With one exception, nothing of the modern excavations carried out in Rennes itself, or elsewhere, is displayed. It is a museum designed by someone with no apparent desire to increase awareness and depth of understanding about Antiquity. With the designer's imprint so heavy it will be difficult to change; let's hope that committed curators will take on the challenge!

Pre-Roman period

The best display is based on the **Paule**–St-Symphorien site, about 12km east of Carhaix, one of the more significant recent Iron Age excavations (1988–95). A video shows the site's evolution through the La Tène period. The existence of farms and hamlets in the region (see PLUVIGNER) has long been known, as have the great enclosures (see HUELGOAT). Despite Caesar's description of Gallic tribal structure as characterised by a warrior elite, it has been difficult to see any reflection of their social status in either kind of settlement. This excavation revealed a 1ha hilltop hamlet with a souterrain, which developed into a much larger centre with a series of timber buildings defended by a massive ditch and ramparts. Finds from inside this 'castle', strengthen the picture of an aristocratic lifestyle: heavy drinking – there were over 300 wine amphorae – and, perhaps Roman influenced, the presence of stone male busts, thought to represent ancestors. One figure is more detailed than others: the **lyre player**. This stone embodiment of a Celtic bard, his neck torc indicating high status, is unique in Western Europe. A display of **Gallic coins** is helped by a magnifying glass, but of course lacks any discussion of their significance.

Roman period

The interface of Gallic and Roman is embodied in the restored large **bronze figurine of 'Brigit'** from Dinéault in Finistère. The swooping crested helmet, crowning a woman's head with a first century AD hairstyle, suggests the Roman Minerva. She is the single goddess in Gaul named by Caesar, yet her portrayal is extremely rare, probably because Caesar was doing no more than indicate the many local goddesses who both protected and sustained. A distinctly rare portrayal of a goose is set below the helmet. Known both for its guard-dog like noisiness and its food potential, it may be reinforcing her roles. Brigit is best known in Irish legend, where her magical skills are stressed and emerge again in the miraculous work of the early Christian saint with the same name.

The clearest evidence for the adoption of Roman religious practice by individuals is the presence here of Roman household gods or *lares*. The fine **bronze dancing figure** from CORSEUL would once have occupied a *lararium*, or shrine, in a fine *domus*. His laurel leaf crown represents an expression of loyalty to the imperial family.

Amongst the general collection of more everyday Gallo-Roman objects are rare candle holders, a folding penknife, a small barrel and wooden spades once used by workers in the tin mines of Abbaretz, 70km south of Rennes. A hoard of silver spoons, bracelets and rings found with 16,000 coins, demonstrates both wealth accumulation and the need to hide it when insecurity became a major problem in the later third century.

The only **honorary statue inscriptions** to survive in Brittany were found in Rennes' late Roman rampart, but no attempt has been made to bring them alive. All five are second century dedications to Mars Mullo, the most widely found Romanised tribal god. They would once have stood outside his temple, no doubt in the *forum*. They tell us how people belonged to a city or *civitas* and also to a *pagus* or sub-tribe within it. Above all, they stress the status of leading men such as T. Flavius Postuminus or L. Campanius Priscus, able to claim and pay for statues and set out all their titles, so perpetuating their personal and family prestige.

The transformation in late Antiquity and the early Middle Ages is barely touched on and the most interesting example of the early Christian world, a stone carved figure of a person with arms outstretched praying, is probably tenth or eleventh century.

Musée des Beaux-Arts
20 quai Emile Zola
35000 Rennes

This contains a collection of Greek, Graeco-Roman and Etruscan material.

Mordelles

14km SW of Rennes by the N24, beside the Allée Gallo-Romain.

Foundations of a *fanum* temple have been preserved next to a basketball pitch on a housing estate. The overgrown outline of a hexagonal *cella* is just visible.

ST-GUYOMARD, Morbihan
IGN 1020 O
GPS 30 T 0536415/5292027

Ossaria.

In the Morbihan mainly away from the coast, over 900 stocky stone pillars have been identified, generally 39–55cm high and 42–45cm in diameter, sometimes with an open 'crown' or ring set on top of the pillar. Many have been found by farms, others in villages; they make attractive flowerpots. First noticed by archaeologists in the 1950s, they were interpreted as rural Gallo-Roman funerary memorials, erected by people isolated from significant settlement, but wealthy enough to be able to afford a local stonemason; some even had simple decoration. Cremated bones were assumed to have been kept in the hollow interior and protected by a lid set on top of the pillar and crown, though only a couple of lids have ever been discovered. There is an absence of datable contexts, the identification being based on comparable monuments found in the Limousin and elsewhere. Outside Brittany, lids are commonplace and the vast majority of *ossaria* have been found in cemeteries.

St-Guyomard. 'Ossaria' in front of Maison Retho

Whilst a 2002 study, *Les Ossaria du Morbihan* (Ce.R.A.A., St Malo), describes all the known examples in the Morbihan and does not doubt their antiquity or function, a 2005 article, *Revue Archéologique de l'Ouest* (22: 221–34), totally rejects this interpretation, seeing them as millet grinders made in the modern era, and thereby explaining why they are found most widely in agricultural settings and also why the lids seem so extremely rare: they were not needed.

There may yet be strong counter arguments for Breton *ossaria* so take the opportunity to examine some yourself at **Maison Retho**. The house stands in the town centre opposite the mairie on the corner of the D139 to Le Cours. Most of this collection (around 25) are pillars, mainly cylindrical, occasionally multi-faced, some refined with a base. The crowns can be simple and undecorated, but some have projections, one where these are shaped into faces, whilst others are no more than handles; a few are dressed to look like capitals. Fortunately, the owner displays a selection of these in front of his house, many sprouting flowers.

ST-MALO, Ille-et-Vilaine
IGN1116ET

Sites, museum and excursion.

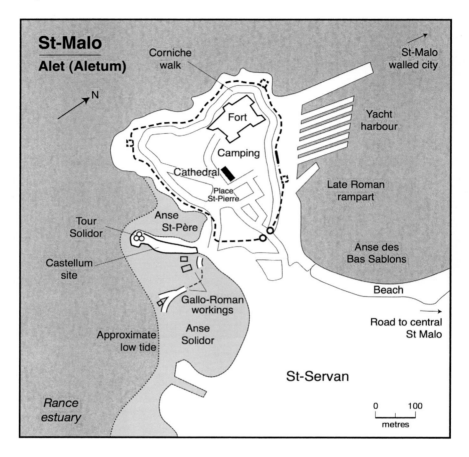

The imposing 'intra-muros' of St-Malo, its walled heart, has a seventeenth century appearance, yet much has been recreated because 80 per cent of the original was destroyed during the second world war. Here you are in a reconstructed shell, peopled by a wandering mass of visitors and a minimum of residents whose livelihoods depend on tourists.

Alet is different. The projecting mass of the Cité d'Aleth (there is no consistent spelling) south-west of the walled city dominates the harbours of St-Malo and guards the estuary of the river Rance. If you walk round the gentle cliff path, where locals come to exercise or dream, past the battered German metal gun turrets and the steep sloping brick walls of the eighteenth century fortress above, it stimulates unforced reflections on the

104

During the early Empire it is clear that Alet was still used, possibly only for provisioning: freshwater supplies were improved by enhancing the Solidor spring with a pumping system. The few houses identified are possibly nothing more than local worker accommodation. Perhaps significantly, it was known as *Reginca*, the Rance's Roman name. It was the internal dislocation and external threats to the Empire of the third and fourth centuries – Saxon and Frank pirates were an increasing problem in the Channel from the later third century – that turned Alet into a major late Roman centre and revived its ancient name *Aletum*. Once again the protection offered by its elevated promontory position became important and it was strengthened by adding 1800m of rampart with towers. Inside, a grid was laid out and the use of imported marble, both from the Pyrenees and the Mediterranean suggests some wealthy inhabitants, though the one hypocaust found was badly made. Pottery and coin finds suggest the 'new' town was occupied from the late third or early fourth century. No doubt many of its new inhabitants came from abandoned Corseul; it is widely believed *Aletum* became the new tribal capital.

Pottery has been found from a variety of sources and indicates that Alet was trading with Bordeaux, eastern Gaul and Britain. But can the latter be linked with possible newcomers? Louis Pape and others, have argued that there was an initial influx of British immigrants under Constantine (306-27) to fill a depopulated countryside and to strengthen the military presence; it could be the black burnished ware from south-west Britain found here came with British troops manning the town's defences. More certainly, the large amounts of Argonne ware, the fourth century version of sigillata, have been associated with the arrival of a legion, the *Martenses*, listed in the *Notitia Dignitatum*. This has been dated to 365–75 when new buildings were constructed in the town including a particularly large structure. Without the known military presence, this would have been seen as a *forum*, though a surprisingly late example, but its excavator Langouët considers this to be a *principia*, a legion's headquarters building.

At the same time, the harbour was fortified with a *castellum* on the rocks of Solidor (the spring was capped). The rising sea level of the period had already helped secure the haven, as it had opened up the sandbank, creating two new harbours, an outer Solidor bay and an inner St-Père, divided by the strongpoint – a role it retained for another thousand years. Yet the *Martenses* troops, their prefect and the command structure including the *dux tractus Armoricani* all disappear in the fifth century. Possibly the troops left to deal with a *Bagaudae* revolt (409) – or joined it – and Alet shrank to a small community squatting in the *principia* and using a corner as a church. The rebirth of the town only occurred in the sixth century during the main wave of British immigrants to Brittany. According to much later saintly lives, 'Maclou' came from Wales to found a religious community on the rocky outcrop that became St-Malo, so attracting fresh settlers to Alet. Once again choosing the *principia* site, these newcomers built a church at the beginning of the seventh century that was to evolve into the Alet cathedral.

Alet
GPS 30 U 0571687/5307618

Roman port installations
Identified by Langouët in the 1970s, these are visible at low tide on the bay shore to the south of the Tour de Solidor. The area then was above sea level and would not have had the worn appearance produced by centuries of tidal flow, but the tracks and basins cut in the rock can still be made out. The wooden pump sections (see diagram), including a massive oak eight cylinder block, were removed from the smaller basin and are now, sadly, hidden away in storage.

St-Malo. The pumping machinery during excavation.
Cliché: Centre Régional d'Archéologie d'Alet

They formed part of a force pump drawing water from a tank at the foot of a channel from the spring. Sailors and locals could fill their buckets, jars and barrels here and then take them down by cart to the boats drawn up on the sandbank, where anchors, net weights and fishhooks were found in underwater archaeological surveys. The larger pool collected water from the spring and supplied the basin. The facilities were in use during the first and second centuries but rising sea levels and then the construction of the *castellum* over the spring and channel put them out of use.

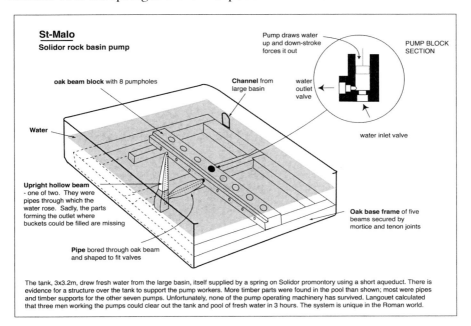

St-Malo
Solidor rock basin pump

Pump draws water up and down-stroke forces it out

PUMP BLOCK SECTION

oak beam block with 8 pumpholes

Channel from large basin

water outlet valve

Water

water inlet valve

Upright hollow beam - one of two. They were pipes through which the water rose. Sadly, the parts forming the outlet where buckets could be filled are missing

Oak base frame of five beams secured by mortice and tenon joints

Pipe bored through oak beam and shaped to fit valves

The tank, 3x3.2m, drew fresh water from the large basin, itself supplied by a spring on Solidor promontory using a short aqueduct. There is evidence for a structure over the tank to support the pump workers. More timber parts were found in the pool than shown; most were pipes and timber supports for the other seven pumps. Unfortunately, none of the pump operating machinery has survived. Langouet calculated that three men working the pumps could clear out the tank and pool of fresh water in 3 hours. The system is unique in the Roman world.

Castellum

Excavations (1980–1) in the Tour Solidor garden forecourt revealed portions of the *castellum* walls and a lean-to hut that must have been one of the barrack houses. It is clear from this that the medieval castle stands on the outermost section of the *castellum*. Elements of Gallo-Roman stonework and tile coursing, forming part of the northern rampart, can be seen in the quay wall leading down to the harbour. Some Gallo-Roman stonework also survives in the base of the tower nearest the harbour.

Principia/early church building

In 1907–8 and again in 1965 excavations were carried out on the early medieval church of St-Pierre, but the crucial work was carried out in the 1970s by Loïc Langouët and his team. The western half of the *principia* was excavated (and the earlier late Roman housing underneath), but it is the cathedral remains on the site that have been consolidated. A column drum and capital, preserved by the altar apse, are believed to come from the *principia*.

Rampart

GPS 30 U 0571847/5387267

Though much of the circuit still stood in the sixteenth century and most has been traced, the only visible section of rampart surviving today lies by the Promenade de la Cornice next to the campsite overlooking the Bas Sablons bay. The worn and weathered stonework, leaning heavily at the start of the slope down to the yacht harbour, shows a length of c.10m of varying height, in clearly coursed *petit appareil*, but without any major distinction between facing and core, 1.5–1.95m wide (thicker at the base), making it only just wide enough for a notional walkway on top of the estimated 3–4m height.

Musée d'Histoire et d'Ethnographie de St-Malo
Esplanade Félicité Lammenais
35408 St-Malo

Hours: 10am–noon, 2–6pm daily. Out of season closed Tuesdays

The fourth floor of the château museum contains the town's tiny archaeological display of Iron Age and Gallo-Roman material.

Centre Régional d'Archéologie d'Alet
Rue de Gaspé
35413 St-Malo

The CeRAA Centre, set up by Langouët, holds a summer exhibition of its archaeological work. There is a library and the Centre can provide guided tours of Alet.

Guernsey excursion
Two hours by daily ferry from St-Malo.

Castle Cornet Maritime Museum
St Peter Port

Hours: end March–end October 10–5pm daily

The museum is well worth visiting for its Roman shipwreck display. The currents and rocks of the Channel Islands made their coasts dangerous, but useful for seaman who knew the waters when gales blew. Guernsey provided the best haven in St Peter Port; an Iron Age settlement developed here into a small Roman town provisioning ships sailing the Channel.

The Roman ship. A video provides good background on the discovery in 1982 by the local scallop diver Richard Keen. As a passionate amateur archaeologist, he recognised Roman pottery sherds when he saw them and reported that the wreck was being destroyed by the new large ferries. Dredging work to create a deeper channel was delayed whilst a team of archaeologists led by Margaret Rule and Jason Monaghan surveyed the wreck. When it was realised how extensive the timbers were (there were

169 major pieces), they were painstakingly raised (1984–5) and then the long-term conservation work began.

Though timbers were 'scattered on the seabed like torn rhubarb' (Rule and Monaghan, 1993, p15), by precisely recording every piece and find before lifting, it was possible to obtain a clear idea of their form and usage, and the techniques used to make them. This was not a sophisticated ship, but though crudely made, it was a practical one. It was a carvel design with oak timbers laid side-by-side, the 'keel' simply three extra large timbers, giving the ship a pretty flat bottom for easy beaching. The hull was held together by cross-timber frames secured by massive nails, hammered through and bent over twice to secure them; wood shaving was used for caulking between the timbers and moss was packed round the nail heads. The 14m keel had stern and bow posts adding another 8m or more, assuming the lost stem section was roughly the same as the stern. A wooden 'step' would have held a single mast, probably rigged with a leather sheet sail. Though the side timbers did not survive to the gunwales, the 6m beam suggests a steep-sided vessel. The excavators believe they have found a typical Armorican design, very like one of those encountered by Caesar at the battle in QUIBERON bay.

The finds. The **pottery** displayed is not cargo but the personal possessions of the three man crew, put together from ports along what must have been their run, from Lusitania (Portugal) to Britannia. The **rotary quern** was for grinding their own wheat which the crew probably stored in a re-used *amphora*. Barrels may have contained stores – or a wine or *garum* cargo. More precious goods might have been salvaged in Antiquity, as the ship went down in shallow waters. The major surviving cargo was pitch, made from pine resin produced on the coast of Aquitania and made into bricks for easy handling. There must have been a major fire on board, melting the **pitch** which in turn destroyed the upper timbers, deck and crews quarters, but, as the pitch hit the water, it spread over the lower timbers, cooling all the time, sealing and preserving them. The nails rapidly corroded away, but their prints were clearly fixed in the pitch. The ship carried spare parts for a **pump**, used to limit water in the bilge: it could not help against fire.

Coins were found in a tight bunch – a crew member's stash? – and the most recent were low value 'barbarous radiate' *antoniniani*. They suggest a date in the late third century. Possibly the ship sank during a raid, or more likely it was an accident, caused perhaps by cooking on board, perhaps a mishap whilst waiting off shore for tides. There is no evidence that the crew failed to escape.

VANNES, Morbihan
IGN 0921 OT

Sites and museum.

The sea on the southern coast of Brittany cuts into the Armorican rocks creating a series of peninsulas and inlets. The two main arms of the Golfe du Morbihan protect its waters from the worst of the Atlantic storms; at their head stands Vannes, deriving its name from the Veneti tribe. As yet, no evidence of pre-Roman Iron Age occupation has been found here, let alone a major *oppidum*, but the location was ideal for Roman needs: a good secure harbour, excellent communications in all directions, and, as the confluence of local riverlets was easily forded, it had potential for growth. The *civitas* capital took the name *Darioritum*, combining *ritum*, meaning ford, with *Dario* perhaps Gallic for 'gurgling', perhaps a Veneti name.

Only the late Roman ramparts have left visible remains and until recently Vannes' archaeological history has not been very impressive. Small-scale excavations and isolated finds during the nineteenth and earlier twentieth centuries gave a hazy picture. Rapid modernisation, characteristic of post-war development, provided little more, as new roads and buildings were driven through with little or no regard for the material heritage. However, during the last 25 years, Patrick André and then Alain Triste have given Vannes a professional archaeological service, discovered the *forum* and significantly deepened understanding of the town's evolution.

Darioritum evolved slowly and never reached great density or size. Current opinion favours an Augustan date for the central grid established in the St-Patern area. It is unlikely that this central area extended very far and the space at the top of Boismoreau hill was only later developed as a *forum*, perhaps under Claudius. Excavations have shown that the sea in Antiquity formed a basin below the ford and that port installations with warehousing and workshops (cloth, leather and pottery) rapidly developed around it. Elsewhere houses and streets were spread thinly over c60ha. Traces of the *forum* were found in the early 1980s, but it was only the 1989–91 rescue digs that confirmed it; unfortunately much of it had been destroyed without record when the Boulevard de la Paix was constructed in the 1960s. Surprisingly, it appears to have been a massively imposing structure (176 x 96.5m) comparable to any north of the Alps. It was abandoned in the later half of the third century. At the end of the 1990s, traces of a theatre (or amphitheatre) were identified and a small *fanum* was excavated in Bilaire, 1.5km north on the road to St Avé; sadly this is now totally overgrown.

Across the Rohan, no doubt soon linked by a timber bridge, Le Méné hill would have had suburban occupation. Here, the low but once sharp slopes made a better site for fortification during the late Roman period. An area of about 5.5ha was enclosed by a rampart c.900m long and 4m thick. This remained the main defence until the fourteenth century when the walls were restored and extended down to the new seafront as the old port area had silted up. This Roman *castrum* was a base for a prefect with a troop of Moorish soldiers under the *Dux Tractus Armoricani*; no doubt a naval squadron operated here as well. Within the walls no late Roman building is known, though it is likely that Paternus, Vannes' first known bishop (450?–470s), had his cathedral here, probably on the site that became the cathedral of St Pierre. Elsewhere, what could be a graffiti *chi-rho* on a fourth century tile has been taken to indicate the site of a cemetery chapel. During the later fifth and much of the sixth centuries Vannes was in the Frank orbit, but as Gregory of Tours reported, it was lost to Waroch, leader of the Bretons, in 578.

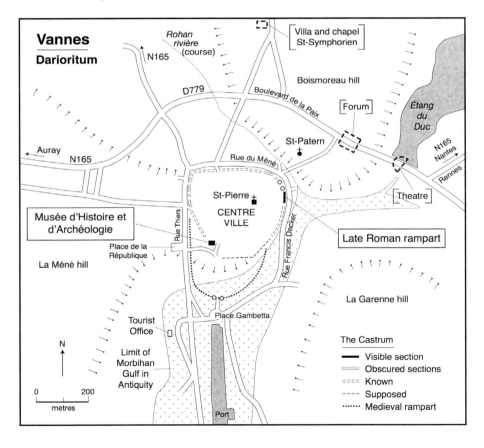

Late Roman rampart
rue Francis Decker

The exterior section of rampart south of the medieval prison gate tower, opposite rue Allain-Legrand, shows very clearly how the fourteenth century construction used the late Roman rampart here. The facing technique is rather different from that at RENNES; the *petit appareil* courses, still visible in lower and upper levels, despite the larger middle-sized stones typical of the late medieval work, are separated by far fewer triple or double brick courses. The late Roman rampart rose at least 7m; the crenellation is medieval but the Roman wall would have had a walkway and U-shaped towers at intervals. Traces of the latter have been found in the medieval tower foundations.

Musée d'Histoire et d'Archéologie
Château Gaillard
2 rue Noë

Hours: Mid-June–30 Sept. 10am–6pm daily
　　　　Oct.–June (school holidays only) 1.30–6pm daily

The Gallo-Roman collection is limited and not representative of work carried out either in Vannes itself or around the Golfe du Morbihan, where the traces of many villas have been found, showing that this was an attractive area for rich and powerful Veneti to live near their capital. All the material is from old excavations and even though objects are numbered only some are given labels. The early Iron Age multiple bronze arm-rings decorated with little balls and the beautiful gold and silver Veneti coins are striking. Another case demonstrates Veneti briquetage and a panel illustrates a rather flimsy looking furnace reconstruction (see SALT, FISH AND ROMAN COOKING). Amongst the bits and pieces representing the region's Roman finds, the most interesting are the seahorse carved schist plaque and the fragments of shell-encrusted painted plaster, survivors from nineteenth century villa excavations.

Arradon
7km SW by D101 and D101A.

Traces of two of the Morbihan's villas are known here; details are available from Arradon tourist office. A small villa bath system has been excavated by the private owner of château Kerran. Le Lodo villa (for site plan see CARNAC museum) has been heavily eroded by the sea, but a small section of stonework still projects by the foreshore path (the rest is under a private garden).

OTHER SITES IN BRITTANY

AURAY, Morbihan
IGN 0821OT

Lomarec Inscription, La Chapelle St-André

1.5km S by D28 towards Crach. La Chapelle St-André is signposted on the left.

On the north interior face of the trapezoidal coffin by the altar is an inscription recently dated on stylistic grounds to the fifth or sixth century. The letters are deeply incised and clear IRHAEMA★I·N·R·I·. Making sense of them is not easy: they could be in Latin or neo-Brittonic (early Breton). Unfortunately neo-Brittonic makes too many assumptions about how the language might have evolved. Even as Latin it is not obvious. Possibly 'Haema' was a person, as such a name is attested in the fifth century. Translated and expanded it would be 'Here lies Haema (buried) on the Ides of November, he retreated in peace'. If, however, the inscriber knew the newly available Vulgate, HAEMA becomes blood, and INRI the standard but late contraction for Jesus. It then reads 'Jesus of Nazareth, King of the Jews pours forth blood'. In Brittany, inscriptions from late Antiquity are rare, compressed and complex, but they show how people were striving to retain ways of expressing themselves in literate form as the old traditions broke down and new languages emerged.

BAUD, Morbihan
IGN 0820 E

Venus of Quinipily

Signposted in Baud. 1.75km SW by D724 for Tenuel, on left.

This curiosity is hard to resist. A 2.2m high granite goddess perched on a pedestal, placed above a classically embellished pool, set in a beautiful garden. Apparently associated with a Gallo-Roman site at Castennec where local peasants saw it as an embodiment of fertility, the statue was saved from a bishop's wrath by the seventeenth century owner of Quinipily château. Certainly old, with thin arms across her body, she is reminiscent of white pipeclay Venus statuettes, but the loin cloth and hairstyle suggest Egypt. Some scholars argued for an Isis cult link, others for a tenth century date. Current opinion considers the statue ancient, but 'improved' over time.

PLUMERGAT, Morbihan
IGN 0820 E

Iron Age stele with Gaulish inscription

By parish church, 20km NW of Vannes by D779 and D308.

The church is surrounded by Iron Age hemispherical stele. Most important though is a squat granite upright dressed in octagonal sections. It was probably moved here in the early medieval period and has two inscriptions and an equi-armed cross. The vertical inscription down one side has been relatively well preserved though it is difficult to read. The word RIMOETE means 'of Rimoeta' and is considered likely to date from seventh to tenth century – when the cross was probably cut. Another older inscription has six lines on the upper part, heavily weathered. Deciphering has been difficult and interpretation has changed; the most recent work considers this to be fourth century and written not in early Breton but in Gaulish. It remains utterly obscure.

Plumergat. Stele with Gaulish inscription

PENMARC'H, Finistére
IGN 0519 OT

Musée Préhistorique Finistérien

33kms W of Quimper by D53 close to Pors-Carn beach.

Taken over some years ago from a local society as a study outpost for
Rennes University I, the museum is generally only open in the summer
months. It contains some Gallo-Roman material, but is best visited for its
Iron Age metalwork and ceramics. The interesting Dark Age burials from
St-Urnel (Plomeur) have been reconstructed here. Even when the
museum is closed, a range of domed and upright Breton stele are on
display in front of the building alongside Neolithic megaliths.

SALT, FISH AND ROMAN COOKING

'A civilised life is impossible without salt' (Pliny writing in the AD60s, *NH* XXXI, 87). Salt has always been essential to human life. It can be directly consumed from raw or roasted meat, but where a diet largely consists of cereals and vegetables, then salt needs to be added. Whilst about six grams a day (2 kilos a year) is sufficient, we generally eat rather more with the associated risks to our health. Of course we do this because salt highlights and enlivens the taste of food. It was the same in Antiquity, but then as today there were more uses for salt than simply as a flavouring. While Cato and Columella writing on agriculture point to some uses for salt, it is the polymath Pliny more than any other Roman writer, who makes clear the range of needs that it fulfilled (*NH*, XXXI, 72–98).

Salt played a major part in Roman medicine. Doctors used it in the treatment of sciatica, jaundice and dropsy; it was part of the mix applied to dogbites and snakebites, sores and boils, and – an Empire-wide problem – eye disorders: Pliny specifically mentions its value for cataracts (*NH*, XXXI, 98). Salt was a significant ingredient in the preparation of many remedies and certainly the antiseptic properties in salt will have helped. Pliny went further: 'for the whole of the body nothing is more beneficial than salt and sun', a sentiment echoed in the nineteenth and twentieth centuries by advocates of sea bathing. Salt was also used in the preparation of cosmetics and perfumes. Equally it had industrial applications: tanners found it helped to make skins malleable in manufacturing leather whilst dye makers added it to various colour preparations.

Without doubt salt's prime importance lay with food. For the malnourished poor, it would give sharpness to their regular diet drawn from cereals and vegetables, such as lentil or bean broth mopped up with coarse bread. It would heighten the flavour of meat. Its relative rarity would have made the distribution of meat after sanctuary sacrifices particularly attractive (see LE MANS). Pork was popular and many classical writers noted how both pigs and wild boars had featured as the main feasting meat amongst the western Celts. In reality significantly less pork was consumed in Roman Gaul than central Italy where a recent bone study put pig derived meats at 65%, compared with less than 40% in Lugdunensis. Here bone studies show that during the first and second centuries, cattle were increasingly bred for meat and over 50% of all meat eaten was beef. There was also the occasional fowl or fish to be seasoned. Palladius, a late Roman Gallic landowner, noted 'There is no housewife who does not know how to keep hens' (*Agriculturae*, 1.XXVII.1) and the cockerel statuettes found on many sites point to their presence as well. Ausonius, the fourth century Gallic poet, is lyrical about the numbers of men and boys out with their rods and nets by the Moselle (*Mosella*, 240–75), while Athenaeus – quoting Posidonius – mentions 'Celts who live by rivers and by the Mediterranean and Atlantic also eat fish which they bake with salt vinegar and cumin' (*Suda*, 4.1512–2a).

Fresh meats and fish become inedible within days, yet can remain palatable if dried, even more so if smoked, but by far the most widely used technique for preserving them was to apply salt. Even cheese, in all its many varieties across the classical world, needed salt when it was not being consumed immediately, and this was particularly true for the long lasting harder cheeses. Salting meat must have been as widespread in western Gaul as it had been for centuries in Italy, where of course ham, bacon and sausages were especially prized: as Martial wrote in the first century AD, 'Let gourmets wolf on ham!' (*Epigrams*, 13.54). All kinds of meat would have been salted to satisfy the Gallic farmers' own winter needs for protein and to sell the surplus in local and regional markets. Indeed, building on Gaul's reputation for feasting on meat and Italy's appetite for smoked ham, even the Menapii of northern Gaul sent their hams to Rome, though no salted pork specialities from the west are detailed by Roman writers.

Salting also dramatically extended the consumption of fish and fish-derived products. Where large shoals of migratory fish spent extended periods of time near the shoreline, fisherman were able to create major industries that flourished in the first and second centuries. In the Black Sea, along the African coasts of Tunisia and Morocco, in western Spain and southern Portugal and along the south-western coast of Armorica the presence of numerous deep plaster-lined basins indicate the many factories devoted to fish processing (see DOUARNENEZ). Tuna and mackerel were the most popular Mediterranean salted fish, but in the Atlantic sardine was just as important. Equally valuable to the producers were the fish sauces and pastes that could be made from the innards of large fish or from pulverised small fish like sardine; these were essential ingredients in Roman cooking and so a requirement wherever there were people who thought of themselves as Roman.

Garum was the crème de la crème of sauce ingredients, adding salt, aroma and taste to any fish, meat or vegetable dish. There were subtle differences between producers and regions, depending on fermentation time, the type of fish, the amount of salt added, even the amount of heat applied and any additions such as other fish or selected herbs; almost all variants commanded high prices. Cooks would select the *garum*, or *liquamen* as it was known in the later Empire, which they needed for their many compound sauces; gourmets would prize the high quality *garum sociorum*, a dark pungent *garum* made from mackerel's blood. *Muria*, was a thinner – and slightly cheaper – product, often added as a condiment. Evidence for them is found on sites all over the Empire. A tablet from Vindolanda fort on Hadrian's Wall records food issued to officers: it included one and a half pints of *muria*.

Iron Age salt production in Western Gaul

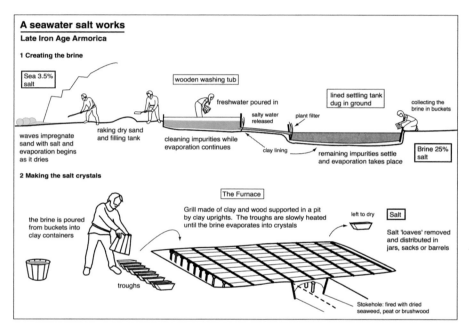

Salt can be obtained directly by mining rock salt or by refining it from naturally occurring brine derived from springs, in concentrations that can reach up to 30 per cent. In Gaul, brine springs in the Seille district of Lorraine were exploited from early times. Salt can also be produced from seawater, where the salinity averages 3.5–3.7 per cent. In the Mediterranean, the hot summers made it possible to collect salt from shallow coastal marshes where the sun could evaporate the water leaving a bed of salt crystals: the Languedoc was famous for its salt 'pans'. On the Atlantic and Channel coasts this was not possible and evaporation had to be assisted. A typical site would use an inlet or shoreline that tended to slow the retreat of tides, so encouraging the deposit of salt.

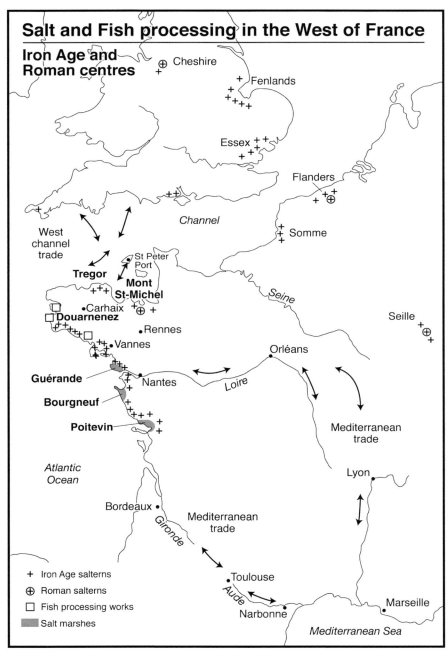

Salt and Fish processing in the West of France

Iron Age and Roman centres

Cheshire

Fenlands

Essex

Flanders

Channel

Somme

West channel trade

St Peter Port

Tregor

Mont St-Michel

•Carhaix

Douarnenez

•Rennes

Seine

Seille

•Vannes

Orléans

Guérande

•Nantes

Loire

Bourgneuf

Poitevin

Mediterranean trade

Atlantic Ocean

Lyon

Bordeaux •

Gironde

Mediterranean trade

+ Iron Age salterns

⊕ Roman salterns

☐ Fish processing works

▨ Salt marshes

•Toulouse

Aude

Marseille

Narbonne

Mediterranean Sea

Manufacturing was in two main stages. Initially, the workers needed to make brine, that is water with a 25 per cent concentration of salt. This would then be slowly heated in a furnace until the water evaporated leaving a crystallised loaf of salt. 'Briquetage' is the word used by archaeologists – both French and English – to describe the roughly fired clay remains excavated at these sites. These largely derive from the second stage of production as the first involved only the most basic structures. The last 40 years have seen considerable progress in making sense of these traditionally puzzling fragments, mixing as they do bits of the rough pottery containers and the furnace framework. Archaeologists such as Nicolas Rouzeau in the Pays de la Loire and Marie-Yvane Daire in Brittany have been able to identify distinct differences in technique, both geographic and chronological. The most widely found technique has been the Armorican or 'Veneti' method. There were strong concentrations in the Morbihan, Guérande and Prigny areas, ending beyond Bourgneuf bay. Furnaces were constructed by digging a rectangular pit that could be filled with a mass of slow burning material. A grid made of clay and sticks covered the pit and each segment would hold a trough with sloping sides. As the brine evaporated, more was added until the troughs were filled with crystallised salt. In the southern Vendée, the 'Pictones' method was characterised by a more complicated furnace briquetage. Shallow ditches in the ground were filled with lines of clay pillars topped with short triangular posts, held in place by T-shaped bricks and the mass of combustible material, generally fragmented charcoal pieces. On top were set the crystallising troughs kept in place by wedges of clay (see the museums in CARNAC, GUÉRANDE PENINSULA and NANTES).

Between Mont St-Michel and the mouth of the Loire, more than 150 pre-Roman coastal salt works or salterns had been identified by the year 2000, the vast majority of them dating to the second and first centuries BC; many more have been identified further south as far as the Charente and east along the Channel shores into Normandy.

Salt works were largely short-term and the activity must always have been seasonal: only the summer's sun provided enough heat for evaporation and the high tides to deposit significant amounts of salt. Farming or fishing must have supported these workers the rest of the year. A British study of fingerprints left on the briquetage suggests it was made by women, implying, at the least, that work at the salterns was shared between the sexes, perhaps based on families specialising in this activity. By the late La Tène there are signs that some salterns were well established within coastal communities. Daire (2003) goes further. She argues that the similarities of workplace organisation and technology means that around the Mont St-Michel bay, on the Trégor coast (Côte d'Armor) and in the Morbihan gulf, salterns could have operated cooperatively in order to provide salt for more than their immediate neighbours and for the two major processed food makers: farmers who specialised in hog meat and fishing communities who wanted to sell fish inland. It is even possible that the Roman Republican trade coming up the Gironde, took, in return for its wine amphorae, barrels of salt as well as ingots of tin.

The salt industry and integration in the Roman world

Demand for salt must have risen with the integration of Gaul into the Roman Empire. The country may have taken many years to recover from the destruction and killing of the Gallic wars, but during the first and second centuries AD the population certainly rose. The absence of tribal conflict, secure sea routes, organised river carriage and the new road system would have made the new *civitas* capitals, the many small towns, the new noble estates and smaller farms far more accessible to the salt producers. Yet, despite increased demand, the majority of these Atlantic and western Channel Iron Age sites seem to have ceased functioning. Occasionally a briquetage site has been radiocarbon-dated to the first century AD, though because such dating is not precise some of these too,could have gone out of use before then. Nor has any tangible evidence emerged, despite archaeological research, to demonstrate that the Atlantic coastal marshes were either fully formed or that people had learnt to adapt techniques used in the Mediterranean to exploit them in the much harsher climatic conditions. Where then did western Roman Gaul get its salt?

The case for outside suppliers

One possibility is that other centres exported to the region. The Mediterranean producers, exploiting their rich and extensive salt marshes, especially in Italy, saw a considerable expansion in their activities during the early Empire; Italian merchants had dominated Gallic long distance commerce before the conquest; it would not be surprising if salt traders now joined their colleagues. Alternatively, salt could have been imported from Britain and Flanders. British research work has shown there were major producers both in the east of the country, where hundreds of salterns have been identified, and in Cheshire, exploiting the brine springs of Middlewich and Nantwich. Belgian and French work has revealed major centres on the Flemish and Somme coasts. However, tracing salt trade routes is in its infancy. Salt leaves minimal traces: whilst the Roman wine and olive trades can be identified through amphorae, jars used for salt were unlabelled, though distribution patterns may eventually be traced through salt corrosion patterns on interior jar faces and by identifying suitable jar shapes for carriage on ships or carts. Even then, much salt will have been transported as loaves wrapped in sacking or carried loose in barrels, the evidence vanishing, eaten or decomposed.

Perhaps the costs of production were significantly lower elsewhere, making it economic to import salt. In addition the State claimed a monopoly and could have favoured suppliers from other regions. Imperial procurators, for a fee or share of the profits, would have contracted out to businessmen willing to invest, much as in mining enterprises. There are hints of an imperial estate in the Fens and suggestions for state control in Cheshire; two inscriptions found in Rimini name an imperial official responsible for administering salt works in Flanders (CIL, XI, 390–391). No record of state involvement in western Gaul has been found.

The case for continued local salt production

However, there is evidence that western Gaul *did* produce salt in the Roman period, though perhaps in more limited quantities and in different ways. Daire's research on the north coast of Brittany led her to identify at least one large Roman salt works spread over 30ha at Hirel, by the Mont St-Michel bay. It alone could have processed as much salt as all the Iron Age salterns in the area; it operated throughout the first three centuries AD. Other abrupt transitions from artisan to concentrated industrial organisation could have taken place elsewhere and have simply not been identified yet. They are the kind of salt works that would have been favoured by imperial officialdom.

The most likely area for Roman salt making must be close to the fish processing installations of the second century AD, particularly the many around DOUARNENEZ bay, but also elsewhere on the south coast of Brittany, such as Lanester on the Blavet river, where salmon, mullet and eel were caught and preserved. Suitable inlets and beaches for salt making were close by and transfer to the fish processing vats should have been easy. Why then have so few possible sites been identified? Whilst it may be because fish processors had to work within an imperial monopoly favouring external salt producers (or because they simply had close links with Italian *salarii*), it could simply be that the sites have not been recognised. Archaeologists have excavated the fish processing vats and their immediate surroundings, but did not search for the salt works or noted only that there was no briquetage.

Sanquer and Gaillou suggested, as long ago as 1972, that the technology could have changed 150 years after the end of Iron Age salt making. They pointed to the use of bricks and cement for furnaces and lead or tin replacing the clay receptacles. In Britain and Flanders lead did replace the clay troughs and new kinds of furnaces were being used. Though rare,

Roman lead pans are present in Cheshire. A German study suggested that one salt works with an 800 year history (Lüneburg) must have used over 340,000 lead pans, yet only one has survived, the implication being that the lead was easily melted down and recycled. Their absence from the Armorican and Atlantic sites could simply be their minimal survival chances. Another factor also has to be taken into account: rising sea levels and erosion. Villas like Mané Véchen (see PLOUHINEC), where a third of the villa has been eroded away, demonstrate how the sea can destroy remains. At Douarnenez, the cliff on which Plomarc'h Pella stands has been seriously undercut; if there was a salt works on the beach below in Roman times it could have been washed away long ago.

A final possibility is that in the districts where the salt marshes evolved, Roman salt workers were active. It is interesting, that the three sites of Langon (Poitevin), Prigny (Bourgneuf) and Clis (Guérande) are all interpreted as small Roman ports in the midst of what had been major districts for Iron Age briquetage operations. Two possibilities suggest themselves: first, there were early Roman salt works using sea salt, now hidden by the marshland; and second, as the marshland grew during the late Roman period, modified Mediterranean techniques were applied to dry and remove the growing salt content. The case for such an evolution has been presented most strongly in the GUÉRANDE PENINSULA area.

Most likely, the western coasts continued to produce salt locally, perhaps even meeting the majority of its needs, but also imported salt from other provinces. In the future archaeologists should be able to demonstrate at least something about distribution routes, undertake new survey work of fish processing sites in the vicinity and extend their research into early marshland history.

ROMAN COOKING AND THE ROLE OF SAUCES

The Roman kitchen in Gaul

Almost any museum with Gallo-Roman material displays a ubiquitous selection from the *batterie de cuisine*, which seem to merit hardly a second glance in their mock-up kitchens with scattered, somewhat dusty artificial foodstuffs. It takes a leap of the imagination to place the pots and pans in their rightful context of a hot, clattering, bustling kitchen. There would be *mortaria*, the heavy clay bowls with a pouring lip, often with grit baked into the bottom to facilitate grinding. These were first exported to the Roman army in Britain in the first century AD, many with a Gallic potter's name, Q. Valerius Veranius, impressed on their rims. The chefs would have needed *pila*, similar to present day small mortars, and a range of oven-to-tableware terracotta dishes, referred to as *patellae* and *patinae* in Apicius (see below). A variety of metal saucepans, casseroles, colanders, straining ladles and skillets were practical and familiar in the labour-intensive preparation of food. Meat carcasses had to be butchered and chopped, poultry plucked and jointed, ovens and fires prepared for slow or rapid methods of cooking and smoking. The poor of course continued to do without a kitchen, using their hearth and the widely found cooking pots to make their broth.

Eating

Food was puréed or ready-sliced into bite-sized pieces which could be picked up with the fingers or soaked up with bread. Knives were of course available when necessary. Spoons (but not forks) are known in bronze and silver, some pointed at the end, allowing meat to be spiked; cheap versions would have been available in wood. Whilst the poorest might eat communally from the cooking pot, the better-off would have provided specialised tableware such as sigillata, whilst the elite used silver plate.

Apicius and Roman cookery

The *De re coquinaria* is an extraordinary compilation of some 500 recipes, gathered together in the later fourth or early fifth centuries AD under the name of Apicius, a renowned chef perhaps living in the mid-first century AD, whose name later became synonymous with any gourmet. The language used is simple and straightforward and was most likely written by chefs and for chefs. These are not recipes for the beginner: they are scarcely recipes at all, in the sense of having detailed weights and measures (which are rare) and instructions for cooking times, but rather are lists of ingredients. Presumably the experienced chef would be expected to know how best to assemble and cook these according to the tastes of the household. This is not food for the poor. The Apician recipes cater for those cooking for the well-off and their guests; those who could afford the lifestyle of a fine mosaic-floored *triclinium* such as that from the Lillebonne villa (see ROUEN museum). At this end of the social spectrum there could be wealth-flaunting delicacies – so despised by Pliny – such as parrot, flamingo and larks' tongues, but many of the other recipes appeal more to taste than ostentatious display.

Sauces

The fact that over 400 of the 500 Apician recipes deal with sauce-making reflects what a vital component this was considered in Roman cuisine: the sauce was the heart of the dish and enhanced any meat, fish or vegetables.

THE SITES OF NORMANDY

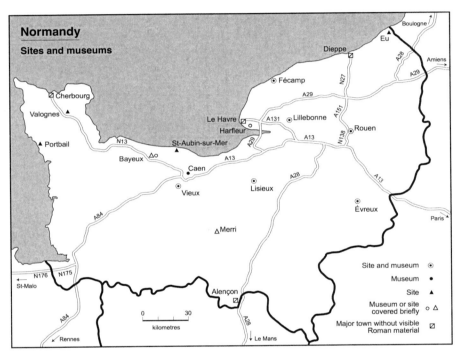

Map 3

CAEN, Calvados
IGN1612OT

Musée de Normandie
Château ducal
Logis des Gouverneurs
14000 Caen

Hours: 1 June–30 Sept. 9.30am–6pm
1 Oct.–31 May 9.30am–6pm closed Tuesdays

Caen itself was a medieval foundation and Gallo-Roman finds here have been rare, but the museum, whilst in no way being representative of Normandy as a whole, does bring together material from some interesting sites. The first four rooms are archaeological.

The late first century AD seated **mother-goddess** is a rare and majestic figure rescued from a well during the second world war (see ST-AUBIN-SUR-MER). This serene goddess is maternal and protecting, with a child by each knee (sadly without heads). Once she would have held a symbol of abundance: a horn of plenty or bowl overflowing with fruit.

A model of the sanctuary at **Baron-sur-Odon** is based on excavations in the 1950s and again in 1969–71. Its extensive polygonal enclosure, reconstructed as a double gallery around a sacred area, and the many surrounding annexes, make the design both unusual and extensive. The site was probably already significant enough to the Viducasses tribe to lead them to choose to build their capital, *Aregenua* (VIEUX) 2.5km away. Beside the model there is a small collection of offerings found at Baron. The bronze rings are mid-first century AD, the white pipeclay figurines second and third century. These include a cockerel, associated with Mercury, a god of abundance in Gaul; a smiling baby; and Venus, in various guises ranging from nubile to mother-goddess. All suggest that worshippers came to Baron seeking well-being and fertility.

The **Giberville bronze tripod**, decorated with claw feet and female heads, embodies luxury living: it would have supported a small table or bowl in a villa reception room. It contrasts with the collection of ironwork, very much the tools of daily rural life. A more personal hint of the people themselves comes in the relief of two men out fishing from a boat and in their footwear, where there are examples of both studded leather soles and wooden pattens. The two small rooms dedicated to the late Roman and Merovingian period embrace a collection of Frankish glass, jewellery and particularly weaponry, enhanced by the **'warrior-blacksmith' burial**, recreated on the floor with his mass of metalwork. One of the major

Bois l'Abbé

The presence of a significant Roman settlement was strikingly demonstrated in 1780 when road builders came upon beautifully inscribed limestone blocks recording the dedication of a *duumvir* funding the embellishment of a theatre. Following a number of nineteenth century digs (legal and illegal), Michel Manard carried out the first systematic excavations in the 1960s and from 1994 onwards a team led by Laurent Cholet has undertaken a major programme of research.

Luckily for the visitor, one aim is conservation and presentation for the public. Current work is focused on the sanctuary. The theatre, obvious despite the vegetation, has had limited sondages in the main body and on the stage area. Sadly, one of the two known baths, although fully excavated, remains closed to visitors. A longer term purpose is to identify other structures in the 30ha zone where Roman traces have been found and even beyond this. Was there pre-Roman occupation here? Was this simply a sanctuary exploited by a small tribe, the Catuslogi, at the juncture of two larger tribes, the Ambiani and Caleti, building on a Gallic tradition for border religious meeting places? Was it a small town with roads, houses and workshops? Or was there a centre in the Bresle valley below the plateau, making a 'bipolar' town with its commercial functions based on the river and road communications there?

The sanctuary

So far there is no evidence that this was a pre-Roman temple site. Gallic-style ritual deposits have been found implying that this was indeed a sacred place, but including bags of coins mixing Gallic tribal coins and Julio-Claudian Roman types; Manard guessed that these might represent offerings from returning auxiliaries who had served in the Roman army.

The creation of a Roman sanctuary began in the late Flavian era when a double wall enclosure was built, named the '*sacellum*' (a shrine) by the excavators. A long and wide **gallery with a large square room** was soon added behind and parallel to the *sacellum*, soon modified by the addition of a *fanum*, apparently joining the *sacellum* and the rear buildings. In the mid-second century, a small temple was constructed in the heart of the sanctuary, only to be replaced in the Severan era by a **grand temple** with a massive central *cella* on a 1.5m high podium with a gallery on three sides and approached by a vestibule. The old *sacellum* had been flattened, but the *fanum* and large room remained standing, now linked by a much narrower apsed gallery. Completion of the work here is sure to expand and modify our understanding of the sanctuary's development.

The enclosure

This banked area c.200m to the south-west, was traditionally seen as a Roman marching camp, but a 1996 sondage disproved this. It could have been a meeting place for pilgrims and/or inhabitants, such as that known on Mt Beuvray (Burgundy).

The theatre

200m to the east, but not quite on the same axis, a theatre was built at the same time as the *sacellum*. It was an unsophisticated affair, using the natural incline of the hillside to minimise building work on the seating area (*cavea*), itself made of rubble, its finishing touches provided by rough cut flint, timber and daub; it had wooden seating and a simple stage. After a fire at the end of the second century, it was replaced by a larger and much more professionally constructed theatre. In the south-west corner, to contain the thrust, internal half circle walls broke up the rubble and external buttressing was added. Two tiers of seating (*maeniana*) were created with a passage between them. The seating must have been accessed by vaulted entrances (*vomitoria*), though little more than suspected gaps imply their existence. This theatre could have held at least 5000 people. In front of the stage building (partially protected by a modern shelter) stand five massive blocks that once supported columns and a wooden pediment that would have held the *duumvir*'s dedication. The lack of any evidence for a platform implies that the orchestra area was used for religious ceremony rather than theatrical performances.

The baths

During the later 1990s two sets of baths were discovered. The larger covered some 4500m² and has so far been explored only with sondages. The smaller was particularly well preserved. It was a simple in-line system, but with a dry sweating room (a *sudatorium*) as well as a wet hot room or *caldarium*. There was a small porticoed garden instead of the usual exercise yard and large numbers of pins and ornaments were found, suggesting this set of baths is likely to have been exclusively for women.

Across the Bois l'Abbé site there was destruction and some abandonment in the late third century, but pottery finds point to continued occupation and use in some places even into the fifth century. Whilst the roots of trees will have damaged the ruins they are not as destructive as modern city foundations or deep ploughing: this is a place with considerable potential.

ÉVREUX, Eure
IGN2013O

Major sites and museum.

Some places demonstrate more sharply than others fundamental issues faced by archaeology. The conflict between current human needs and the desire to retain our past is a perennial dilemma; the struggle to give meaning to the past is another, especially when there is a complete absence of written sources. 'L'Affaire Évreux' highlighted the first with stark clarity: should an exceptionally rich Roman public baths, revealed in a 1993 rescue dig, be preserved for all to see, or should a new hospital maternity wing be given priority? Le Vieil Évreux, 6km east of modern Évreux, epitomises the second: identified as one of the largest Roman sanctuaries known in Gaul, it remains a major enigma, despite research going back two centuries.

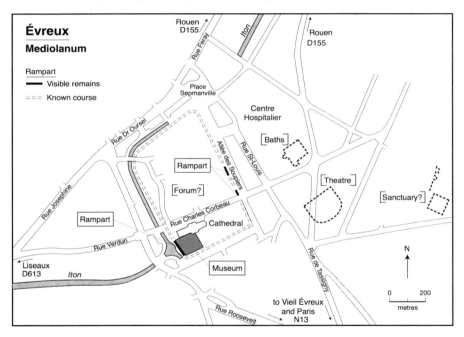

Modern archaeological work has significantly increased our knowledge of Évreux's Roman past. It was at a crossroads for routes linking the Paris basin and Chartres plain with both upper and lower Normandy; the river Iton joins the navigable Eure and Seine here, and the surrounding land allowed mixed farming in the alluvial valley and on the plateau. There was a small settlement here before the conquest. The local tribe, the Aulerci Eburovices, though mentioned by Caesar, had not been a leading tribe in the Gallic wars and no pre-Roman *oppidum* has been identified with them.

Mediolanum's grid was laid out in Augustan times, then modified under Claudius when there was an upsurge in building. Gravel and then paved streets were laid, porticoed with both timber and stone columns. The rue de la Harpe excavations (1989) showed wealthy houses with wall painting, finely paved courtyards and fountains. An aqueduct is likely though there were many wells. *Mediolanum* was a production centre for metals and cloth (indicated by a fuller's inscription). To the east of the town there was a large theatre with a capacity of over 6000, and a *forum* has been identified by the rue de la Petite Cité. Yet the town never covered more than 40ha.

The public baths found in 1993 were second century, richly decorated and equipped with two large cold basins in the *frigidarium*, two separate *caldaria*, a dry sweat room, and, instead of an open *palaestra* for exercise, an inside gallery around a porticoed swimming pool. And their fate? Following passionate debate in both the local and national press a 'compromise' was reached. Évreux mothers have their babies in modern facilities, the excavated remains are covered with sand and the hospital foundations have been constructed around them. I must admit to siding with those who regret that no other site could be found for the maternity wing: at the very least, no one in my generation will see this part of everyone's heritage.

There is evidence that the town began to contract before the mid-third century and that the destruction levels of the later third century were especially extensive: it is no surprise only 9ha were enclosed by the late Roman rampart. The enclosed area follows a playing card design, similar to that of Lisieux; the 1981 Palais épiscopal and rue de la Petite Cité excavations revealed its construction methods. No towers or gates are known but the river may have been diverted to form a moat. There is little evidence of occupation continuing outside the rampart. The 1990 cathedral excavation failed to show evidence of a late or sub-Roman church, but a hexagonal Roman fountain basin found here has been interpreted as being re-used for a font in a sixth century baptistery.

Rampart remains

Allée des Soupiers. An 8m stretch cut across by the rue Charles Corbeau is largely mortar and rubble core. North along the Allée a further low stretch with outer facing stones reaching the first brick course joins the modern walling.

Iton basin. Retained as part of the Palais épiscopal wall, this 6m high section overlooks the pool created between the rue Charles Corbeau and the rue de la Harpe. The finely cut outer *petit appareil* and the brick courses have survived; large block foundations are equally apparent.

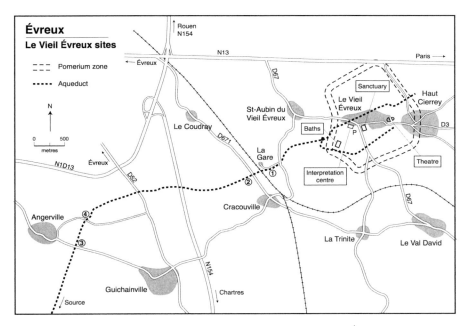

François Rever, antiquarian and professor at the new École Centrale in Évreux, was the first to examine seriously the evidence for ancient ruins at le Vieil Évreux. During the Napoleonic era between 1801 and 1804, bringing his students to dig for him, he recorded many remains in and around the village, later producing a *Mémoire* of his discoveries illustrated with engravings (1827). Others were stimulated to explore further. Most important was Rever's ex-student, Théodose Bonnin, whose writings and especially plans (1835-42) formed the basis for all subsequent work until the 1970s. Yet Bonin's plans for all their detail, were often found by later excavators, such as Emile Espérandieu (1912 to 1914), to be erroneous and even included whole buildings for which there was no evidence. A new start was needed.

A group of concerned local archaeologists set up Archeo 27 in 1973 to put this in hand. Modern techniques were applied to the baths site and in 1976 Roger Agache, who had already revolutionised knowledge of ancient settlement in the Somme, was called in. His and Archeo 27's own aerial photography and follow-up sondages produced a far more accurate picture of the known structures, some chronology, and an entirely unexpected feature, a habitation pattern unlike any known elsewhere in Gaul. Their initiative culminated in the decision (1994) to make le Vieil Évreux the Eure's prime example of Roman heritage with an on-site centre to co-ordinate a major programme of excavation, research and presentation.

A sanctuary stood on the southern edge of the modern village. No evidence has been found for a Gallic predecessor; finds suggest that the earliest remains were Augustan. It must have grown significantly during the first century – better dating evidence will clarify this as current excavation results are published. North-east of the sanctuary a settlement developed with a road grid and a large stone structure, suggesting a public building of some kind – popularly named a *forum*.

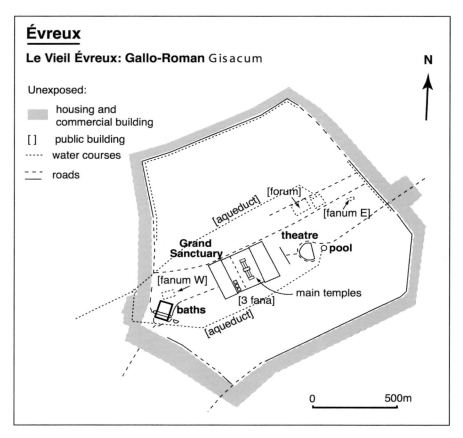

Under Trajan a dramatic transformation took place: an irregular polygonal 230ha zone was created by constructing a road and water course around the sanctuary forming a boundary or *pomerium* to a sacred zone. The settlement was flattened, though the public building was retained and expanded. Domestic habitation was transferred to the exterior of the polygon, with buildings of various sizes but constructed with standard façades and porticos looking inwards across the boundary. A theatre was erected and an aqueduct built bringing water from springs 20km away to supply not only the needs of a baths complex, but also various water features and the most important houses in the south-west corner of *Gisacum*. The monumental scale of the site culminated under Severus with the Grand Sanctuary, its temples, enclosures and portico spread over 8ha. The baths and their *palaestra* covered almost another hectare.

The sanctuary itself was expanded into a grandiose expression of status with at least three enclosures. If Bonin's plans prove correct, the three *fana* (now covered by the village sports centre) were probably superseded by the massive new complex and its three temples. In the west, near the baths, was another *fanum* and near the eastern edge of the zone yet another. Which gods were worshipped here? An inscription '[A]ug[ustus] deo Gisaco' (CIL XIII 3197), is one of two mentioning Gisacus, a local god certainly, but identified on the basis of the crowned statue found here, as an embodiment of Apollo. Another god must have been Jupiter, on the basis of the bronze statue found here, but no other deities are known at the time of writing.

Understanding *Gisacum* is much more difficult! The scale suggests that this was not a sanctuary dedicated only to gods of particular value to the Aulerci Eburovici tribe; after all, Baron-sur-Odon, seen as the main sanctuary of the Viducasses, an equally small Normandy *civitas*, covered just 4ha (see VIEUX) and in Brittany the Curiosolites' sanctuary, the apparently massive Haut-Bécherel, fills just one hectare (see CORSEUL). Was it then a famous healing sanctuary perhaps attracting pilgrims from around the Roman world? A massive sacred area, the presence of Apollo and extensive water network make suggestive comparisons with Grand in eastern France, a place once visited by Constantine. Yet the zone enclosed here by the *pomerium* is over twice the size of that at Grand.

Another approach has been to focus on the extensive evidence of habitation here. The old theory that the sanctuary was the original tribal capital and was replaced by Évreux with its more logical communications links has been ruled out by the discovery that the two settlements existed in parallel. Could *Gisacum* have been a summer capital? But why would such a small tribe do something that seems so exceptional in Gaul, and even more curious, how could they have afforded such a massive investment? Was there imperial involvement? A last puzzle: how do we explain the existence at Cracouville, only 2 km away, of a further sanctuary with a large *fanum* and annexes (no longer exposed)?

Undoubtedly as work proceeds, the accumulation of well-dated and better identified structures will increase understanding, but inevitably also generate new questions.

Centre d'Interprétation Archéologique
rue des Thermes

As its name implies this is not a museum. The artefacts displayed are disappointingly few: fragments of décor from the Grand Sanctuary, typical small finds from the public baths – pins, board game counters and rings – and some domestic artefacts including a rotary quern and a thimble. There are wall panels, photographs and large models to explain the main sites. The effect is functional but surprisingly dull; worst of all, the display lacks any clear indication of where things are in relation to the modern surroundings.

Jardin Archéologique: the baths
5 minutes walk from the car park.

Since Bonnin's day, the baths have always been the best-known site at le Vieil Évreux and the re-excavation of the eastern half of the central bath system by P Rossel (1973–8) made this the obvious choice for public presentation. More excavations were carried out on the main block 1996–8 and non-invasive techniques, for example geophysical surveys, were applied to the rest of the site.

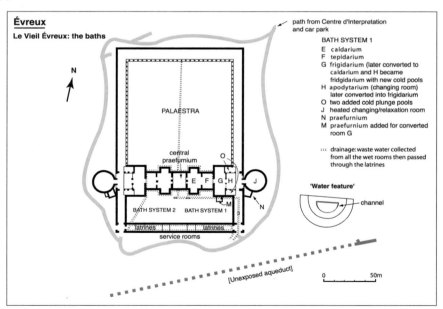

Évreux
Le Vieil Évreux: the baths

path from Centre d'Interpretation and car park

BATH SYSTEM 1
E caldarium
F tepidarium
G frigidarium (later converted to caldarium and H became fridgidarium with new cold pools
H apodytarium (changing room) later converted into frigidarium
O two added cold plunge pools
J heated changing/relaxation room
N praefurnium
M praefurnium added for converted room G

::: drainage: waste water collected from all the wet rooms then passed through the latrines

'Water feature'
channel

N

PALAESTRA

central praefurnium

O

E F G H J

M
N

BATH SYSTEM 2   BATH SYSTEM 1

latrines   latrines
service rooms

[Unexposed aqueduct]

0   50m

The exposed remains were then sealed with 'geotextile', floors were covered over and finally walls and hypocausts were reconstructed 30cm above the preserved originals. The western half of the central system has been completely sealed under a representation of the rooms; the portico is

142

rectangular cut stones; they are some 2m thick and still rise 3–4m. The interior is paved with marble and the walls are plastered. Outside, there is a line of large grooved blocks – which perhaps held wooden frames – and a low wall beside a pathway. One of the curved buttress walls is re-emerging along the line of temples. Further discoveries are likely to lead to significant re-interpretation of the remains.

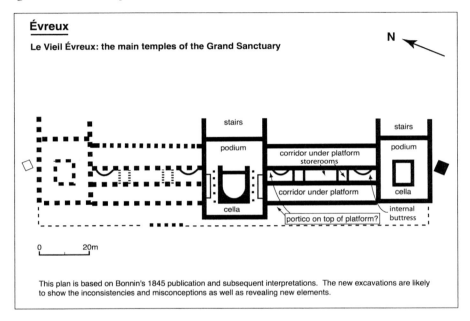

Évreux

N

Le Vieil Évreux: the main temples of the Grand Sanctuary

stairs

podium

stairs

podium

corridor under platform
storerooms

corridor under platform

cella

cella

internal
buttress

portico on top of platform?

0   20m

This plan is based on Bonnin's 1845 publication and subsequent interpretations. The new excavations are likely to show the inconsistencies and misconceptions as well as revealing new elements.

Theatre
GPS 31 U 0370993/5429506

500m from car park, turn left, then immediate right towards Haut Cierrey. The theatre is on the left.

The grass covered *cavea* (seating area) is still obvious. Looking from where the small stage building once stood, on the right two thick masses of masonry that supported the seating are exposed. The theatre perhaps held 7500 people. It has not been excavated since Bonnin's time, when his cursory look resulted in the mistaken reconstruction straightening the sides (Rever got the horseshoe shape right) and inserting seven *vomitaria*. Certainly there was at least one at the rear centre, allowing those taking part in any ceremony to enter the orchestra directly from the grand sanctuary. The theatre was in use during the second and third centuries. The southern branch of the aqueduct ended in a pool behind the stage, now a charming pond with reeds and willow trees.

Aqueduct

The aqueduct traces noted by archaeologists are no longer as clear as one would like, despite an 'aqueduct circuit' signposted for cyclists, which lacks any panels at points of interest. The following numbers are marked on the map above. (1) By the road down to La Gare in the final 100m before the road turns to the hamlet, there are occasional rubble core remains of the channel, frequently overgrown. Passing through Cracouville, take the D671 towards Évreux. At (2), the channel embankment is clear crossing the fields west of the road coming from La Gare. Returning to Cracouville, take the road to Guichainville, crossing the D52 for Angerville; more aqueduct channel embankment is visible 1.5km after Guchainville (3) and again (4) by turning right at the T junction and coming back towards the east and the D52.

FÉCAMP, Seine-Maritime
IGN 1809 OT

Hillfort and museum.

Camp du Canada
GPS 31 U 0313593/5513333

3km from the town centre by rue G. Couturier to roundabout then take D926 SE towards Yvetot. The road climbs, skirting the eastern flank of the hillfort; c1200m from the roundabout, there is a track up into the *oppidum* by a parking pull-in.

The Camp du Canada promontory was created in the Caux chalk plateau by the Valmont river valley to the north, the Ganzeville tributary to the west and a torrent in the now dry ravine to the east; a narrow segment in the south-east links it to the main plateau. Its height, outlook, and implicit security attracted occupation from the Neolithic onwards and during the later Iron Age lay in the territory of the Caleti tribe. This site more than any other in France, except perhaps Camp d'Artus (see HUELGOAT), is associated with the great British archaeologist Mortimer Wheeler. His 1938 and 1939 expeditions to Normandy and Brittany provided the foundation for all subsequent analysis of fortified *oppida*.

Wheeler's excavations here established that the defences represented a particular form found east of the Seine amongst the tribes referred to by Caesar as Belgae. The Fécamp type is always on a high, steep promontory overlooking a river or the sea - both in the case of Camp du Canada. They are separated from the rest of the plateau by a huge rampart, simply made of rubble and earth largely drawn from a wide flattish ditch, and often have one or two more much smaller banks and ditches. Finally the main entrance is built with interned arms lined with a stone border and a wooden gateway that would have allowed a parapet structure above. The Wheeler expeditions identified 16 'Fécamp' *oppida*; the term is still used today.

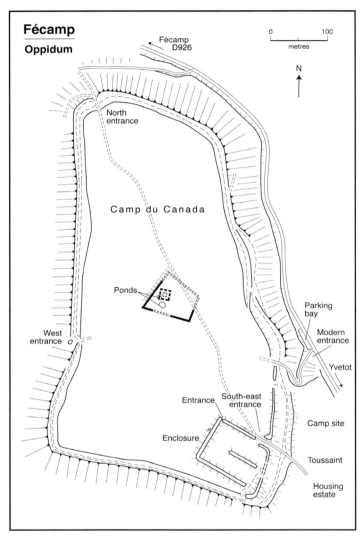

Of course more recent work, here and elsewhere, has modified and expanded Mortimer Wheeler's summary – but not by much. Monique Remy-Watté's excavations in the late 1980s showed that the stone borders were in fact full-scale facings and that these might have been used more widely; similarly Wheeler missed the evidence for the use of tree trunks to stabilise the dump material, however, clearly these were never used in the intensive, coherent way of *murus gallicus*. Wooden gateways, marked by the post holes found by Wheeler in the south-east entrance, are now seen as not simply supporting parapets but towers. Remy-Watté confirmed that the occupation in the south-east corner was largely post-conquest to mid-first century AD (as was the possible *fanum* he noted in the central enclosure). This date supports Wheeler's contention that the ramparts were a late Iron Age work and that there had been little time to create a settlement within; the obvious context is Julius Caesar's invasion, the wide ditches being designed to keep Roman siege equipment back.

Visiting

Though the path up from the D926 is steep, it is the easiest to find. The plateau slopes are tree covered, but much of the interior of the *oppidum* is grass and ferns. It is straightforward to cross to the **pools** (modern), where the *fanum* enclosure is just visible. In the south-east corner, the **enclosure banks**, identified by Remy-Watté, are more evident; she excavated a number of huts here. Were these the homes of early Caleti collaborators modelling their inner enclosure on the camp design used by Roman military auxiliaries found at other 'Fécamp'-type sites, such as la Chaussée-Tirancourt (in nearby Somme)?

The south-east entrance (GPS 31 U 0313431/5513175): guarding the most vulnerable side, the scale of the ramparts is striking, reaching heights over 5m. A modern track enters the *oppidum* by the old passageway. Outside, the trees fail to hide the dramatic slope up from the ditch base and the smaller external banking is still apparent. A path at the foot of the ditch takes you back to the parking place.

Musée Centre-des-Arts
21, rue Alexandre Legros
76400 Fécamp

Displays include finds made at the *oppidum*. Fécamp was an important Roman port, but finds are still mainly from the large cemetery found near Fécamp and excavated by Abbé Cochet in 1852. The collection includes moulded pipeclay models, a hipposandal and an attractive bronze bowl and tripod. Perhaps most interesting is still the fourth century burial found by Cochet in 1872. The grave of a young girl, perhaps with a Frank background, produced a fine trumpet fibula, a long decorated silver pin, a Rhineland glass goblet and a silver gilded bronze bowl.

town contained a large villa with its own baths, but also traces of the road grid and first century timber and cob housing. The building of the new Hôtel de Ville, allowed Follain to re-explore the Roman walling first noted in 1821 and reveal the foundations of a large peristyle house here.

Like many other cities, Lillebonne experienced both decay and damage during the third century, but without re-emerging as a new administrative and religious centre in the late Roman and early medieval periods. The lack of new building under the Severans suggests that the city had supported its opponents too long, a mistake it perhaps repeated at the end of the century in its loyalty to Carinus (283-5), a bitter foe of Diocletian, and shortly after its support for the rebel fleet commander Carausius (286–93). Equally, the gradual rise in sea levels may have undermined the city's harbour facilities and it was also vulnerable to Channel piracy; serious fire damage noted in the town may well be the result of the documented barbarian raids into Gaul. Lillebonne was fortified (in the early fourth century), but the rampart took in only 1.5ha of the higher ground and turned the theatre into a massive strongpoint with its entrances blocked off.

This decline in public life, symbolised by the house built within the theatre's arena, is confirmed by the city's loss of status. The more secure centre of Rouen became the diocesan capital for both State and religion, ensuring that Lillebonne never recovered its regional role. If the purely stylistic dating for Lillebonne's finest mosaic, known for its hunting scenes (see ROUEN) is correct, and it is fourth century, then possibly some wealthy citizens maintained houses outside the ramparts, but the majority must have left for their estates or transferred to Rouen.

The Theatre
Place Félix Faure

There is a good general view of the theatre from the Place. At the time of writing only approved groups could go on site and these had to be arranged in advance through the Musée des Antiquités in Rouen or the Musée de Lillebonne.

The theatre was recognised as such in the eighteenth century and intrusive trees, bushes, huts and houses began to be cleared. Archaeological exploration began in 1812 and gradually replaced ransacking for stone, though study tailed off in the later nineteenth century. In the 1930s Albert Grenier, the author of the Gallo-Roman sections of Déchelette's *Manuel d'Archéologie*, did three seasons' work here. More recently, Eric Follain has sorted out some confusion over the position of the stage building.

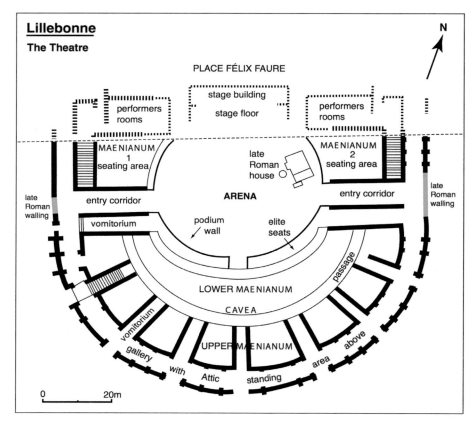

Lillebonne

The Theatre

N

PLACE FÉLIX FAURE

stage building

performers rooms

stage floor

performers rooms

MAENIANUM 1 seating area

late Roman house

MAENIANUM 2 seating area

late Roman walling

entry corridor

ARENA

entry corridor

late Roman walling

vomitorium

podium wall

elite seats

passage

LOWER MAENIANUM

CAVEA

vomitorium

UPPER MAENIANUM

area above

gallery

with Attic standing

0   20m

The original theatre was built in the middle of the first century. Some authors, including Grenier, have argued that this structure was not a theatre, but an amphitheatre and that only in the second century did it become a theatre-amphitheatre. Others, such as Provost, are convinced that this was the design from the beginning, typical of the Gallic mix (and British – as at St Albans). The variations in the precise terminology for these mixed theatres, depending on the size and shape of the arena-orchestra, the *cavea* and the stage building, led Provost, amongst others, to focus on function, seeing them as centres of 'spectacle' with a range of activities. Certainly this is what it became when reconstructed in monumental stone during the second half of the second century. Prior to Follain's work the new seating – *maenianum* north 1 and 2 – had been confused with the stage building, but this is now recognised to be entirely under the Place Félix Faure. When the most recent work is published, it should provide a picture of how this centre of 'spectacles' operated.

Fountain base

Jardin Jean Rostand

By the Jardin gate beside the Place Félix Faure, are the re-sited foundations of the fountain found in the rue Pigoreau next to the Alincourt baths. This plinth supported upright slabs set in the inner grooves forming a basin 4.75m by 1.56m where people could come and fill their jars. Traces of red mortar show that it had been made watertight. A pipe would have filled the basin at the rectangular end and the overflow would have fallen into a gutter taking the water into a channel set in from the edge and then into the wheel-design drain, which in turn fed the water into the baths' sewers.

Forum

Place Sadi-Carnot

The decision to renovate and pedestrianise the town square allowed Follain to prove that the monumental stonework found previously did indeed belong to a *forum*. Despite both destruction by fire and removal of stone for rampart construction, it was possible to identify a road and the distinctive foundations of a surrounding *forum* precinct with three of its rooms, probably shops. They have been restored in outline as a decorative feature with a re-erected column, dedicated to Carinus. It is unreadable, not the result of time, but deliberate defacing – a sign of damnation by order of the victorious Diocletian (284–305). It may even have been deliberately set up in the *forum* as a warning to the town.

Musée Municipal

Place Félix Faure

Hours: May–Oct. 10am–noon, 2–6pm daily
         Nov.–April 2–6pm closed Tuesdays

'Lillebonne au temps des Gallo-Romains' constitutes the ground floor exhibits in the old Hôtel de Ville. The display is modern but uninspired. There are a few architectural pieces from the theatre, and, despite being incomplete, the Dionysic faun, seahorse and dolphins are good Roman relief work. There are also some fragments of the mosaics that once decorated the Alincourt baths. A fine original bronze lamp hangs from its chain in a display largely of bronze copies (the originals are in ROUEN).

The most interesting exhibit is the rich and eclectic collection from **1864 tomb**, found by Abbé Cochet near the lycée villa site. The lead coffin held a glass jar containing the ashes, but was accompanied by more than the usual food and drink offerings. Amongst them are a glass perfume phial, dolphin-shaped in a rich deep black with a gilded tail, resting on its fins; a finely made bronze jug in the shape of an adolescent youth that would have contained exercise oils; and a handsome oval silver bowl with edging reliefs of isolated temples, animals and plants. Most enigmatic is the massive wide knife with its fragmented ivory handle.

LISIEUX, Calvados
IGN 1712 E

Sites and museum.

The Armorican Lexovii tribe are assumed to have had their main *oppidum* at the massive Camp du Castellier, 3km south-west of Lisieux, and it was from here that they were tempted out only to be destroyed by Caesar's general Sabinus in 56BC. However, there was already Iron Age occupation by the Orbiquet at its junction with the Touques, and the rivers would have provided a link with the sea; this became the urban centre of *Noviomagus* and late Roman *Lexovios*.

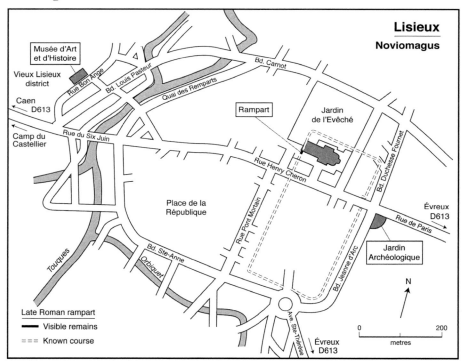

Relatively little is known of the Roman town. Established under Augustus, it perhaps grew to about 20ha during the second century. Traces of an amphitheatre/theatre along with a healing sanctuary survived in Vieux Lisieux until the eighteenth century, but the only public building known in

Lisieux itself is a bath complex. Wharves were constructed on the Touques, and scraps of road and porticoed pavements are known. Wells supplied most water though there is evidence for an open channel aqueduct. Workshops engaged in making metal and bone artefacts have been found in the late Roman cemetery site of Michelet, by rue Guilloneau. The usual pattern of major fires in the third century was followed by the construction of a rampart enclosing 8ha, half the size of Rouen. Little is known of either late Roman or sub-Roman Lisieux and no bishop has been identified earlier than 538.

Jardin Archéologique
Corner of boulevard Jeanne d'Arc and rue de Paris.

The construction of the Centre Hospitalier in 1967 revealed major remains in this area, but it was not a period friendly to archaeological research. In 1978–82, Claude Lemaître examined the zone between the hospital and the roads. The excavation revealed two substantial houses had been constructed at the end of the first century on either side of a secondary *cardo*. In the final years of the second century the northern house was rebuilt as a public baths with separate men's and women's facilities, whilst the southern house was modernised with a heated room and new decoration. During the third century the house was deliberately dismantled and the public baths were destroyed by fire.

The buildings' walls are recreated with hedges and the road using gravel: it is not very inspiring, though panels help in understanding the site. Ten tonnes of painted plaster recovered from collapsed walls and ceilings have been painstakingly restored and are now displayed in the museum.

Rampart fragment
Exterior south tower of the cathedral.

A tiny section of foundation walling projects from the tower. It is only about 1.5m high and little more than 2m thick.

Road fragment
Mediathèque de Lisieux
Place de la République

A short paved section of the Roman road to Vieux (*Aregenua*) survives here. An incomplete memorial was found nearby. Inscribed IA PROC HERMADION, it is believed to be dedicated to a procurator of Greek origin.

Musée d'Art et d'Histoire ("du Vieux Lisieux")

38 boulevard Louis Pasteur
14100 Lisieux

Hours: 2–6pm closed Tuesdays

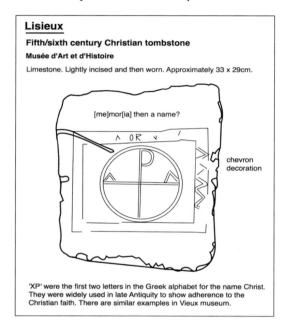

Lisieux

Fifth/sixth century Christian tombstone

Musée d'Art et d'Histoire

Limestone. Lightly incised and then worn. Approximately 33 x 29cm.

[me]mor[ia] then a name?

∧ OR ∨

chevron decoration

'XP' were the first two letters in the Greek alphabet for the name Christ. They were widely used in late Antiquity to show adherence to the Christian faith. There are similar examples in Vieux museum.

The beautiful half-timbered building contains a small Gallo-Roman display with some exceptional restored wall paintings. Much of the collection comes from the two cemeteries. Most interesting of the early Roman finds are the pipeclay models of animals and birds. From the late Roman fourth and fifth century burials, come delicate glass goblets and a lead coffin decorated with three vine-covered busts, its small size showing that it was for a child. Amazingly long pins made of silver, some with gilded bronze, were used by women to support their hair styles. They are considered German in style and hint at the unromanised families of soldiers recruited from outside the Empire (see THE DEFENCE OF WESTERN ROMAN GAUL). A tombstone records an early Christian burial.

The **wall paintings** all come from the Jardin Archéologique. Putting the fragments together took years of intensive work. The fish decorated the late first century southern house, but the others are all Severan. The white painted plaster delicately patterned with garlands and floral patterns come from a corridor and small room in the house and from the vaulted ceiling of the women's *caldarium*: perhaps the leading citizen who paid for the baths conversion also owned the house. The most impressive decoration recovered comes from the *tepidarium* walls. Two strongly outlined and delicately shaded faces are very well preserved, one with a laurel leaf crown. It is believed that there were once nine of these muses.

PORTBAIL, Manche
IGN 1211 OT
GPS 30 U 0594490/5465604

Early Christian baptistery.

On W coast of Cotentin peninsula, 46km N of Coutances. D15 to lower town centre, signposted 'Le baptistère' N on rue Lechevalier. 150m after the mairie by the basketball court.

Early Christian baptisteries are extremely rare is northern France and even more so outside a cathedral city. The rural masses only became widely Christianised by the eighth century and only then were parish priests taking on the role of giving the sacrament of baptism. Yet Michel de Boüard, the original excavator (1956), plumped for a sub-Roman sixth century date, though 'avec beaucoup de réserve'. However, his case seems strong.

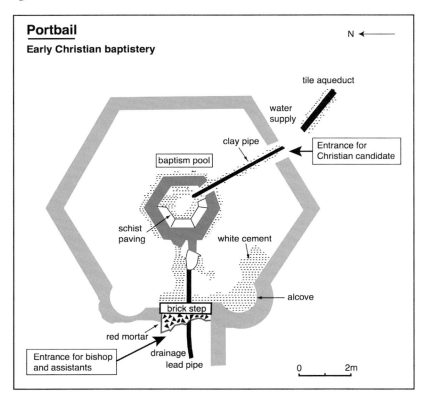

The external wall and the baptism pool are hexagonal, a typical shape for both late Roman and early medieval periods, but the bricks, tiles and mortars, the pool's schist paving and the clay pipe and the aqueduct supplying water, all reflect Roman rather than Merovingian techniques. The pool could be part of a pre-Christian building, subsequently converted for baptism (see ÉVREUX), though no evidence for such a structure has been identified.

Why then was it built here in such a relatively isolated spot? It could have formed part of an early monastery, the missionary role of monks was of major significance in the conversion of western France, but there is no real evidence for this. Hints at another answer come from the early episcopal history of the Cotentin peninsula. Portbail was in the diocese of Coutances or *Constantia*. According to the *Notitia Dignitatum*, *Constantia* was a late Roman base for a prefect in charge of *tractus Armoricani* troops and a centre for *laeti* or soldier settlers, yet it has barely any evidence of occupation in either the late or sub-Roman period. Whilst there could have been an episcopal organisation for the diocese in the fourth century, the first named bishops are in the sixth century, the most eminent being Lauto, who was active in Church councils in the 530s and 540s and later better known for his missionary zeal as St Lô. Interestingly he is described as bishop of *Constantia* and *Breviorum*, a small town to be later named after the saint. Perhaps one way to make sense of this evidence is that there was no real urban centre in the diocese; for a bishop lacking a firm base, Portbail's baptistery could have been built where the bishop perceived the most need for converting pagans.

Baptism in a society where many were still pagans was an adult experience, a decisive step – indeed the only step – by which the convert could be forgiven his past sins and enter the Christian world. The holy sacrament of being bathed in flowing water, recalled the Jordan river. The candidate at Portbail entered the baptistery from the small south-east door undressed and approached the pool. The bishop waited opposite, probably under a canopy, on each side of him stood assistants using the alcoves for altar tables and the holy oils with which the convert was covered before plunging into the water. The bishop would question the candidate on the tenets of faith and then anoint him or her with more oil; finally the assistants would help the purified Christian to dress in a white garment symbolic of his/her new status.

Guernsey excursion

Sailings once a week from Carteret (9km north); three a week from Dielette (32km north). For site details see ST-MALO.

ROUEN, Seine-Maritime

IGN 1911 ET

Museum.

During the last decade of the twentieth century Rouen became a leading centre for urban archaeological research where numerous excavations have been carried out by teams of archaeologists. It marks a return to the dynamism of l'Abbé Cochet, who worked so tirelessly in the middle years of the nineteenth century to reveal Seine-Maritime's archaeological past. Cochet was also the curator of the Musée des Antiquités 1867–75 and it too has been reinvigorated in recent years, publishing a whole series of new guides to its Gallo-Roman collections. Yet for the visitor, despite the increase in knowledge, there is little more to see than there was 25 years ago: virtually all the excavations were 'rescue' digs and at the time of writing gallery space in the museum has not been expanded to accommodate displays reflecting the new discoveries.

The Belgic Veliocasses tribe occupied the Vexin and Rouenois regions at the time of Caesar's conquest. When Augustus created the Gallic provinces their territory was allocated to Lugdunensis and work began on developing a Romanised urban centre at *Rotomagus*. A terrace on the north bank of the Seine was chosen as the point where sea-going ships would transfer goods to river craft and people could cross the river with relative ease. Evidence of a late Bronze Age site has been found here, but so far, there is little sign of Iron Age occupation. Timbers dated by dendrochronology show moorings along the Seine being constructed 5–3BC and subsequently expanded under Claudius (AD41–54). Across Rouen, the recent excavations have demonstrated the first century town was largely made of wood.

The second century saw the city's transformation into a much closer approximation of the Mediterranean model. A formal grid was created. Roads were built to standard widths of 5–10m with gutters and drains, while stone became a prime construction material for both the new public buildings, such as the baths found when excavating the rue des Calmes area, and noble houses, such as the peristyle *domus* found in the cathedral excavations. Both a *forum* and amphitheatre (or theatre-amphitheatre) are known to have existed. An enormous structure found in the place de la Pucelle may have been a commercial centre. Many workshops are known, ranging from fullers to jewellers. Though temples are lacking, the base of what was probably a Jupiter column has been identified and the Espace du Palais rampart excavation revealed so many blocks taken from one building that, with brilliant ingenuity, it was possible to reconstruct 'virtually' an enormous mausoleum that could have functioned as both a private temple and funeral banquet hall: it must have stood on the edge of town overlooking the Seine. There do not seem to have been any aqueducts, but then artesian wells and springs on the higher slopes ensured a good water supply for baths and fountains.

A common feature of the excavations has been the presence of fire damage, especially from the mid to later third century. It is not possible to say that this was the result of barbarian attack, but undoubtedly the decision was taken to build a rampart enclosing about 16ha using the standard stone and brick method. Only two sides of this have been fully traced. Archaeometric dating of the bricks puts them at 268–303, Construction could then have begun soon after Probus' sweep through Gaul following the 276 Germanic invasions. The design is broadly similar to that found at Bayeux, Liseux and Lillebonne, though here a circular tower differs from their U-shaped forms. Evidence of abandonment outside the rampart is not surprising but even within the walls land in the north-west and south-east corners lay empty and in the fourth century on the cathedral site cob building succeeded the burnt *domus*: perhaps the news that the town would become the capital of an enlarged *civitas*, as Lillebonne lost its urban status, made the authorities over-ambitious for *Rotomagus*.

However, after Diocletian's administrative reforms, the late Roman town was successful enough to be chosen as the capital of the new province of Lugdunensis II and the natural centre for an episcopal see. A bishop Avitianus is known at the 314 council in Arles, but it is really bishop Victricius at the end of the fourth century who emerges as a leading figure, acquiring Christian relics and taking advantage of Theodosius' decision in 395 (*De laude sanctorum*) to try to destroy local paganism. Victricius had personal links with the Pope, the fervent bishop Ambrose of Milan, and more locally, the missionary Martin of Tours. He is credited with building the *basilica* church, found in the cathedral excavations. Though little is known of sub-Roman and Merovingian Rouen, the bishopric continued to function here and the *basilica* roof was even leaded in the sixth century.

Public fountain
EDF Office entrance
9, Place de la Pucelle

This is a real rescue case. Excavated when building work began in the square in the 1990s, the fountain has been partially restored as a window display. The original must have been imposing, almost a monumental *nymphaeum*. The basin, surrounded by a hexagonal frame, has been reconstructed along with the steps that led down to this open well, its cellar-like position necessary to reach the natural water level. The excavation revealed that it had a chamber behind it, and, from the amount of broken stonework still with traces of paint, it appears that garland and foliage decorated columns once supported a roof over the pool.

Musée Départmental des Antiquités

198 rue Beauvoisine
76000 Rouen

Hours: 10–12.15pm, 1.30–5.30pm closed Tuesdays
        2–6pm Sundays

The rooms are small and the displays inevitably limited but there is material here of real interest. In the 'Protohistoire' section, there are the finds (1983) from La Mailleraye-sur-Seine on a plateau by the Seine, today in the Forêt de Bretonne: it is the epitome of an **Iron Age warrior burial**. Caesar wrote, 'Funerals there (in Gaul) are splendid and costly. Everything the dead man is thought to have been fond of is put on the pyre … (*BG*, VI, 19). A glass urn cremation was placed under an upturned bronze cauldron, itself encircled by metal chariot wheel-rims. Piled up with them were other precious objects marked by burning: three swords, four shield bosses and five lances; fire dogs and a hooked chain, tools and brooches; and an extremely rare second century BC Syrian yellow glass bowl, which must have been very valuable indeed. The coin and **jewellery** room contains a touching group: a signet ring, a signed gold ring with garnets, beautiful emerald and gold earrings and a granulated gold necklace. They were found originally in an iron box, which must have been a woman's jewel box, hidden but never recovered.

The main room contains one of the best mosaics to have survived in the region. Discovered in Lillebonne in 1870, the **hunting mosaic** contains a heavily and badly restored central medallion of a god propositioning a nymph, but a fascinating surround illustrates a stag hunt. The mosaic was once much bigger, both wider and significantly longer, with a section for the diners to lounge in and admire the rest of their host's floor. Hunting has always been central to aristocratic living, but these four scenes provide a special perspective on Gallo-Roman noble practices in the late third century. The first shows the sacrifice to ensure a successful hunt: a priest stands by an altar in front of a statue of Diana on her pedestal. He has two small assistants, possibly children. Hunters look on and a man on the right holds a rein attached to the jaw of a captive stag. This animal will be bait to tempt a wild stag to challenge him; the season must be right for rutting. The next two scenes show the hunters on their way: the right has a (restored) mastiff leading the way; the left shows the captive stag, followed by a man carrying a roll, probably rope decorated with feathers to help stop the wild stag using tracks away from the captive deer. The final scene shows a hunter drawing his bow, facing the wild stag followed by his doe. The **Orpheus panel mosaic** with animals and seasons brought to the museum in 1844 from a Forêt de Bretonne villa site was severely damaged. Only the central panel of Orpheus and the panels of the lion and one season (summer) are original mosaic.

Rouen. Tombstone relief of a shopkeeper at work. Musée Départmentale des Antiquités, Rouen. Cliché Yohan Deslandes

Much more interesting is the large **tombstone relief**, which had been re-used in the Lillebonne theatre fortification. Both the man and his wife wear the popular Gallic long fringed tunics, while she has a cloak and carries a *mappa*, a napkin evoking the funeral feast. On the reverse there is a glimpse of the man's life as a shopkeeper/workshop owner; given the size of his tombstone, a prosperous one. He holds a stylus on a writing tablet and reaches up with his other arm; behind him are a series of hammers and above these boxes and jars, on his right a fragment shows the damaged figure of a young woman holding a little dog: a symbol of early death. In

162

surviving traces. It is a story of courage on both sides, for a German actively to delay military construction work and for French people to expose themselves to accusations of collaboration. Even the State comes out of it well: when the overpowering feelings were gratitude to the Allies for liberation and shame about any cooperation with Germans, Eble's work was published under his name in the pre-eminent and government funded journal, *Gallia*. They deserve to be remembered.

St-Aubin-sur-mer. A copy of this original lifesize mother-goddess statue is displayed in St-Aubin (Musée de Normandie, Caen)

VALOGNES, Manche
IGN 1211 E
GPS 30 U 0611865/5484995

Baths.

21km SE from Cherbourg by the N13. Take the N2013/Boulevard Leclerc from the centre ville 500m SE, then 500m E by rue du Balnéaire to rue Pierre de Coubertin.

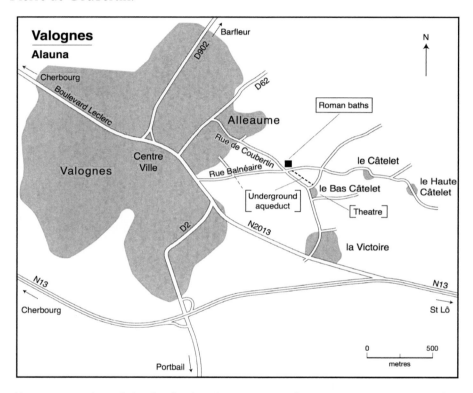

Alauna, mentioned in both the Antonine and Peutinger Itineraries, has since the seventeenth century been identified with the small town of Valognes. No inscription has ever confirmed the identification, but the eastern suburb of 'Alleaume' was suggestive and in 1692, excavations initiated by the same Caen Intendant Foucault – who began the investigation of VIEUX – revealed public baths, a theatre and a spread of Gallo-Roman finds demonstrating that this was indeed a Roman town. It is widely considered that this was the first *civitas* capital of the Cotentin tribe, the Venelli, mentioned by Caesar as one of the Armoricans. Though modern work has been intermittent at best, it is clear that there was Iron Age occupation here, that there was a formal grid and that settlement town, no more than a scatter of houses retained any inhabitants, and became the medieval village of Vieux; the rest, a deserted urban wasteland, by the eighth century had returned to agricultural use. This is therefore a prime green-field site for modern archaeologists and, despite limitations, it does indeed offer great potential.

One limitation has been its early recognition. In 1702 Nicolas Foucault was Louis X1V's Intendant, the chief royal administrator for Normandy. He had an antiquarian's fascination with the past and decided to investigate Vieux's Roman inheritance. Hundreds of workers uncovered extensive remains of a baths and theatre (1703-5) and an illustrated book subsequently proclaimed his achievement. Unfortunately one print mis-labelled the baths as those of Valognes (the subsequent correction slip being ignored), causing considerable confusion for 250 years. In addition, the baths themselves were so inadequately recorded, they had to be found again in the 1840s, but yet again they were so badly located that they needed to be rediscovered by aerial photography in the 1980s! There have been many other less dramatic examples of bad record-keeping and confusion. Predictably, much material has been removed (and lost) both in clandestine digging and in the considerable number of organised excavations during the nineteenth and twentieth centuries. At last, however, the situation has been transformed.

A professional archaeological service was established in 1988 dedicated to Vieux with clear research objectives, including presentation to the public. Pascal Vipard and his team have provided a comprehensive plan of the known city, including its road grid, a full excavation and the only complete plan of a *domus* or noble townhouse north of the Loire, whilst at the same time creating the best archaeological museum in the region. The work continues.

The Viducasses are not mentioned by Caesar, but occur in the writings of Ptolemy (*Geography*, II.8, 2) and Pliny (*NH*, IV,107), whilst *Aregenua* appears as '*Civitas Viducassium*' (Vieux is a corruption of the name) in the Peutinger Table. It is thought that they had been a tributary tribe during the Gallic wars, but under Augustus claimed independent status. Their territory was small, probably little more than the Caen plain with a short stretch of Channel coastline. The town has a Gallic name, but no evidence has so far emerged for any pre-Roman settlement. It seems most likely the site was chosen for its proximity (2.5km) to what may have been the tribal sanctuary at Baron-sur-Odon (see CAEN). *Aregenua* lay on the Chemin Haussé, a route linking the eastern Loire cities with the Cherbourg peninsula and near the navigable river Orne.

The orientation of buildings suggests that from the start the town was laid out using the cardinal points, but streets were a late addition: not one *cardo* (A–F) or *decumanus* (G–K) has shown a stratigraphy earlier than the start of the second century. Other urban development was almost equally tardy. Even in the second century, many *insulae* were thinly occupied and buildings were still typically wattle and daub, only a few having stone foundations. However, the theatre was probably a later first century construction of stone with wooden seating, haphazardly modified in the second century to function as an arena-theatre, with a capacity of at least 5700. A small *fanum* has been identified but little is known of any other temples. Vipard has proposed that a building described in the nineteenth century as the 'northern baths' might really be a *basilica*, in which a stepped semi-circular room would have been a council chamber (*curia*) rather than a pool and which would have been part of the *forum* which is currently being excavated. The southern baths, the notorious lost baths, were extensive and perhaps a double system with men's and women's sections. They are thought to be late Antonine or even Severan, but, like the 'northern baths', need to be re-investigated.

By the end of the second century, *Aregenua* had reached its peak and included a few large *domus* for the elite. They, along with the public baths, were supplied with running water from the three small-scale aqueducts, though most also still had wells, the only source of water for their poorer neighbours. Their homes and workshops were in many cases still wooden with wattle and daub walls, though their Roman appearance was enhanced with tile roofs and lean-to porticos. It is not surprising evidence of textile working has been found at a number of sites, but more unusual are the glass workshops, of which there are at least three, suggesting that the needs of the elite were being met in part from local providers.

From the 230s, *Aregenua* decayed. There is no sign of the mass destruction associated with barbarian marauders, but new building seems to stop, the quality of repairs declined, fires were more frequent, rubbish was dumped more widely and *insulae* were abandoned. An attempt at regeneration seems to have taken place in the early fourth century when roads were repaired and one or two new ones built. It failed. No ramparts were constructed. Small quantities of Argonne pottery produced in eastern Gaul indicate some occupation continued, but urban life had disintegrated. A poor community survived on the northern periphery, but the wealthy moved out to defended urban centres or their villas. By the fifth century the town was an abandoned ruin. The Merovingian village roads ignored *Aregenua*'s grid; the ruins were only visited by groups looking for ready-made building materials. The occasional passer-by is represented by lost belt buckles and a Frankish axe head.

Grand Peristyle house (formerly known as 'Bas de Vieux')

From the car park continue on the path past the museum to Chemin Haussé and turn right. At the crossroads turn left. The site is c.50m on the right.

This *domus* was excavated over three years, 1988–91. The consolidation of the remains secured them from weather and vandals, but has produced a rather soulless effect. Use this visit to identify rooms, what is known about their use and how the house functions as a whole; the museum is essential to breathe life into it.

The archaeologists distinguished six building phases beginning during the early first century AD. No substantial structures were erected until phase IV (120s), when the roads were laid, forming the *insula* here, and the first definite stone walling was used (see Room 17). In the 150s (phase V), a developer/owner constructed two similar side-by-side houses, but twenty years later, during phase VIa, the western house was levelled to construct a new aisle of large rooms and a bath system, a small central peristyle was created and the rear was remodelled to integrate the two sides. The modifications made in phase VIb represent the house at its peak (190s–230s): these are the exposed remains.

Guests arrived via a **monumental entrance** (not restored) with twin arches supported by double portico pillars; across the pavement, decorated pilasters framed the porch. Let through the door by the porter, they would have been equally impressed by the rich reliefs on the vestibule walls. A staircase in the **porter's lodge** once led to the upper storey and balcony looking inwards over the garden. Another staircase must have led to household accommodation (bedrooms?) above the west wing. A wall, once under the balcony, is believed to have been an **altar**, identified by comparison with Pompeian examples and the scatter of earthenware statuettes found nearby. The **peristyle** columns around the garden were covered in foliage relief whilst the enclosing wall was painted with a blue frieze decorated with fish. Water flowed from piping into the pool at its edge and bubbled out of the central fountain and into a drain: only the wealthiest had running water like this linked no doubt to a mains pipe and an aqueduct. Close examination of the columns identified grooves that must have held wooden shuttering; in the winter this would have helped keep rain and draughts out of the rooms facing the court.

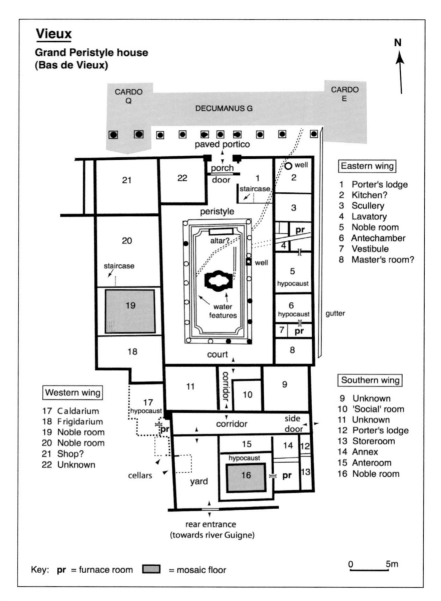

Vieux

Grand Peristyle house (Bas de Vieux)

N

CARDO Q

CARDO E

DECUMANUS G

paved portico

porch

door

21

22

1 staircase

peristyle

altar?

20

staircase

water features

19

18

court

Western wing

17 hypocaust

pr

cellars

yard

11

corridor

17

10

corridor

15

hypocaust

16

14

12

pr

13

rear entrance
(towards river Guigne)

well

2

3

pr

4

5 hypocaust

6 hypocaust

gutter

7 pr

8

9

side door

Eastern wing

1 Porter's lodge
2 Kitchen?
3 Scullery
4 Lavatory
5 Noble room
6 Antechamber
7 Vestibule
8 Master's room?

Southern wing

9 Unknown
10 'Social' room
11 Unknown
12 Porter's lodge
13 Storeroom
14 Annex
15 Anteroom
16 Noble room

Western wing

17 Caldarium
18 Frigidarium
19 Noble room
20 Noble room
21 Shop?
22 Unknown

Key: **pr** = furnace room ▢ = mosaic floor

0   5m

The **kitchen** unit (Rooms 2+3) is very likely to have been based round the well. No seats survive in the **lavatory**, but running water from the garden drains under here and the furnace room next door (accessed from outside). **'Noble' rooms** clearly played a significant role in the life of the master, his household, his guests and his 'clients'. Here they seem to be in pairs. Rooms 5+6 and 19+20 were perhaps respectively the winter and summer reception rooms with their anterooms. A more private pair

Musée de Vieux

Hours: July–August 10am–6pm daily
Sept.–June 10am–6pm Saturday and Sunday
9am–5pm Monday, Tuesday, Thursday, Friday

It is a rare pleasure to see a museum where money to display archaeological material has been spent with pride and vivacity. Daylight floods in. There is a good introductory film available in English (13 minutes) and English summary panels occur frequently. It also has an excellent interactive website (http://visites-virtuelles.vieuxlaromaine.fr).

Most of the displays derive from the discoveries made at the Grand Peristyle site, but the first part of the museum provides a more general picture of the town's development. The major exhibit is a copy of the **Thorigny marble**. The original, found at Vieux in 1580, is now in St Lô museum. It probably stood in the *forum*, as a pedestal for a statue of Titus Sennius Sollemnis (born c180, died 237). The main inscription outlines his distinguished career, four times *duumvir*, he was not only a delegate to the Imperial Cult at Lyon but was elected Grand-Priest, the highest possible reward for a Gaul without taking up a career in Rome. He was also companion to a military tribune in Africa and client/adviser to two governors of Lugdunensis, both of whom provided commendations inscribed on the pedestal. It is unlikely any other Viducassian rose so high.

The nature of the **Grand Peristyle house** is tackled in a variety of ways. Models and pictures provide an overview and the status of the owner is implied by the crowned **head of Tutela** with her fragmentary cornucopia. Wealth and taste are most vividly portrayed through the shattered entrance **reliefs** and garden columns and pilasters with their delicate and intricate portrayals of animals, birds and human figures – such as the **satyr** with his stick – all surrounded by luxuriant foliage settings. The beautifully **painted peristyle fish** are just as striking. Reception room 19 has been partially reconstructed to show the mosaic, the layering of wall masonry and plaster, and the painstakingly put together **painting**, a scene depicting three figures one with armour. Possibly it derived from the Iliad, and shows Thetis saying farewell to his son Achilles, who departs with his female slave. Everyday experience in the *domus* is presented in imaginative ways: **handling boxes** allow visitors to relate directly to Gallo-Roman life, for instance by guessing herb and spice smells and what they might have been used for; there is even a 'try to use a Roman key box'. The 30-odd keys on display make a further point: the need for extensive security, at least in the latter days of the house. A 3D **virtual garden**, based on the excavation, was added in 2012.

OTHER SITES IN NORMANDY

BAYEUX, Calvados
IGN 1512 OT

Rampart and museum.

Bayeux remembers its medieval rather than Roman past. *Augustodurum* was the *civitas* capital of the Baiocasses - thought to have been a *pagus* or minor tribe in the Iron Age but raised in status by the Romans. Visible remains are confined to fragments of the rectangular late Roman rampart in front of the cathedral and along the southern walling in the car park off rue Duhomme, behind the rue St-Malo. The collection of the **Musée Baron Gérard** (rue Lambert Leforestier) includes a reconstructed pottery furnace, a Severan milestone found in the rampart, material from the baths, belt buckles and other burial goods from the Germanic fourth century Pouligny site and a trumpet *fibulae* found at St Vigor-le-Grand. At Le Manoir, 9km east of Bayeux, an 1839 copy of a Claudian milestone stands on the find site by the D12.

HARFLEUR, Seine-Maritime
IGN 1710 ET

Musée du Prieuré
55, rue de la Republique

Harfleur has been identified as the town *Caracotinum*, mentioned in the Antonine Itinerary. Gallo-Roman housing, a *fanum* and a pottery works have been found but the most important excavation (1962–85) has been in the Mt Cabert necropolis, used from the first century AD into the Merovingian period. The fifteenth century museum building contains **the finest Roman glass** in Normandy. Note the globular flask with dolphin-like handles and the ribbed jug with the elegantly angled handle. Really exceptional, however, are the first century Italian deep blue jug and the translucent yellow late third/fourth century trailed Rhineland beaker. Other material in the collection includes an unusual pipeclay donkey and a good, simple display of Frank weapons.

MERRI, Orne
IGN 1614 E

'Le Camp Celtique'

2.5km from Merri. Approaches signposted. Car park below hill by D245.

South-west of Bierre is a low U-shaped promontory fort hidden amongst deep ravines and woods. Occupied from the Neolithic, it became a major settlement during the late Bronze Age and early Iron Age, when the principal rampart was first built completely enclosing the roughly rectangular end of the hill. This was reinforced at the end of the Iron Age and extended with further enclosures. Thousands of rough-cut stones cover the slopes. Merri was not an important Gallo-Roman site, but was certainly used during the troubled late and sub-Roman periods and once again in the tenth century. The site was first seriously excavated in the 1830s with modern work from the 1960s to 1980s. It is today being restored by local volunteers, whose panels covering history, environment and nature dot the site.

THE DEFENCE OF
WESTERN ROMAN GAUL

In part the importance of late Roman ramparts is due to their survival. On occasion, in western France they are the only visible Gallo-Roman remains, though, happily for us, these include the magnificently preserved ramparts at Le MANS and JUBLAINS. Yet even more notable perhaps, is what these ramparts meant for the people who built them and the society they lived in.

For three hundred years of Roman rule the cities, villas, farmsteads, small towns and ports of western Gaul had been without defences: settlements were 'open'. Apart from the frontier zone, far away in the Rhineland, defended sites had been almost as rare elsewhere in Gaul, the nearest being Autun and Boulogne. Autun was the capital of the Aedui, the most important tribe to have backed the Romans in the Gallic wars. Their Augustan ramparts were undoubtedly a privilege granted in recognition of their key role in securing Gaul and asserted a status equivalent to the *coloniae* of southern Gaul, such as Nîmes and Orange. Boulogne was equally exceptional. As the headquarters of the British fleet, securing the Channel crossing for troops to move between the frontier zones of Britain and the Germanies, its fortifications were the only ones on the north coast of early Roman Gaul.

Civilian and military ramparts differed markedly from their predecessors, but little from each other, though the latter tended to be narrower (see St-MALO and Ste-GEMMES-Le-ROBERT).

Foundations

Trench depths could vary significantly depending on the nature of the subsoil. Sometimes, where buildings had existed before and there were already solid footings, none were dug at all, in other places, where crossing sodden ground, wooden piles were driven deep to stabilise the substructure. Trenches were generally filled with durable material such as pebbles or mixed clay and cobbles. To provide a strong footing, large stonework was laid. The number of courses varied but generally rose at least a metre. With urban ramparts, this *grand appareil* was often *remploi*, re-used monumental material – not simply large blocks but also architraves, capitals, column drums and reliefs: many of the inscriptions and tombstones that now fill museums were found in ramparts. At military sites *remploi* is infrequent, but they were less likely to have public buildings nearby.

Walls

The two faces consisted largely of *petit appareil*, but unlike the early Empire ramparts, courses of brick broke the stonework into bands, a style called *opus mixtum*. The width of both stone and brick bands varied. As the rampart was built up, the core was filled with 'blockage', a concrete-like mix of rubble and mortar. It was usually allowed to set after one or two facing courses had been added which helped prevent the wet blockage pressing down and forcing the facing stones outwards. Occasionally builders chose to use timber framing to contain the pressure, allowing them to complete more courses at a time. At some sites, brick courses were completed over the whole width, so perhaps helping stability, but normally they only extended horizontally a couple of bricks and were concentrated on the outer face. Put-holes, the size of a facing stone, extended into the rubble core. Poles could rest here and secure scaffolding close to the rampart, enabling the builders to work easily at the higher levels. Upper tiers survive rarely and original crenellation is totally unknown in the region. At Le MANS it is clear that the parapet walkway was marked out by 6–7 courses of brick, but elsewhere it may have been indicated by projecting stonework.

Towers and gateways

For towns like Le Mans, towers could reach as much as 13–14m up to the roof, allowing space for one and probably two rooms above walkway level. They could house catapults and a troop of soldiers. Illustrations show that some indeed had roofs, but others were crenellated providing space for further catapults. In the lower courses most towers were solid, making it more difficult for attackers to undermine them. Gateways were narrow and functional, generally with one passageway for carts and people protected by massive towers. Unfortunately, traces only survive under later medieval constructions (see NANTES). Postern gates normally nestled by a tower. They allowed for small-scale military sorties and for inhabitants to reach wells, farmland and workshops that lay outside the walls so avoiding long walks to the main gates. For defenders, easy access to rampart and towers was provided by a road running parallel to the internal face.

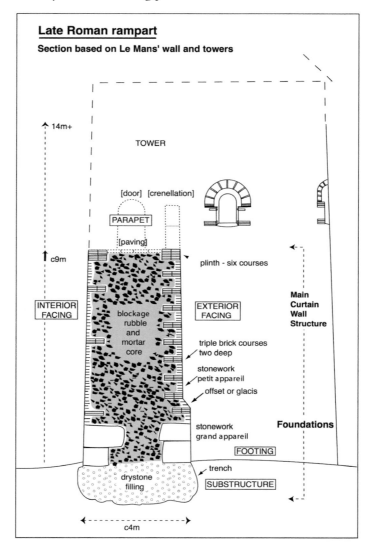

Late Roman rampart

Section based on Le Mans' wall and towers

14m+

TOWER

[door] [crenellation]

PARAPET

[paving]

c9m

plinth - six courses

INTERIOR FACING

blockage rubble and mortar core

EXTERIOR FACING

Main Curtain Wall Structure

triple brick courses two deep

stonework petit appareil

offset or glacis

stonework grand appareil

Foundations

FOOTING

trench

drystone filling

SUBSTRUCTURE

c4m

Funding rampart building

The costs must have been huge. Who then took the initiative? It may be that local feelings were so strong that the *decurions* pressed governors and Emperors to have their ramparts built, but there was a strong incentive for Emperors as well: they could demonstrate their concern for the urban population and their all-embracing power, so much greater than that of the separatist Gallic Empire (260-74). Certainly Verona proudly pointed out that its ramparts were funded by the city (CIL V.3329), on the other hand a Grenoble inscription (CIL XII.2229) shows that in some instances – in this case Diocletian – Emperors were prepared to fund construction. But military expenditure took by far the largest allocation of taxation (whether in money or kind) without adding the cost of new urban defences. Whilst the imperial input may have been at its greatest with *castella* like Brest, Ste-Gemmes and Jublains, and may have been important at harbours like St-Malo and Le Yaudet, funding the *civitates* capitals and towns such as Lillebonne must then have been a matter of balancing local and imperial interests: getting towns to pay as much as possible without bankrupting themselves, which would have severely limited their capacity to pay taxes. What is clear is that no town could build defences without imperial approval and, when the military situation was not threatening, provincial governors would surely have counselled spreading construction over an extended period.

When were the ramparts built?

In his seminal work on the history of Gaul published in the 1920s, Camille Jullian presented a picture of extreme crisis during the 270s. The Gallic Empire collapsed, but Aurelian's subsequent victories were short-lived. In 275-6 came a terrible invasion involving both Alemanni and Franks, for Jullian an unprecedented calamity when all Gaul's cities were occupied and pillaged by the enemy. However, Probus (276–82) 'a man renowned for his military reputation … restored the Gauls' (Eutropius, *Breviarium*, 9.17). The *Scriptiones Historia Augusta* (Probus, XV.3) elaborates: 'sixty of the most prestigious towns had been taken away from enemy oppression and all of Gaul completely restored.' This was given more weight (the SHA is notoriously unreliable) when the Emperor Julian (355–63) commended his work in restoring the cities (*Convivium*, 314b). With a Gallic population in panic and material available from the ruins for ramparts, Probus, Jullian argued, had reason to act quickly and initiate a huge and rapid programme of rampart construction.

Until the 1980s, most scholars willingly accepted Jullian's dramatic narrative. However, doubts grew as archaeologists found scanty signs of massive destruction that could be linked to a major barbarian invasion and scholars pointed out that sources frequently overstated the military threats faced by Emperors to make their achievements seem greater. Detailed examination of the ramparts themselves revealed little or no evidence of haste but highlighted the scale and complexity of the tasks involved in building them. Modern archaeological dating, though still frustratingly incomplete, has increasingly supported the belief that a significant number of ramparts were being built after Probus. Inscriptions found in the *remploi*, plus coins and pottery found in building contexts, provide a *terminus post quem* showing they could not have been built before the 270s. However, this neither shows when building actually began nor when it was finished. In addition Jason Wood's study of Tours (1983) demonstrated that the ramparts here were built in the 370s, a hundred years after Probus. Orléans is now considered to be mid- or later fourth century and some archaeologists consider that the mid-320s alterations at Rouen in fact date the circuit as a whole. The dating of Vannes' defences has been questioned, though the local archaeologists consider them to have been begun in the 280s. Archaeomagnetic dates obtained from rampart bricks at Le Mans, Jublains and Angers, all point to the 280s as a time when the bricks were being fired.

The modern consensus is that most town ramparts were the result of construction work in the later third and early fourth centuries. The historical evidence supports this. The knowledge that the eternal city, Rome, had been constructing its enormous circuit, must have given prestige to cities that followed in its footstep. The troubles in western Gaul associated with the revolt of Carausius (286-93) and the *Bagaudae* (see HISTORICAL DEVELOPMENT) would have been constant reminders about the practical value of ramparts, but there would have been many years of peace when building work could go forward with imperial prompting. Diocletian (284–305) and his co-Emperor Maximian believed in the value of strong walls, as their Empire-wide intensive fort building showed. Even if Constantine (306–27) had less confidence in defence and relied more on mobile forces, this policy assumed hinterlands like Gaul would be penetrated: for the inhabitants, strongholds would have had even greater relevance. Most of the ramparts in western Gaul would therefore have been built by the 320s. Renewed barbarian incursions in Gaul, provoking the need for Julian's campaigns in the 350s and those of Valentian I in the 360s and 370s, would have stimulated the late builders of Orléans and Tours.

The effectiveness of the new ramparts

When the Gallic Empire crumbled in the late 260s, Autun declared for

Claudius II, the legitimate Roman Emperor. Prematurely, as Victorinus besieged then ransacked the city. Yet it stood out seven months defending ramparts constructed 250 years before. Late Empire ramparts were far stronger, their ability to withstand both mining and battering rams was much greater, and direct assault was far more difficult. One factor, as their windows show, was that they were designed to allow artillery to be used. By the second century, Roman forces were equipped with new and better bolt-firing torsion catapults, *cheiro* or *manu ballista*; they were made with a metal spring frame, replacing the older wooden *scorpio*. Reconstructed modern versions have shown that these *ballista* could deliver a more accurate and deadly bolt at greater distances than even the *scorpio*'s maximum 400m. The *Notitia Dignitatum* designates Autun as an armament manufacturing centre where machines could be made, but were they available to the troops scattered around western Gaul and any town volunteers there might have been? And how long did the skills and resources to make them remain when, as modern experimental work has shown, even a single bolt took an hour to produce?

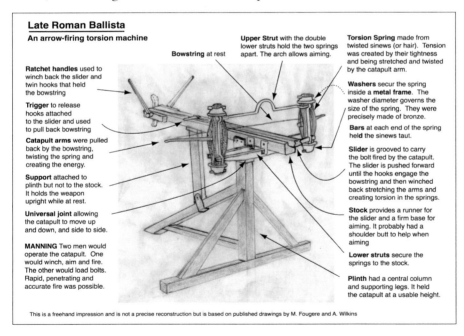

Late Roman Ballista
An arrow-firing torsion machine

Bowstring at rest

Upper Strut with the double lower struts hold the two springs apart. The arch allows aiming.

Torsion Spring made from twisted sinews (or hair). Tension was created by their tightness and being stretched and twisted by the catapult arm.

Ratchet handles used to winch back the slider and twin hooks that held the bowstring

Trigger to release hooks attached to the slider and used to pull back bowstring

Catapult arms were pulled back by the bowstring, twisting the spring and creating the energy.

Support attached to plinth but not to the stock. It holds the weapon upright while at rest.

Universal joint allowing the catapult to move up and down, and side to side.

MANNING Two men would operate the catapult. One would winch, aim and fire. The other would load bolts. Rapid, penetrating and accurate fire was possible.

Washers secur the spring inside a metal frame. The washer diameter governs the size of the spring. They were precisely made of bronze.

Bars at each end of the spring held the sinews taut.

Slider is grooved to carry the bolt fired by the catapult. The slider is pushed forward until the hooks engage the bowstring and then winched back stretching the arms and creating torsion in the springs.

Stock provides a runner for the slider and a firm base for aiming. It probably had a shoulder butt to help when aiming

Lower struts secure the springs to the stock.

Plinth had a central column and supporting legs. It held the catapult at a usable height.

This is a freehand impression and is not a precise reconstruction but is based on published drawings by M. Fougere and A. Wilkins

It is more likely that the walls and towers would have been defended by men armed with bows, slings, javelins and swords. However, capturing a walled town by storm was exceptional. The western enemies of Rome were rarely equipped with suitable siege machinery and no bandit could hurt those inside the walls when the gates were shut. Through the fourth and fifth centuries towns were not taken; they fell through the absence of defenders, panic, subterfuge or starvation. Ramparts worked.

The significance of the new ramparts

It is a sobering thought that during the late Empire ramparts are almost the only public buildings constructed in the west of Gaul. They also represent abandonment: the area they enclosed was rarely more than a third of the existing Roman city – NANTES is an exception at more like a half – but then Rezé on the opposite bank of the Loire was not fortified. This did not mean that people were absent outside the ramparts, or that new building did not sometimes take place there (as it did at RENNES), but, as many late Roman cemeteries on previously urbanised land show, this was normally suburban and small scale. These constricted Roman towns became the heart of medieval and early modern towns, a heritage fortunately largely preserved, but which makes comment about Roman occupation largely supposition. Maligorne (2006) considers that the elite would have made sure they had houses in defended towns, whilst of course retaining their estates. The *Notitia Dignitatum* lists many of the towns as the headquarters of various troops of soldiers: were they in barracks, as the late fourth century *laeti* were at Arras (Pas-de-Calais), or living on land granted in return for service? Did their commanders have mansions or simple lodgings? Were there storehouses placed here for security? Traces of the earliest churches identified, despite their frequent status as cathedrals, show that they were tiny and poorly built. What is certain is that traditional Roman monumental buildings were rarely in use and rebuilding was virtually unknown.

At ÉVREUX, the *forum* may have been within the walls, but the theatre, public baths and a major sanctuary were not; at LILLEBONNE the theatre was made into a fortress, the *forum* left outside and a large baths built over. At TOURS the amphitheatre was also converted into a fortress then bastion, the site of the *forum* is unknown but probably outside; at both ANGERS and Le MANS the *forum*s were not included and public baths were pulled down to clear space for the ramparts. At VANNES the walled town was across the river from all the major public buildings; at RENNES, the *forum* may have been inside, but public baths were destroyed and probably the Mars Mullo temple too.

Remploi shows the use of *any* suitable monumental stone: not just columns and entablature, but the finest reliefs and sculpture; not just milestones, but inscriptions recording leading citizens, their mausoleums and tombstones. These communities abandoned not just many key public buildings, but the life and relationships they embodied. This demonstrates a deep social and cultural change.

The immediate cause for the construction of ramparts can only have been an increase in the perceived threat from invaders and the vulnerability of citizens to loss of life, home and possessions. But the ability of the *civitates* elites in particular, who had embraced so much Romanisation, to show so little interest in preserving the forms of culture built into *forum*s, temples, public baths and burial demands explanation. If there was no panic building, then it must be that they no longer cared. Whatever the reasons, plague, taxation, economic recession and more, nearly all the towns of the west had experienced contraction in the third century. Of course decay and destruction levels are difficult to interpret. Fires were an ever-present threat to all pre-modern communities. Lillebonne undoubtedly declined because of the rise of Rouen. Local factors most easily explain how Valognes became a backwater. But, with few exceptions, the picture is of a Severan peak followed by a cessation of new building and then, from the 250s onwards, widespread fire damage, *insulae* abandoned and buildings going out of use.

Significant as economic changes are, it is the social implication of ramparts that is the most interesting. To turn your theatre or amphitheatre into a fortress means that the relative importance of performances there has declined markedly; meetings in the baths or *forum* no longer play the role they once did; recording your achievements and gifts to the community is no longer significant (the small number of inscriptions after the 240s is very obvious in Gaul). Despoiling ancestors' memorials would just be the last step. Throughout the Empire, despite imperial claims to be 'restoring' the old, there was a trend to seek new gods or even one God. The cannibalisation of old public monuments to create new ones – and undoubtedly having a rampart now gave urban status to a settlement – denoted a real break. It is no surprise then that western Gaul, however slowly, was prepared to absorb the culture and society associated with the late Roman adoption of Christianity.

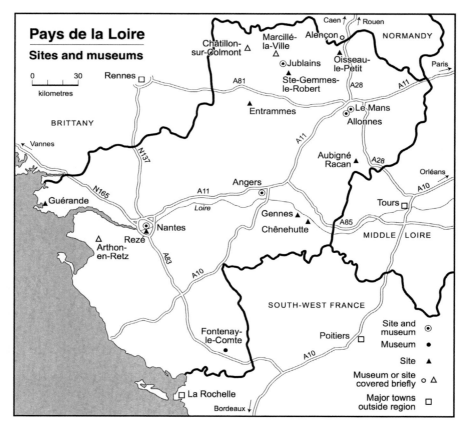

Map 4

THE SITES OF THE LOIRE VALLEY

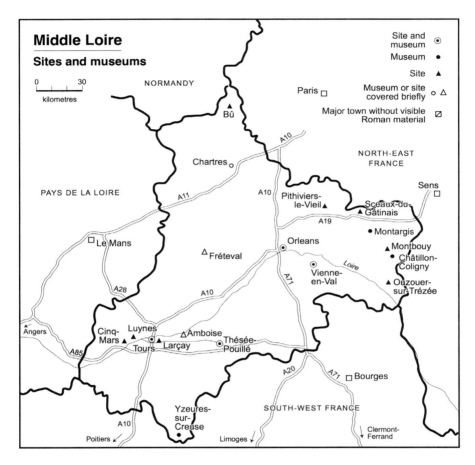

Map 5

ANGERS, Maine-et-Loire
IGN 1522 O

Site and museum.

Of all the urban centres that began as Roman *civitas* capitals in western France, only Chartres exceeds Angers in preserving less of its ancient Roman past. There is nothing here to touch the sinister grandeur of the Angevin castle or the wonderful late medieval tapestry inside; simply a stretch of late Roman rampart and a rather limited collection in the museum.

Caesar mentions the Andes as one of the Loire tribes amongst whom Legion VII wintered and foraged during his Armorican campaign. They supplied men for the failed attempt to rescue the inspirational Vercingetorix and the Gallic forces surrounded at Alesia in 52BC, but it was only in 51BC that they made any major effort to resist Roman conquest when Dumnacus led them to help the Pictones faction besieging pro-Roman supporters at Poitiers. After the legions arrived and killed 12,000 retreating Gauls, Dumnacus fled, never to be heard of again.

Whether the Andes – or Andecavi as they were called by later writers like the Elder Pliny – had a central *oppidum* is uncertain. However, recent work in the château has revealed that the Angers bluff overlooking the Maine had a defended settlement during the late Iron Age. For the Romans, it provided a strategic centre for the road network linking Lyons and Armorica at a place that could control river communications on the Loire and the major northern tributaries including the Maine, Loir, Sarthe and Mayenne. The old fords were replaced by bridges across the Maine and the Loire (Les Ponts-de-Cé, 10kms away). Road building, the earliest housing, pottery finds and the name *Juliomagus*, commemorating his father by adoption, point to an Augustan foundation date. The town developed quickly but tailed off after the 150s, using a grid parallel to the river, eventually covering some 60ha. Though archaeologists were active in the later nineteenth century and did extensive work in the 1970s and 1980s only fragmentary remains have been identified: an amphitheatre, known since the Middle Ages; four bath systems; some housing; various workshops, indicating this was an active production centre, at least during the first century AD; and two large cemeteries. Excavations continue, the most important discovery (2010) being the first undoubted temple of Mithras known in western France. Built in the early 3rd century, it was still in use in the fourth.

Mausoleums and monumental buildings were plundered to construct the foundations of a fortified zone on the main promontory 35m above the river. The western end was destroyed by the castle, but the rampart must have stretched 1220m and enclosed c9ha. Though people still lived outside the walls in the fourth and fifth centuries, insecurity and instability grew. Gregory of Tours describes (*History of the Franks*, II.18) how the ramparts were held in 463, but breached in 469 when Saxon pirates based on islands in the river Loire entered Angers. Frank and 'Roman' forces retook the town in 470 with considerable fire and destruction. However, the 'Roman' count Paul, probably no more than a local strongman, was killed and Childeric, the Frankish king, gained control of the city. Another of Gregory's stories (X.14) also mentions the rampart. In the 590s, Theudulf, a swaying, swearing, drunken deacon, fell to his death from the bishop's oratory constructed on top of the walls. By then Merovingian rule had lasted over a hundred years. The first known bishop came in 543, although the town probably had a bishop earlier. So far, archaeology has added little to our picture of Angers in the fifth and sixth centuries.

Rampart
Rue Toussaint

Next to the tourist office, street widening exposed about 200m of the southern rampart wall rising some 8m. The external facing has rather irregularly cut *petit appareil* separated by brick courses. Behind lies the usual blockage and an internal facing without bricks, making the wall over 4m thick here. A poorly finished stretch in the centre, about 10m wide, hints at a tower that once projected from the face. No precise dating has been achieved. A gate once stood across rue Rangeard, opposite the rue du Musée.

Musée des Beaux-Arts
14 rue du Musée

Hours: June–Sept. 10am–7pm daily; Wednesdays to 9pm
         Sept.–June 1pm–6pm Wednesdays to 8pm closed Monday

A bronze '*protome*' – the upper body of a griffin – is striking. This would have decorated the top of a cauldron and is evidence of Etruscan or Greek goods reaching into the Loire valley during the early Iron Age c600BC. A bronze dish handle in the shape of a warrior, also found near the Loire–Maine junction, suggests that exchange continued into the fourth century BC.

Everyday Roman life is hinted at via pottery: imported sigillata with the occasional finely decorated bowl (for example the athletes on one from Lezoux), obscure graffiti names scratched on sherds and even a reconstructed furnace. Homes are represented by roof antefixes, door keys and lead piping, their owners' possessions by high value coins and bronze statuettes, such as the **gilded Apollo**. A mould taken from a Lyon burial inscription records an Andecavi name: possibly a shipper along the Loire–Rhône route or maybe he was on a visit to the annual games there. The 1879 excavation of Place Raillement is attractively represented by contemporary photographs, a floral and geometric carpet-type **mosaic** in a late second century Rhône valley style, some fragments of painted plaster of high quality and bronzes presented with nineteenth century labels.

A modern excavation produced exciting finds embodying late Roman Angers. The **Goth *fibulae* and belt buckles** were found in burials and most likely belonged to warriors and their wives recruited into the Roman army in its last phase and probably based in the city.

AUBIGNÉ-RACAN, Sarthe
IGN 1721 E

Sanctuary settlement.

40km S of Le Mans by N138/D30 to Vaas, then 6km EW by D305 to signposted site (Michelin maps: 'Cherré'). Parking N of road.

Appearances possibly mislead. The visible remains here imply that this was purely a rural sanctuary, having the excavated remains of a sacred area with temple, theatre and baths. Less usual are the exposed foundations of a building that must once have been very impressive, whose plan takes the form of a *macellum* (an enclosed market) or a small *forum*. The sites are in two groups, but aerial photography, field walking and sondages have shown that there were streets and other buildings now hidden by the soggy grass fields, suggesting that the site is probably best classed as a *vicus*, though its religious role is likely to have remained its key element.

Support for this interpretation comes too from the **Butte de Vaux**, a hill 2km south along the D188 overlooking the Loir river, which was settled from the late Bronze Age, fortified during the Iron Age and then abandoned. C. Lambert and J. Rioufreyt, the excavators of both Vaux and Aubigné (1970s-1990s), discovered that the flat meadows where the Gallo-Roman site developed were already being used for both ritual gifts – they found more than 50 fourth and third century BC sword fragments – and burials from at least the early Iron Age. The theatre and the *macellum* were built over a cemetery, the foundations of the former even being designed around megalithic stones, whilst by the temple there were three final Iron Age (first century BC) burials; it all suggests that the meadows were sacred to the pre-Roman local inhabitants. Yet it was the emergence of the new

Gallo-Roman religious rites with its combination of Gallic and Roman practices, including the need to make sacrifices at the home of a god, to cleanse worshippers and for ceremonial and entertainment: these required dedicated specialised buildings. These were provided here from the mid-first century and, as elsewhere, coin evidence suggests use peaked during the second century.

The *vicus* is considered to be within Aulerci Cenomanni territory, though no inscriptions indicate who funded the sanctuary, whether *civitas*, *pagus* or leading citizens. Its frontier position serving both the Andes and the Turones tribes, its river traffic access and its closeness to the main Tours–Le Mans road, probably encouraged large numbers to come here. Even so, there is little evidence that it continued to function in the fourth century, though early medieval burials cluster around the temple area and might imply that this still had a religious aura.

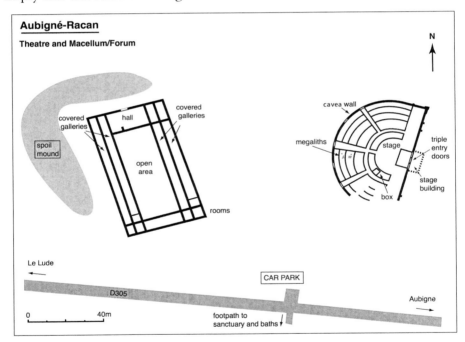

Theatre
GPS 31 T 0292486/5282627
North of the D305.

The theatre was discovered and described (inaccurately) in the nineteenth century, but became overgrown and forgotten. Revealed again in aerial photographs, it was re-excavated in the 1970s. Dated along with the temple to the second half of the first century, it was probably Flavian and so typical of a period when many *civitates* were adopting Roman forms. It took its final form at the end of the second century. Whilst the flat ground undermines its impact (though some walling exceeds 2m high), this is almost a Gallo-Roman theatre type-site.

Aubigné-Racan. The cavea foundations with a box for high status onlookers

The sweeping *cavea* (seating area) wall with inset *petit appareil* courses, some with white sandstone forming simple patterns, and the semi-circular walls within would have provided support for timber floors and seating. Note how the rubble foundations on the west side of the *cavea*, must have lifted the main structure over the megaliths. An inner area around the orchestra provided places for the privileged, though the purpose of the box on the southern side is unknown. Roman theatres had stage buildings along the whole face, but here, and at many other sanctuary theatres, there is only a small structure behind the buttressed enclosing wall. It has a central alcove and a projecting stage set. Possibly the entertainments provided included some Roman style spectacles (pantomimes?), but many must have tied in with sanctuary ceremonial; the theatre could hold an audience of 3000 or more.

Forum/Macellum
North of the D305

Best seen from the spoil mound, this really is no more than a plan; a few centimetres of walling with the zones defined by sand and gravel. It looks like a market place and perhaps it had a dual role as a communal and

196

commercial focal point, with an open central area and long narrow covered galleries, perhaps porticoed, and a few rooms at one end. These foundations are too thin to be load bearing and indeed, hundreds of nails have been recovered: the superstructure must have been wooden. Thermoluminescence dating of the roof tiles indicates a first build around AD110 with a rebuild in the early third century. The discovery of numerous cattle, sheep and pig bones from the discarded less edible parts, strongly supports the idea that at least one function of the building was as a meat market. The rarity of this type of structure made the excavators think it may have had a part in the distribution of food to worshippers rather than simply supplying provisions to the inhabitants.

Sanctuary and enclosure
GPS 31 T 0292447/5282242

South of the D305

Today we have only fragmentary remains, but to the contemporary eye, the sanctuary must have appeared very Roman. A square zone (90x90m), now marked out with gravel, is surrounded by a thick wall decorated with *exedra* (recesses). It seems likely that there was an entrance on the eastern side opposite the temple steps, but no traces survive. To further confuse the visitor, a pool was later constructed astride where the path presumably ran. Only the lowest courses of the temple survive, though enough to show that its dimensions and external form were very similar to the classical temples of southern Gaul.

Framed by a stone base are the foundations of the temple's enclosing wall, constructed with an outer face of large blocks and an inner face of *petit appareil*, once covered with painted plaster. Only traces of the staircase survive and the *pronaos* or porch is represented by an open space; fragments of curved stone suggested to the excavators that a colonnade defined the *pronaos*, whilst collapsed walling indicated the rear walling was decorated with various coloured stones forming simple patterns. Inside was a *cella*, not the classic rectangle but the square Gallic *fanum* form with a typical passage around it. The ritual would then have been Gallo-Roman, though, sadly, no evidence has been found of the god(s) for whom it was built.

Baths
South of the D305

An aqueduct drew off water from a nearby low-lying stream feeding the Loir to supply a simple linear system constructed beside a small *palaestra* (courtyard), more probably used by officials and privileged pilgrims to chat and walk under its portico than to do strenuous exercises. The baths were completed after the temple around AD90, then remodelled and enlarged during the second century. The access area on the southern side was enlarged with two small rooms and a large chamber, possibly the apodytarium (changing room) or an indoor exercise hall.

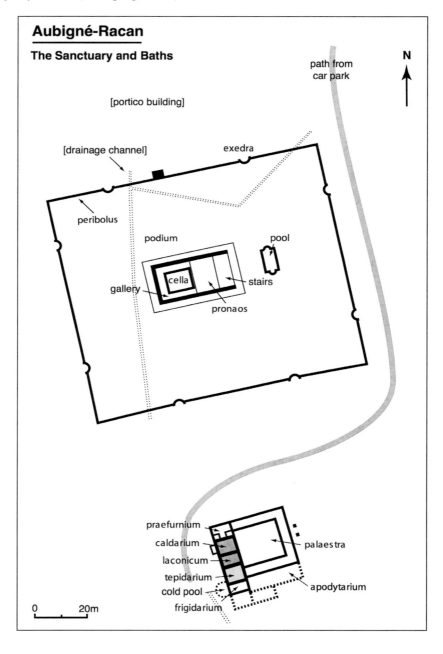

CHÊNEHUTTE, Maine-et-Loire
IGN 1623 E

Oppidum and settlement.

Chênehutte-les-Tuffeaux is a typical Loire village straggling along the D751, the south bank road between Angers and Saumur. Steep cliffs rise behind it, cut by a ravine through which the Fontaine d'Enfer stream bubbles down from the plateau. To the north of the stream is le Chatelier promontory. Its strong position overlooking the Loire, where a ford almost certainly existed, made it attractive in prehistory and Antiquity. Despite recognition as a 'Camp de César' in the eighteenth century, modern excavation has been limited, but the site offers an appealing walk along good tracks.

Important work was carried out by Gilbert Boisbouvier in the 1980s, who revealed occupation from at least the late Bronze Age which intensified during the final stages of the Iron Age with a 9ha *oppidum* secured by a rampart. Aerial photography has made quite clear that, unusually, settlement continued here. By the Flavian period, a small Romanised town filled the site with regular right angle roads, a central square, some large buildings, possibly public, varied housing and workshops. Boisbouvier's research also revealed a *fanum* in the Fontaine d'Enfer valley and suburban occupation along the short Roman road linking the *vicus* to the much older 'route de crête' linking Poitiers and Angers, recalled today as the Chemin de Saumur.

It is likely that the town was *Robrica*, named in the Peutinger Table as a stop between Angers and Tours. First suggested in the nineteenth century, this was disputed by many because the main Roman road clearly ran north of the Loire. However, the discovery of timber piles in the river during a summer drought in 1993, subsequently dated by dendrochronology to the early first century AD, proved that the town could be reached easily by this bridge and that the distances, given by the itinerary's writer, at last made sense. The bridge would also have enabled travellers to visit the amphitheatre at GENNES sanctuary, only 7km away, no doubt the religious centre of the local *pagus*. The town declined from the late second century, revived in the fourth, but was then abandoned.

The sites. Coming from the D751 there are two possibilities: (a) from the church, take the steep narrow rue du Castellane passing Le Prieuré hotel. Opposite the cemetery a track leads up to le Chatelier *oppidum*; (b) take the rue J-F Bodin, or D214, c.400m to the local primary school and then use the path up the hillside.

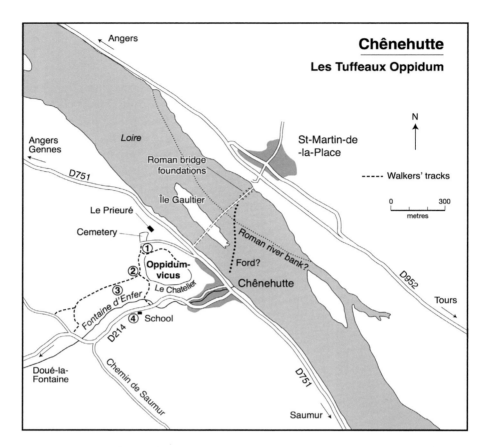

Chênehutte

Les Tuffeaux Oppidum

Angers

Loire

Angers Gennes

D751

Roman bridge foundations

Île Gaultier

Le Prieuré

Cemetery

① Oppidum- vicus

②

Roman river bank?

Ford?

③ Le Chatelier

Fontaine d'Enfer

④ School

D214

Doué-la- Fontaine

Chemin de Saumur

D751

Saumur

St-Martin-de -la-Place

N

- - - - Walkers' tracks

0   300
metres

Chênehutte

D952

Tours

1 Rampart and *oppidum*. GPS 30 T O714679/5243376. A line of trees defines the *oppidum*, at first hiding the rubble embankment of what was once an earth and stone rampart; neither precise building methods nor dates are known. The open meadow of the interior evokes where the town stood, but there are no visible remains; perhaps in the future there will be.

2 Roman road. GPS 30 T 0714514/5243262. First studied and recorded by J-F Bodin in 1812. To counter the slope a 2m high bank supported a rubble core cover with brick fragments; it is still used as a popular track for Sunday walkers.

3 Roman houses. By the south side of the road, c100m along, are the remains of two houses excavated by Boisbouvier. The western house has no more than the rough-cut stone foundations of a one room structure, it may have been a farm labourer's home. The eastern house was larger with two rooms, the front wider and gallery-like, its façade now lost. The walling was thicker and better made, the floor paved

Though two coins found in 1770 implied a later second century date, the immediate area has been dug over many times with little success, until 2005. Then a two month excavation by Emmanuel Marot revealed a sunken chamber behind an enclosing wall just north of the tower. The chamber was empty, but nearby his team found a statue of a heavily bearded figure in a Phrygian hat: only the eastern god Jupiter-Sabazios combines these features. It is equally exceptional as the only full-size representation of the god found in the Empire. His cult had a following in Rome where it was associated with wild practices similar to Dionysic rites (smearing with mud, noisy repetitive dirges, dancing with snakes, and the suspicion of debauched sexual behaviour). The god also safeguarded the well-being of believers.

The most convincing interpretation of this evidence is that the tower was a memorial proclaiming a rich and cosmopolitan landowner or a family's ancestor who came from Rome itself. The 'mosaic' décor combined with *opus testaceum* (brickwork finish) is characteristic of Latium rather than the Loire valley and the owner is most likely to have become a follower of Sabazios through direct contacts in Rome. Mausoleums along the Appian Way asserted the status of the families that built them. It may be that the enclosure here was a family burial site on the edge of an estate, the tower erected to proclaim their importance to travellers both on the river and on the major Roman road running beside it. Perhaps the estate was administered from the villa identified at nearby L'Homme d'Or.

ENTRAMMES, Mayenne
IGN 1519 O
GPS 30 U 0670318/5318491

Baths.

8km SE from the centre of Laval by the N162; take D103 to the parish church.

In 1987 restoration work began in Entrammes church. When the nineteenth century plaster was removed from the south face there was astonishment at finding not the expected sixteenth century structure, but a magnificent Roman wall, 21m long and over 8m high. Jacques Naveau, the Mayenne departmental archaeologist, excavated the nave (1988–90) as far as the transept – which was still being used for worship – and revealed that the original church had been constructed using the core rooms of a Roman bathhouse.

The building would have tempted early church builders because most of the walling must still have been standing and perhaps even the roof was in good condition (no traces were found as debris). A further attraction must have been its 'in-line' design, making it straightforward to convert by simply knocking down the partition walls between the rooms.

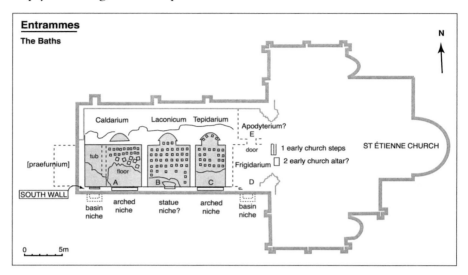

In the *caldarium*, **Room A**, many of the hypocaust pillars have survived, despite the thick *suspensura* floor having collapsed in places. Bathers could immerse themselves in hot water in the large tub or *solium*. This was positioned to retain the maximum heat, as the furnace would have been immediately outside the west wall. Box-tiles (*tubuli*), used to carry hot fumes up the walls and out of the baths, survive only to *suspensura* level. Slaves would have helped bathe visitors using the niche basin and a shallow pool in what was probably an *exedra* in the south wall, represented by the large arched niche. **Room B** was the *laconicum* where the heat was dry; here slaves would have oiled the skin and then scraped away the sweaty mixture. The niche on the south wall may well have been decorated with a statue. **Room C** was the *tepidarium*. Bathers could relax here in the lesser heat (furthest from the furnace) before moving into **Room D**, the unheated *frigidarium*. Unfortunately, two thirds of this is hidden, but no doubt it had a large and bracing pool. Here are traces of the early church: (1) two steps on the north side that would have led to a presbytery and (2) a block in the centre, possibly an altar or an ambo, used in early churches for reading holy works. The only door identified suggests that beyond lay a changing room (*apodyterium*) **Room E**, although this remains uncertain.

It is of course the **south wall** that impresses. Most noticeable is the extensive use of brick, not just in double or triple horizontal courses, but

204

around the niches and, the (much rarer) high circular windows: presumably this brickwork was exposed, even when *tubuli* and painted plaster covered the stonework in the hot rooms.

No useful archaeological dating evidence was found at all: no coins and only one sigillata sherd. The profusion of brickwork suggests a date in the second century, but earlier and later uses are known. Certainly more excavation would increase our understanding of the baths: were there, for example, exercise areas, such as an outdoor porticoed *palaestra* or even an indoor yard? (see AUBIGNÉ-RACAN). Other examples of churches constructed on bath sites are known (see JUBLAINS), but quite when this happened remains obscure: sixth or seventh century? The context of the baths is now emerging. Archaeologists have recognised that the junction of three Roman roads by the baths represents the centre of a widely spread *vicus*, no doubt representing a transfer of population from the large Gallic *oppidum* identified at Port-du-Salut overlooking the Jouanne river.

FONTENAY-LE-COMTE, La Vendée
IGN 1527 O

Museum.

The Vendée had no great surge of archaeological activity in the nineteenth century and even in the twentieth century discoveries were limited. The most important excavations have been of Iron Age salt production sites, there being a large group of them in the Golfe des Pictons marais region. Over the years, a significant number of Gallo-Roman villa sites have been acknowledged, but few excavated and none preserved. Since the 1970s many 'enclosures' have been identified by aerial photography, but equally little to show on the ground. It is surprising then to find that the museum has a room filled with an exceptional display of Roman glass.

Musée Vendéen
Place du 137ème RI (by Notre-Dame church)
85200 Fontenay-le-Comte.

Hours: May–Sept. 2.30–6pm closed Mondays
Oct.–April 2.30–6.00pm Wednesday, Saturday, Sunday

Presented here are finds from two excavations together with prints and photographs depicting the archaeologists who carried them out. Benjamin Fillon and Frédéric Ritter excavated an extensive porticoed villa at **St-Médard-des-Près**, 2kms from the centre of Fontenay, in 1846. In the following year they found a burial chamber containing a young woman's coffin surrounded by grave goods. Crumbled wood and rotted fabric proclaimed her three clothes boxes. It quickly became known as the tomb of 'la femme artiste' because of the metal box with brushes, mixing cup, tiny spoons and various minerals, the presence of phials with traces of resin and colours and a pestle and mortar. Revisionists suggest it could equally have been her make-up set and body oils. *Amphorae*, earthenware plates and around 80 pieces of glassware filled much of the remaining space. The finds suggest a late second century date.

In February 1914, F and A Huguet carried out a 2½ week dig on what turned out to be a third and fourth century cemetery at **Bouillé-Courdault**, 12km south-east of Fontenay. Once again the first tomb contained the body of a young woman, this time in a very rare stone sarcophagus, buried with a small animal – her pet cat or dog? There were vases inside the sarcophagus and more around it, many of the highest quality imported from the Rhineland. Further burials included glassware amongst the grave goods, though not in the profusion associated with the initial discovery.

Whilst the second century **glassware** is largely colourless or green the most attractive being the small phials and scent jars, the third century material presents beautiful yellow glass plates, beakers and flasks, decorated with the typical white and blue snake-like trails associated with the Köln workshops. Amongst the elegant jugs, cups and dolphin bottles are two flasks, one made to look like a bunch of grapes, the other blown into a mould to form a back-to-back shell shape, which may be local.

GENNES, Maine-et-Loire
IGN 1623 O

Amphitheatre-theatre.

31km E of Angers by D952, crossing the Loire at les Rosiers-sur-Loire, or 15km W from Saumur.

The belief that water from particular springs gave protection has considerable antiquity and was a widespread focus for Gallo-Roman culture; even in the nineteenth century the local tradition that 'St Fort' would make a baby strong if sprinkled in Chapeau spring water survived in Gennes. In 1812 Roman walling was recognised in Gennes, marking the first step in the realisation that here too, 'holy' water preceded Christianity. The Gennes sanctuary is likely to have been the most important religious centre for the tribal sub-group or *pagus* which occupied the south-eastern territory of the Andes *civitas* (see ANGERS), accessible to travellers and

buttressed wall supporting the eastern side of the *cavea*, though still finding no evidence of a western *cavea* wall. He was able to correct d'Achon's inaccurate plan of the *cavea* wall as well as exposing two additional rooms on top of the one in the centre, the drainage system, and exposed the fine stone (sandstone and tufa) and triple brick courses.

The *cavea* is unlikely to have had stone seating, except perhaps for those privileged to be closest to the arena. Access round the *cavea* was never more than by an arching road, cut into the rock itself at the top centre. The three rooms (A,B,C) would have held performers who could have moved along the hidden corridor entering the arena by doors through the high podium wall that protected the spectators sitting on the front seats above. The arena, made of a deep fine rubble, was drained by gutters into a tiled channel running down the centre of the corridor. Dating evidence was rare but though the brick courses suggest the second century on grounds of style, archaeomagnetic dating of sample bricks gave mid-first century dates. If this date is accurate, the amphitheatre was contemporary with the early investment in public building at Angers. Cost cutting features suggest funds must have run low. Perhaps rather than fund long-term construction work, leading citizens preferred to pay for spectacles at major religious festivals that would more obviously enhance their prestige. During the Merovingian era the amphitheatre was used as a small cemetery.

GUÉRANDE PENINSULA, Loire-Atlantique
IGN 1023 OT

Museum and site.

The salt marshes of the Guérande peninsula have a calm, almost mystical atmosphere, especially in the spring and autumn when the roads and villages around the coast and across the marshes are emptier, even so the sun can still sparkle across the salty white impregnated embankments outlining the separation pools and the water itself. Le Croisic and Batz–sur–Mer were once granite islands off the coast, but around 10,000 years ago, a gradual climate warming began, associated soon with a rise in sea levels. It is estimated that during the last 2000 years alone the level has risen 1.5m. Sand banks formed to make the Penbron peninsula and the La Baule dunes, forming the shallow and increasingly saline Guérande bay.

During the La Tenè Iron Age and particularly the first century BC salt processing using furnaces to crystallise the salt (see SALT, FISH AND ROMAN COOKING) proliferated in the region. Some sites, like Dousseille and Kerrande, are now covered by saline pools, whilst others have been found along the coast and some inland, where the settlements' salt artisans must have been supplied with brine.

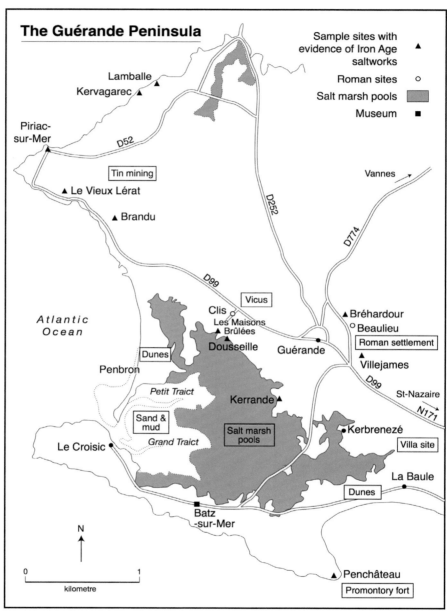

A few sites, such as Les Maisons Brûlées, show continued use of the furnace technique during the first two centuries of the Gallo-Roman era. At Clis, during the late nineteenth century, Léon Maître discovered enough Gallo-Roman settlement evidence to consider this a *vicus* of some 20ha and to suggest, from wreckage found in the marshes, that Clis was a port with a channel across the bay to its mouth near Le Croisic. Excavation in the 1990s revealed another Roman settlement 5km away at Beaulieu where the roads into the Guérande from *Darioritum* (Vannes) and *Condevicnum* (Nantes) met. Housing plots (including a *domus*) and a *fanum* were found, but it seems to have depended not on salt but on the land's rich farming soil.

The problem grappled with since Maître proposed it is whether Roman initiative marked the replacement of furnace heat for salt processing with the warmth of the sun. Unlike the salt pans of the Mediterranean, this entailed developing a much more complex system, moving the water through a series of pools and gradually concentrating the brine until a salt scum formed that could then be skimmed off by a salt worker with a wooden rake. Gildas Buron, curator of the Batz salt marsh museum, argued strongly that it was indeed the Romans who brought the concept of modifying the marsh itself, but that it was Guérande initiative that made the essential adaptations for the Atlantic climate.

Buron's case is based on analogy and linguistics. By the 1980s research in Flanders had shown that saltern techniques were being modified at a time when they were under Roman supervision, by the construction of large timber enclosed pools to facilitate the creation of brine, though furnaces were still used to make crystals. Buron considers that in the Guérande they carried experimentation further and that between the second and fourth centuries the new method had replaced the need for furnaces as well. He points to the late Latin origin of workers' names (including the general term 'paludier', from *palut* or marsh), some of the processes used, and various technical terms, such as 'scanne', a saline embankment derived from *scannum*, the late Latin for dyke. The word 'aderne', used to describe a brine reservoir, he thinks came directly from the local term for the brine tub used on the beaches in the briquetage method.

So far, there is little archaeological and no historical evidence to support this undoubtedly logical thesis. Late Roman material is scarce but not unknown, ranging from a hoard found in Le Croisic to three cisterns in Batz (which *may* be Roman and *may* be linked to the new techniques). Sub-Roman and early medieval material is also thin. During this period the Guérande might have harboured a Saxon pirate base, but the district was soon absorbed by the Merovingians to form part of their border with independent Brittany, until, with the break-up of the Carolingian Empire in the ninth century, it was taken by the Bretons. Only then do contemporary sources demonstrate that salt pan exploitation had become a major activity with an important export trade. Answers may be found amongst the salines themselves, though further rises in the sea level will make this increasingly difficult.

Batz-sur-Mer
GPS 30 T 0540063/5242196

Musée des Marais Salant
29bis rue Pasteur
44740 Batz-sur-Mer

Hours: July–Sept. 10am–12.30pm 2–6.30/7pm daily
June 10am–noon daily; Sunday also 2–6.30 pm
Oct. to May 10am–noon; weekends 2–6pm
Open daily in school holidays.

The museum is dedicated to the people of the salt marshes. Downstairs presents their traditional costumes and homes, upstairs the history and methods of salt making. Buron has suffused the museum with a love for a way of life embodied by the paludiers and their close relationship with nature. The video depicts this extremely well and is an excellent introduction to saltmaking techniques. There is a fine large-scale reconstruction model of the Piriac-sur-Mer saltern site, excavated by Nicolas Rouzeau at the beginning of the 1980s. Panels make clear Buron's view that there was a local evolution in saltmaking from salterns to marsh pools and that it took place in the Roman era.

Clis
GPS 30 T 0540063/5242196

From Guérande 4km by D99 to Clis; turn south towards Les Maisons Brûlées; c.400m on the left is a small sign to 'Villa Grannon' and a track.

The only visible Gallo-Roman remains in the region are the 20m of walling on the north side of the track with further traces in the enclosing walls surrounding the field behind the garage. Excavated by Maître in the 1880s, these are the visible traces of a large terrace (the field area), buttressed in the south and with an apse in the north equipped with an aqueduct and drain. Not enough was found to identify this as either a *forum* with a decorative fountain, or a bath complex, but it was certainly some kind of monumental public building.

network was not laid out until the later first century AD. The grid was based on the road running south 1000m from the reconstructed Roman style sanctuary (c.AD65) to the new theatre (*cardo* A); a *forum* was constructed on the Tonnelle site halfway between them. There was at least one public baths on the church site and another is hinted at in an inscription. Housing and shops have been identified, but few *domus* though a villa has been confirmed in the suburbs, along with evidence for a variety of workshops. The grid would have covered 25ha, but not all *insulae* were used. Occupation must always have been limited and from the mid-second century some parts were being abandoned.

Jublains was not walled in either the third or fourth centuries – though it did have its fortress. The town slowly decayed to no more than a village in which imported pottery is notable for its rarity. The sanctuary was in ruins by the later fourth century, and, at some point, the *civitas* lost its independent status, being administered from the Aulerci Cenomanni capital and bishopric at Le MANS. Jublains can then be classed amongst the ephemeral Roman cities of Gaul.

Recent work elsewhere has cast fresh light on the Diablintes tribe and the evolution of their *civitas*. Caesar only mentions them once, as allies of the Veneti in 56BC (BG,III.9). However, Ptolemy, writing about 150 years later, described them as one of three allied tribes in the Aulerci confederation, along with the Cenomanni and Eburovices. In Caesar's account then, the Diablintes appear to play a minor role in the Gallic wars and Ptolemy implies some loss of status, which is of course confirmed by the city's rapid decline in the late Roman period. *Noviodunum's* ephemeral existence, it was argued, could be best explained as the result of the relative poverty of Diablintes territory: the country they occupied was a borderland, then as today; a land of barren soils covering the granite, limestone, sand and schist of the underlying Armorican massif; a land of high rainfall and low yields.

A new discovery dramatically undermined this explanation. In the 1970s, Naveau had excavated Moulay, a promontory site 10km away, where he found Iron Age occupation behind a rampart enclosing 12ha, but nothing exceptional. In 2004, work began on a major new road outside the hillfort and immediately late Iron Age material appeared. Over the next seven years a huge team of archaeologists from INRAP revealed that next to the promontory fort was another rampart enclosing 135ha, of which 80ha at least was occupied, divided by a series of roads into districts with housing, workshop zones, religious centres, etc. Here was the largest *oppidum* in all of western France and undoubtedly the Diablintes' Iron Age centre of power. Why then was Jublains at its maximum so much smaller than

Moulay? Was the Mayenne valley always a more natural centre of population than the more barren plateau on which Jublains had been established? What could have happened to Moulay's inhabitants at and after the conquest? Was there unrecorded slaughter, or were its people dispersed with perhaps a few forming the early residents at Jublains? Was there a deliberate Roman policy to curtail the status of the Diablintes by linking them with the Aulerci?

For all Jublains' failure as a long-term city the positive benefits for archaeologists and visitors are substantial. Here remains really have been 'rescued': excavation has been followed by conservation including three public buildings, – and there is the 'fortress'. It has not been possible to preserve major housing, but you can always visit the *domus* at VIEUX, another ephemeral Roman city emerging as a major site for visitors.

The site

Roads and grid
Outside the large sites of southern France it is very difficult to grasp the scale and nature of Gallo-Roman grids. At Jublains, gravel has been used to show many of the central blocks, revealing that the surveying must have been rather rough and ready as *insulae* often vary in size and regularity. They are aligned with road A which must have followed a track down to the theatre where a lone Iron Age stele stands in the orchestra, suggesting a pre-Roman link between the sanctuary and theatre sites. The original roads also varied in quality, but the best were equipped with granite cobblestones, gutters, wooden drains and pavements. They were re-laid at least three times. The Tonnelle building (erected 1878) is believed to embody evidence of a monumental building that might have been a *forum*. Despite modern study this has not been confirmed.

The Sanctuary
The pre-Roman site. Geophysical survey work across the courtyard and sondages in the temple revealed an early ditch and evidence of a palisade, but nothing of its form; its religious nature was confirmed by the discovery of a deliberately bent sword, typical of late northern Gallic La Tène ritual.

The *Peribolus*. A gravel path defines the portico around an almost square, open, flat courtyard, created on the gently sloping hillside. Today only lower courses survive of walling (originally buttressed on the south side) that must have hidden the interior. Granite blocks indicate the porch outside the west entrance, originally used for placing offerings. Little survives of the eastern entrance, certainly the main way in, emphasised by the second portico.

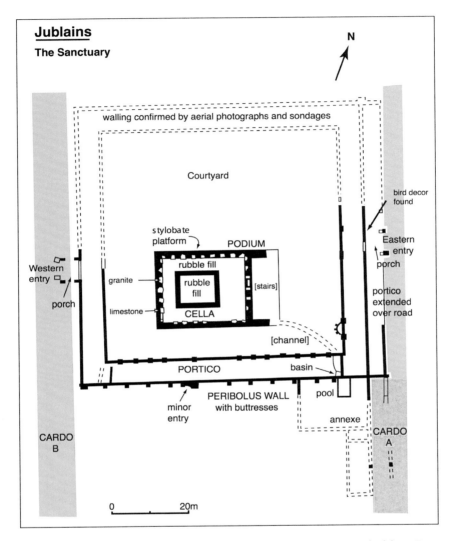

Jublains

The Sanctuary

N

walling confirmed by aerial photographs and sondages

Courtyard

bird decor
found

stylobate
platform

PODIUM

Eastern
entry
porch

Western
entry

granite

rubble fill

rubble
fill

[stairs]

portico
extended
over road

porch

limestone

CELLA

[channel]

PORTICO

basin

minor
entry

PERIBOLUS WALL
with buttresses

pool

annexe

CARDO
B

CARDO
A

0   20m

The Temple. A mass of stonework was carefully disentangled by Naveau's excavators. Set asymmetrically in the courtyard, the temple had been built by cutting foundations down to the granite bedrock for two enclosing walls. Only the lower courses of the outside wall survive, made from a mix of alternating well-cut limestone and rougher granite, suggesting it supported a *stylobate* and its columns. The inner wall formed the base for a *cella*. At some point this was filled with rubble, like the space between the walls, to form the solid core of a podium. The temple was entered from the east by steps up to a *pronaos* or porch, no doubt also decorated with columns.

The Annexe. Traces of a basin inside the portico and a pool outside,

217

supplied with drainage water from under the temple by a short vaulted aqueduct, suggest that an annexe was added to the sanctuary's south-east corner. Remains of a hypocaust (not visible) hint that these were rooms for priests or worshippers to wash in before entering the sanctuary. Perhaps the concentration of coin finds here were lost payments to the attendant.

The God(s). No readable inscriptions survived, but in the temple rubble tiny fragments of a seated goddess were found, reminiscent of that found at ST AUBIN-SUR-MER (now in CAEN). The concentration of pipeclay 'Venus' figurines and *fibulae*, found both at the porch and near the south-east corner, equally point to a mother-goddess who, like many later saints, also had healing qualities – see the bronze votive eyes in the museum.

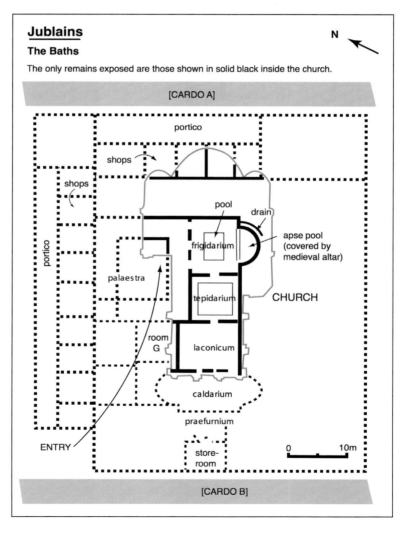

218

The Baths

By the early 2000s much of the baths *insula* was known. Whilst the bathhouse occupied the centre between roads A and B, the *insula* also contained rows of portico-fronted shops and other buildings. Like the better preserved example at ENTRAMMES, the in-line system of baths must have offered, by knocking down partition walls, an easy way of creating the church nave (perhaps in the fifth or sixth century), though here the nineteenth century church removed the elevations and left both the *caldarium* and *praefurnium* outside.

Constructed in the late first century, the baths were modified over time. The frigidarium's original main pool filled the northern end. Then, in mid-second century, it was replaced by a new central pool, drained on the east side around the second smaller pool in the apse. The last change came when in the late third century finely made schist pavings were added to the central pool. The *tepidarium* is unusual as it is only heated by hypocaust around its circumference. The laconicum provided hot dry heat to facilitate sweating. 'Room G' could have been added later, as an extra hot room. The Merovingian stone coffins (mainly seventh century), along the west side, were found in the adjacent early churchyard.

The Theatre

Identified by Magdelaine, partially exposed by Barbe and fully excavated in the 1980s and 1990s, it is now clear that the remains represent two theatres. The first, built at the same time as the sanctuary (considered Flavian), was paid for by a wealthy citizen, Orgetorix, whose broken inscription was found here; the second, larger structure, enclosed the first in the later second century. Neither effort shows much sophistication but, on site, each seems to fit the plateau edge reasonably well.

Theatre 1. A hollow has been created, then a circular wall marked out the *cavea* with curved buttress zones added to resist the pressure of the hillside. A 26m wall cut off a segment of the circle at its base and a semi-circular podium wall built to create the orchestra area. The theatre building itself was a simple projecting apse. The seating must have been wooden; the balance of opinion is that the stone *vomitaria* were second theatre additions replacing wooden staircases.

Theatre 2. This appears to have been constructed to enlarge the performance area, allowing more space for spectacles, whether religious ceremonial or hunting displays. The wooden posts that marked this 'arena' are recalled by reproductions. At the same time, a new *cavea* was fashioned, this time using a segmented double wall for strength and to support an external access gallery for the audience; its lack of symmetry smacks of local builders. Later agricultural use destroyed the south-west *cavea* segments and made it impossible to distinguish the restructured stage area.

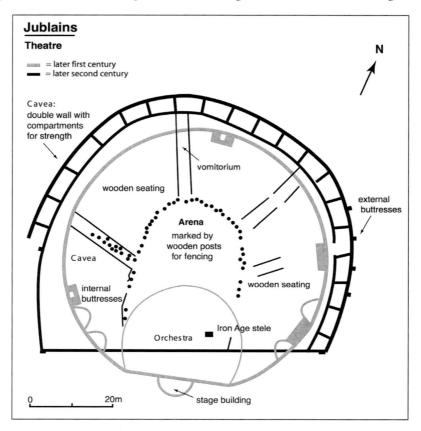

The Fortress

Magdelaine certainly 'revealed' the fortress in 1839, in the process removing 3000 cartloads of rubble, a loss deeply felt by later archaeologists! However, following René Rebuffat's research (in the 1990s), there is no doubt that construction took place in three stages: the central building, then the earth rampart and last, the trapezoidal stone rampart.

Central building. Immediately striking are the substantial **granite blocks** used to face the exterior; they are mainly cut in regular shapes although some are not, yet these are neatly notched and appear to fit almost Inca-style. Some show leverage and lifting holes used in the quarry and construction work. Whilst robbed for medieval building, enough blocks survive to indicate that this building must have given a massive impression of forbidding strength as the walls rose at least 6–7m high and, with the rubble core and internal *petit appareil* facing, were over 2m thick. At the corners, forming an 'H' design, towers rose at least 8–9m. The **main entrance** was wide enough for a small cart, but there are two **posterns** for pedestrian access to the towers; holes in the walls show that they were secured with massive beams. Arched brickwork above doorways seems a minor concession to decoration. The central *impluvium* must have helped in collecting rainwater – drainage was a serious problem all over the site – but its main function would have been to bring some light to the courtyard as the stone bases for thick posts indicate the yard was roofed, probably with an intervening storey as well.

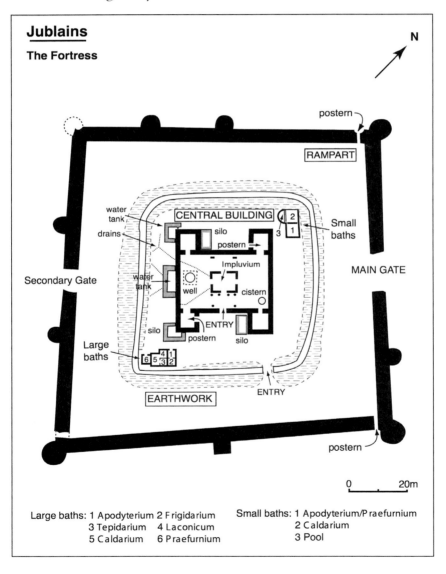

Jublains

The Fortress

N

postern

RAMPART

water tank

CENTRAL BUILDING

2

3 1

Small baths

drains

silo

3

postern

Impluvium

MAIN GATE

Secondary Gate

water tank

well

cistern

silo

ENTRY

postern

silo

Large baths

6 5 4 1
3 2

ENTRY

EARTHWORK

postern

0   20m

Large baths: 1 Apodyterium 2 Frigidarium
3 Tepidarium   4 Laconicum
5 Caldarium   6 Praefurnium

Small baths: 1 Apodyterium/Praefurnium
2 Caldarium
3 Pool

This is clearly not a *quadriburgium* type fort, like Le Rubricaire (STE-GEMMES-LE-ROBERT), the towers do not project on all sides. Parallels have been found in Hungary and Egypt (in paintings) where such buildings are linked to farming and were used as barns.

Despite the contrast with conventional warehouses, the most convincing interpretation seems to be that it was designed as a military supply stronghold: it could undoubtedly have withstood attack by either bandits or even quite large forces lacking siege equipment. The collection of supplies, to become a tax-in-kind – the *annona militaris* – became more systematic during the third century from the Severans onwards. Though Rebuffat found no strong dating evidence he considers the building to have been early third century. It may also have played a part in the *cursus publicus*, the imperial postal and fiscal service, by providing accommodation in the towers for officials; it may equally have operated as a base for a detachment of *benificarii*, the soldiers policing the service and countering brigands. The provision of two **bathhouses**, one with a full set of bathing rooms in miniature, the other only a hot room and bath, have an 'officers and men' look to them.

External additions and earthwork defences. The earthwork was a later construction than the central building because it covers drains from the *impluvium* and elsewhere; this was quite definitely defensive, dated to some time after the latest coins found under it (Tetricus 271–273), and was perhaps contemporary with the silos and water collectors added to the exterior of the central building. Its wide entrance and grooved stone pavings suggest that large carts could be brought in and parked here with fodder and water for the animals. The defences were being strengthened with a ditch (not visible today) cut into the solid granite when, almost finished, this was abandoned as new much stronger defences were decided upon.

Stone rampart. This was a typical late Roman project, 4.8m thick with circular corner and semi-circular intermediary towers, the latter added to the rampart when it was finished. Like many city defences it has foundations and lower courses with re-used column drums and mouldings brought from the town. The carefully cut small stonework and regular decorative brick courses of the exterior are marked by equally unnecessary trowel-picked mortar joints. The two entrances raise the question why are they simply openings? It could be that they have been robbed out, but there are no lintels or pavings either and the adjacent rampart facings show they were ready for towers, but without any trace of them. Even the postern doorways have not been provided with any locking devices. For Rebuffat, the implication is that this rampart was never finished. The

Jublains. The dodecahedron. PRISMA, Musée Archéologique de Jublains

The town as a whole is represented by a large-scale model which is being modified as research continues, and there is a large screen 'virtual tour' of the fortress. There are samples of finds from the many excavations. From the sanctuary, there is a delicate **pigeon painting** found in the portico east entrance, a bronze **votive eye tablet**, and numerous pipeclay Venuses. The broken Orgetorix theatre inscription – note his unromanised name – and a column fragment decorated with a **theatre mask**, were recovered from the fortess rampart foundations. From various habitation and workshop sites come fire rakes, local pottery, loom weights, evidence of glass production, jeweller's tools, an intaglio and **coiner's moulds** – evidence of a strictly illegal practice and punishable by death, but found widely during the inflationary third century. Most interesting perhaps, is the **dodecahedron** (a 1995 find in a luxury goods shop). No ancient author describes these enigmatic twelve-sided objects, each face is formed by a pentagon and punctuated by holes of varying sizes. Theories abound, but a mystical religious interpretation seems the most plausible. Most have no pictorial decoration, but one found in Geneva had signs of the zodiac on each face: a divinatory dice seems as convincing an explanation as any.

LARÇAY, Indre-et-Loire
IGN 1822 E
GPS 31 T 0332125/5248357

Late Roman fort.

12km E of Tours by D976, turn S at Larçay by rue de la Croix, signposted
Bellevue Bureau de Poste. At the roundabout, take rue du Castellum c.50m
to small roundabout; follow road 100m, signposted La Tour and
Castellum.

The fort sits on a bluff facing north, high above Larçay village and the river
Cher. Despite its proximity to a modern city, the hamlet of La Tour is
surprisingly rural. The few houses are covered in flowers and it is
birdsong, not traffic, that makes the most noise. The western half of the
fort's southern face is obscured by the farmhouses built in and over the
rampart and towers – one is now a wine cellar, but the eastern half still
presents 5–6m high walls and two massive towers. The *petit appareil* and the
brick courses of the external facing has been heavily robbed out, but on the
eastern side, the wider footing of *grand appareil* is quite clear.

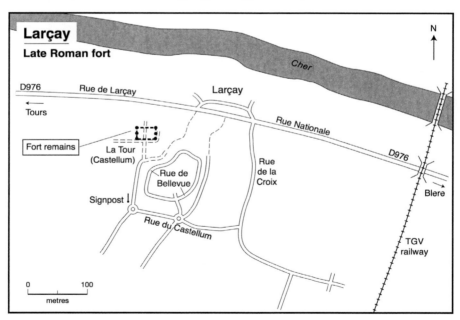

The fort overlooked the main Roman road linking Tours and Bourges and
a north–south road down from the Loire. The northern wall of this
irregular trapezoid fort was understandably built to a minimum thickness
(only 2.2m), whilst the southern was double that; the east and west walls
in-between. There had been a villa close by at Bellevue, occupied certainly

during the first and second centuries, and this had been plundered for stone and brick – the fort's foundations include column half drums and sculptured pieces. However, no dating evidence has emerged from any of the fort excavations, the most extensive having been Jason Wood's in the 1980s.

Though obviously late Roman, the fort's purpose is obscure. The interior has provided no help here, any buildings must have been constructed of wood and have left no trace. Certainly any force based here would have been small as the fort is only a third of a hectare (similar to Le Rubricaire at STE-GEMMES-LE-ROBERT). Obviously the troops could oversee road and river movements between major centres, providing escorts for transporting supplies, perhaps protecting materials moving between Tours and THÉSÉE; but at less than one day's march away it is surprisingly close to Tours. Another possibility is that it formed part of a system of outer defences for Tours, along with the supposed *castellum* at LUYNES to the west from Tours. This would make sense perhaps if these forts were built in the late third century when only the amphitheatre in Tours had been fortified and before the city's ramparts were constructed during the second half of the fourth century, so removing the need for dispersing troops in this way. A further possibility is the fort was part of a strategy that was suddenly changed: Wood thought the northern wall may never have been finished. Without contemporary written evidence or appropriate archaeological material the real purpose of Larçay's fort will remain a matter for speculation.

Le MANS, Sarthe
IGN 1719 E

Major rampart and sanctuary site.

For the motoring enthusiast Le Mans is synonymous with the 24-hour race and the Renault factory; for the casual visitor the town is always surrounded with heavy traffic and impossible in mid-June. But for anyone interested in Antiquity, it is its magnificent late Roman ramparts, whose brick and mortar led to Le Mans' medieval nickname of the 'red city' which make it such a worthwhile visit. Now there is an additional reason for coming here: in the Allonnes suburb is one of the most revealing modern excavations of a major Gallo-Roman sanctuary anywhere in western France.

The promontory sites of Le Mans and Allonnes are 5km apart, both looking down on the Sarthe river. During the nineteenth century there was much debate on the early occupation of the sites, seemingly equally appropriate as possible Iron Age *oppida* and/or Roman *civitas* capitals. Subsequent work has clarified the role of Allonnes. At La Forêterie, from at least the fifth century BC, there was a sanctuary of some kind. In the Roman era this became a major enclosed temple site dedicated to Mars Mullo and broadly comparable to that at CORSEUL.

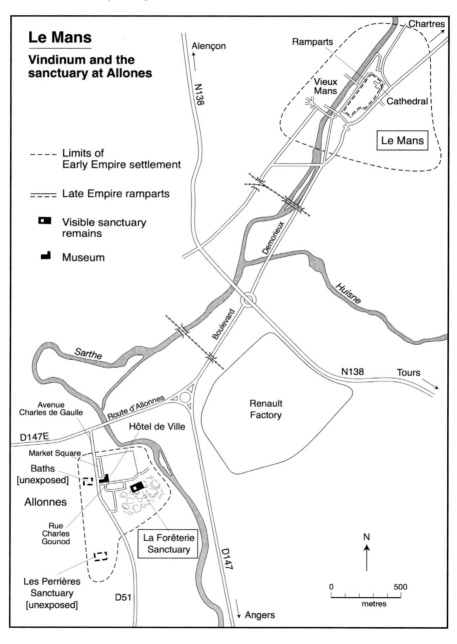

Close by at Les Perrières there was another sanctuary, there was a large bath complex in rue Pasteur, and, enough evidence of other occupation at Allonnes to justify identifying this as a sanctuary-*vicus*. Surprisingly, in Le Mans itself, even with extensive research since the 1960s and the occasional find of La Tène material, there is no case yet for seeing a pre-Roman Cenomanni *oppidum* here, despite the site's suitability and its subsequent Celtic name. What cannot be doubted is that from the Augustan era onwards *Vindunum* (Le Mans) was the Cenomanni's political capital – a hub for the Roman transport network with links by road or river to the Loire at both Tours and Angers, to the eastern and southern Gaul via Orléans in the middle Loire, to north-eastern Gaul via Chartres and west to Jublains and Brittany.

The Cenomanni occupied an ill-defined and not particularly productive territory between the more sharply differentiated Armorica and the northern plains and Paris basin with their Belgic tribes. Caesar links the Cenomanni with the Diablintes as 'Aulerci', but this was probably his way of suggesting that there was some loose federation of *pagi*, pulled, in the way border regions are, by external pressures that made it easy for Augustus to create two *civitates* and for the later bishopric and county of Maine to be split again into the departments of Mayenne and Sarthe.

Vindunum grew slowly. Evidence of Augustan and Tiberian houses and workshops is preserved especially well in the damp valley left by the 'lost river' Isaac and revealed in the many rescue digs that characterised the 1980s and 1990s; they showed few signs of Romanisation in construction. Provost (1993) postulated some of this early housing was deliberately destroyed, perhaps during the AD21 revolt (see HISTORICAL DEVELOPMENT). Certainly it was only under Claudius the slopes of the old town were first terraced, stone foundations were utilised and the first known public building was constructed – the baths in rue École des Beaux-Arts. It is unlikely the town ever had a coherent grid because of the uneven topography. Modern estimates suggest by mid-second century it covered some 40ha, small but still markedly larger than the Diablintes capital at JUBLAINS.

No *forum* site or temples have been firmly identified, and whilst a theatre of some kind was revealed in 1792, almost all traces were subsequently destroyed and are only recalled in the 'rue du cirque' street name. Finds of architectural fragments and sculpture have been rare. Two short aqueducts (1.5 and 4km long) and numerous wells have been identified. Whilst evidence of noble houses has been found, they were not on a truly grand scale. Perhaps the latter were built on Vieux Mans hill and are hidden today by medieval building or lie untouched by archaeological survey in the suburbs, maybe on the right bank of the river Sarthe, which was certainly crossed by a bridge in the Roman era. Alternatively -though less likely - the Cenomanni elite expressed their status simply by creating communal sanctuaries: it is now known that Allonnes was not the only grand sanctuary site outside Le Mans, as c.10kms north, a vast temple complex was revealed in 2010 by INRAP at Neuville-sur-Sarthe.

The upsurge in rescue digs in Le Mans also showed that some zones were abandoned in the late second century. The third century culminated with the decision to build the ramparts, enclosing the part of the city that offered most security, Vieux Mans, some 9ha. Their construction involved the destruction of many buildings and only modest occupation continued outside them between the fourth and seventh centuries (see RENNES where recent work has shown a significant quarter of urban living outside the walls). Nevertheless, *Civitas Cenomannorum* or *Cenomanos* not only retained its status as a local capital, but also took over control of the Diablintes, a change of status marked most clearly at JUBLAINS by the fortification of a single building. The *Notitia Dignitatum* notes that Le Mans was the headquarters of a prefect responsible for *laeti* and *Suebi gentiles*, perhaps these 'barbarian' settler troops supplied some of Le Mans' garrison forces. The Germanic Suebi, generally ex-prisoners, may have been cavalry: they were best known for being horsemen and their topknot hairstyle.

A saintly bishop Julian, mentioned first in the sixth century, is believed to have brought Christianity to the city in the fourth century; certainly Le Mans bishops figure at Church councils from the mid-fifth century. An early episcopal church is presumed to exist under the cathedral, but no excavation has taken place to prove this. As at Angers, a bishop had an oratory built on top of one of the towers by his cathedral; sadly, all traces of this tower have been lost under the 'jet d'eau' fountain. Equally, no traces appear to have survived of other early churches.

Ramparts

The western rampart overlooking the Sarthe is spectacular; the eastern and northern ramparts are more typical survivals; the south and south-west defences are simply known from now hidden traces or logical deduction. The ramparts once had between 42 and 48 towers, and probably two main entrances, one on the narrow northern side and another on the east facing the old heart of the Roman city; no vestige of either exists. Four postern gates have survived, but there were probably double this number.

The following should be read in conjunction with THE DEFENCE OF WESTERN ROMAN GAUL. It is there you will find what for me are fascinating questions raised by these and other Roman rampart remains in the West. How were they actually constructed and what governed their design choices? Who decided to build such defences and when? How were they manned and used by defenders? What are the implications posed for us by these ramparts when we reflect on late Roman society?

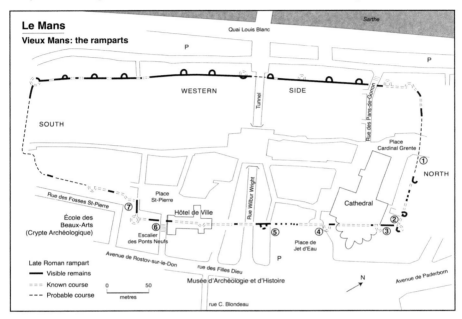

Le Mans
Vieux Mans: the ramparts

The western face.
Use parking areas off quai Louis-Blanc.

Here is the best preserved and most impressive stretch of late Roman city defences anywhere in France. Like Carcassonne in the south, the hilltop position and clear ground in front accentuate their impact; but unlike Carcassonne, these defences have been far less modified by either medieval repairs or romantic restorers. Though no original crenellation survives, curtain walling still reaches walkway level, in many places touching 7–8 metres above the foundations, and a number of towers rise many metres above this. Further pleasures are the almost fanciful bands of patterns that decorate the facings and the pink glow, most apparent in afternoon sunlight.

Generally late Roman ramparts are above all practical. The aesthetic appeal is restrained though present. Different rock types for the *grand* and *petit appareil* contrasted the foundations and the walling above or sharpened the appearance of corners. Even the widespread use of brick courses cannot be explained by the need to stabilise walling (brick courses rarely cross the

231

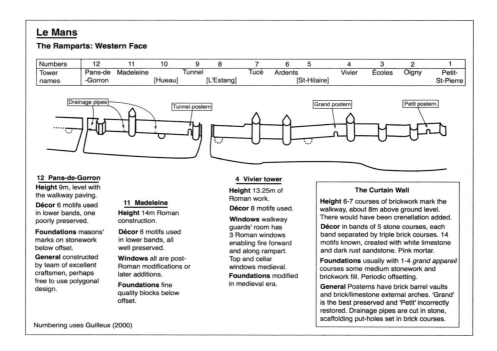

Le Mans

The Ramparts: Western Face

Numbers	12	11	10	9	8	7	6	5	4	3	2	1
Tower names	Pans-de-Gorron	Madeleine	Tunnel [Hueau]		[L'Estang]	Tucé	Ardents	[St-Hilaire]	Vivier	Écoles	Oigny	Petit-St-Pierre

12 Pans-de-Gorron

Height 9m, level with the walkway paving.

Décor 6 motifs used in lower bands, one poorly preserved.

Foundations masons' marks on stonework below offset.

General constructed by team of excellent craftsmen, perhaps free to use polygonal design.

11 Madeleine

Height 14m Roman construction.

Décor 6 motifs used in lower bands, all well preserved.

Windows all are post-Roman modifications or later additions.

Foundations fine quality blocks below offset.

4 Vivier tower

Height 13.25m of Roman work.

Décor 8 motifs used.

Windows walkway guards' room has 3 Roman windows enabling fire forward and along rampart. Top and cellar windows medieval.

Foundations modified in medieval era.

The Curtain Wall

Height 6-7 courses of brickwork mark the walkway, about 8m above ground level. There would have been crenellation added.

Décor in bands of 5 stone courses, each band separated by triple brick courses. 14 motifs known, created with white limestone and dark rust sandstone. Pink mortar.

Foundations usually with 1-4 *grand appareil* courses some medium stonework and brickwork fill. Periodic offsetting.

General Posterns have brick barrel vaults and brick/limestone external arches. 'Grand' is the best preserved and 'Petit' incorrectly restored. Drainage pipes are cut in stone, scaffolding put-holes set in brick courses.

Numbering uses Guilleux (2000)

rampart's thickness), instead the builders clearly enjoyed the opposition of colours and textures in brick and stone, just as the framing of windows and doors went beyond the essential.

Here at Le Mans is something on a totally different scale. The array of **decorative patterns** and colours is startling and beautiful. It surely could not fail to impress anyone, hostile or benign. There are exuberant bands of chevrons, diamonds, triangles, circle-like hexagons, alternating lines, white diamonds separated by hourglass forms – and more. All created by setting courses of dark (sandstone) and white (limestone) in rose mortar.

Why here and not on other ramparts? It is likely that the decision drew upon two strands. First, military men could see it as an assertion of confidence and intimidation, like the bright colours on the planes of First World War fighter aces; occasional examples have been noted elsewhere on British Saxon shore forts and the Köln rampart. Second, there is evidence that Cenomanni craftsmen liked this sort of décor: traces have been observed on the theatre and temple at AUBIGNÉ-RACAN, fragments on the Rennes rampart suggest that they worked there as well. Nowhere else has such a display of exuberance survived.

hypocaust. The suspended floor is covered by a mosaic, not quite aligned with the eight walls. The geometric décor survived but not the central emblem, probably a figure of some kind.

Musée d'Archéologie et d'Histoire
Le Carré Plantagenêt
2 rue Claude Blondeau
72000 Le Mans

Hours: 10am-6pm closed Mondays

This sparkling contemporary museum is dedicated to the city's rich archaeology with material from prehistory to the medieval era. New Gallo-Roman material from the many recent excavations is now on display, integrated with the nineteenth and early twentieth century collections.

Iron Age. INRAP rescue digs along the A28 in Sarthe as well as revealing how dense the Gallic farm network was also found iron mines and smelting remains which stimulated the museum to organise a presentation around the theme of ancient mining. A **coin hoard** found in 1997 the Sablons district of Le Mans, is a glittering example of late Gallic coining, particularly the Alexander style heads (obverse) and the dislocated chariots (reverse). Most of the coins are Cenomanni, some are possibly Diablintes.

Gallo-Roman. *Vindunum*'s ramparts have a significant place in the displays, with a wall panel, video and a model which shows men at work constructing two towers and a section of curtain wall. Other models evoke the AUBIGNÉ-RACAN and Allonnes(see below) sanctuaries. For me though, the **moustached head**, a lone survivor of what was probably a large statue, is the most interesting exhibit. Despite the Gallo-Roman provenance, the head with its moustache, large eyes, bulging cheeks, heavy head and hair in crude stylised rolls is distinctly and attractively Gallic. Was it the embodiment of an ancestor kept by a noble family? The main interest of the late Antiquity material (fourth to eigth centuries), drawn in the main from rural cemeteries, is in the fact that it does not appear, in any obvious way, Christian.

Allonnes
GPS 31T 0288479/5316728

From Le Mans take the D147/Boulevard Demorieux across the Sarthe and follow the D147E/Route d'Allonnes. At roundabout, turn left for Allonnes centre/Avenue Charles le Gaulle; after 600m, turn left on rue Charles Gounod for 200m to a parking area between tower blocks. Climb any track

50m through the trees for La Tour-aux-Fées, the local name for the sanctuary at La Forêterie.

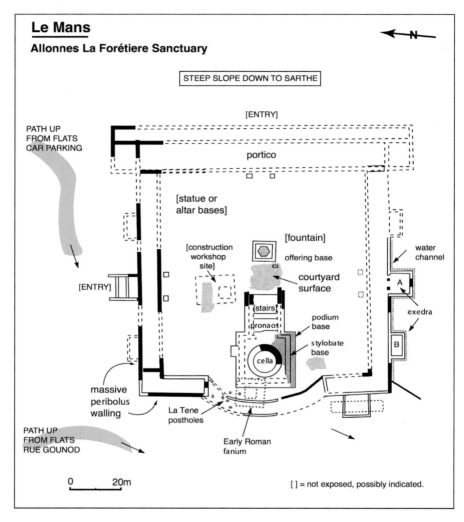

Le Mans

Allonnes La Forétiere Sanctuary

N

STEEP SLOPE DOWN TO SARTHE

[ENTRY]

PATH UP
FROM FLATS
CAR PARKING

portico

[statue or
altar bases]

[fountain]

[construction
workshop
site]

offering base

water
channel

[ENTRY]

courtyard
surface

A

[stairs]

podium
base

exedra

pronaos

stylobate
base

cella

B

massive
peribolus
walling

La Tene
postholes

PATH UP
FROM FLATS
RUE GOUNOD

Early Roman
fanum

0   20m

[ ] = not exposed, possibly indicated.

Ancient ruins were first noted here in sixteenth century quarrying, but serious excavations only took place when Pierre Térouanne, the son-in-law of the then proprietor, recognised its potential and began many years work here (1953–79). He revealed the site's main features, despite the removal of so much of the sanctuary fabric previously. However, real advances in understanding have taken place since 1994, when the team directed by Véronique Brouquier-Reddé and Katherine Gruel began work. Their sensitive awareness of the opportunities offered here helped them treat the site as more than a collection of structures and finds, but rather a place which people had once shaped, used, modified and abandoned as their needs evolved. Most striking has been the sophisticated treatment of the La Tène deposits and the precision of their closely dated stratigraphic phases for the Gallo-Roman period. Work continues and certainly more will be learnt, but parts of the site have already been prepared for presentation.

The Iron Age sanctuary
The pre-Roman wooden sanctuary is hinted at by modern markers.

So far, it has been possible to distinguish two phases prior to the first century BC. Initially, a palisaded enclosure surrounded two round buildings, later replaced by rectangular structures. Unstratified metalwork finds show that people were here at the end of the fifth century BC during La Tène A. So far neither buildings nor finds demonstrate in themselves that this was a place of worship, though this seems very likely as the La Tène B and C finds (late fourth to early third centuries BC) are much more typical of other sacred sites, with fragments of ten swords, brooches and bracelets: typical 'warrior' gifts.

The period from the early first century BC (La Tène D) to the Augustan era brought significant changes. The site was levelled – mixing the finds mentioned above – and a rectangular wooden *fanum* temple was built. Clustered around it were found more than 500 Cenomanni coins together with Roman imperial coinage and some military equipment; the excavators tentatively suggest that this material may represent service by Cenomanni leaders in Roman auxiliary forces, a common way by which local elites adapted to the new order.

The Roman sanctuary

The stone *fanum*. Using the same dimensions and lying on top of the wooden structure a new stone *fanum* was constructed, dated by a coin to Claudius (41–54) and so contemporary with the beginning of stone building in *Vindunum*. This remained in use until the AD80s/90s. Nearby, three inscriptions on bases dedicated to Mars Mullo were found. He is certainly a regional god, being the most important deity amongst the Redones too (see RENNES). Considering the later embellishment of the site and its proximity to *Vindunum*, Mars Mullo must have been the Cenomanni *civitas* deity as well, and, given the stone *fanum*'s imprint on the wooden, Mullo is likely to have been the earlier tribal god.

The new sanctuary. The overall plan derives from the Templum Pacis in Rome begun by Titus after he crushed the Jewish Revolt (71AD). This Flavian model spread throughout the Gallic provinces in the first and second centuries (see JUBLAINS and CORSEUL). The design was characterised by a *peribolus* or external wall which formed the outer part of a portico, enclosing an inner courtyard. Typically, the court incorporated statues of leading citizens, altars with dedications, a fountain, and a central base where offerings could be made. These elements are found in all such sanctuaries; the large number of *exedra* or recesses in the *peribolus* here, where there could be elaborate décor and seating, was less usual.

Some sanctuaries had the temple integrated in the portico, like the original in Rome, in others it was quite separate and many, like this one, had a temple framed by an apse. Only part of the podium survives, but enough to indicate the design. The strengthened base for the *cella* shows that it was circular within a square frame. A still visible internal wall suggests that this was the foundation for a *stylobate* or base for a line of columns around the cella. The less well preserved front clearly extended into the court and is likely to have supported a *pronaos* or pillared entrance hall approached by a steep staircase. The podium alone would have risen 4m and the *cella* could have been as much as 17.5m high (based on comparisons with Corseul).

Construction. The sanctuary was built between AD80/90 and 160. Within this period the archaeologists were able to distinguish five sealed and firmly dated strata. This has enabled them to follow in detail the construction process and to conclude that the sanctuary took around 70 years to finish, raising interesting questions about the accessibility of money and skilled labour for projects such as this; obviously the Cenomanni lacked the resources available in Rome, where it is believed the Templum Pacis took only 6–7 years to build, but it also implies that rapid completions in the Gallic provinces have been assumed too easily.

The masons set to work first on constructing the new temple. The waste from their work is scattered to the north of the building where they must have refined and finished the blocks. At least three different kinds of stone were used brought from various quarries by river, then up the steep road to the site. They would have fitted together the podium and then the *cella* and its surroundings, with the architectural specialists coming in last. This work took over 20 years. The carpenters, tilers and metalworkers then moved in. The latter had a workshop in what became the courtyard. Here, as well as the cinders and metal fragments, a rubbish pit shows that they were drinking wine, eating imported olives and living on site. They would have been making all the decorative fittings for the interior and exterior of the temple. They stayed for at least 20 years. Finally, work began on the courtyard and its surroundings around 140. The workshop was flattened and the uneven ground levelled, the drains were laid (rain and a clay bedrock made water a serious problem); masons and labourers were brought in to construct the foundations and the massive holding walls of the *peribolus* and portico (see the north-west *peribolus*); and last the panellers, plasterers and painters arrived to finish the work, especially on the monumental entrances and *exedra*. There was at least one other workshop outside the *peribolus*. This work was completed by 160.

Use. From the later second to early fourth centuries this was primarily a state ceremonial sanctuary. There will have been key occasions when the leading citizens came to make offerings to their god and the Emperor. There are few sealed strata from this period and the pottery is far less easy to date precisely. Nevertheless the archaeology is revealing: in *exedra* A floor remains were preserved and outside the northern entrance finds were equally extensive. Clearly many congregated there to prepare offerings and to eat – possibly at the major religious festivals. Sigillata plates and common ware are plentiful as well as the bones of meat consumed. There may have been a shop too and perhaps people camped here.

Abandonment. Only ceramics and coins from the first half of the fourth century are known and in declining numbers. A thick layer of cinders in *exedra* A has been dated to the 330s suggesting a major fire and hinting at systematic destruction. By the mid-fourth century the site seems to have been totally abandoned. Possibly this was the result of direct Christian pressure, but others factors may have been in play: this was a time when the elite withdrew from traditional public display and towns became strongholds. There was a ruthless dismissal of the ways of the past, epitomised by the new ramparts at Le Mans and a forlorn Allonnes sanctuary.

Allonnes exhibition
Centre Archéologique P. Térouanne
72700 Allonnes

Hours: 9am–noon, 1.30–6pm weekdays
　　　　9am–noon Saturday

Many of the La Forêterie finds and a few from elsewhere (e.g. Les Perrières) are displayed in the Hôtel de Ville (Rue Charles Gounod). However, further down the road there is a centre for archaeological research (CERAM). This is used to process the finds made locally, holds regular exhibitions and has planned a permanent museum.

The main Iron Age and conquest period finds from La Forêterie sanctuary are the swords and scabbard remains, and a sample of the Gallic and early Roman coins. The key finds associated with the first century AD *fanum* phase are the **dedications to Mars Mullo** by Crescens, a public slave, set on a short round column. Whilst dedications by slaves were not unusual, public or communally owned slaves are rarely found in Gaul. The other inscription records Severus Niger, a common enough name for a Romanised inhabitant.

The remaining displays, largely in simple glass cases, focus on the enlarged sanctuary. The architectural stonework is fragmentary, but there is a reasonable Corinthian capital from the *stylobate*. Evidence of the extensive panelling and paving is supplied by pieces of schist, fine limestones and various marbles, some from Greece and North Africa. Tiny painted plaster samples represent the considerable quantity of plaster necessary to secure the mortar from rain damage. Entrances and some *exedra* had **relief work**: the best surviving pieces are heads that are interpreted as **Mars**, his upturned pose and helmet showing clear Graeco-Roman origins, and an **old woman wearing a turban**, taken to be a wet nurse, often present in mythological scenes. It is a type of décor that hints at the sanctuary's role in state-inspired worship.

It is sad that so many of the later second and early third century inscriptions are no more than scraps, even if specialists have been able to show that they nearly all represent civic and imperial dedications. One set of fragments combined suggests a career inscription to a senator and a governor of Lugdunensis, but no more. It is a pity too that the metalworkers left such scrappy remains of their important work! The pipeclay figurines are mainly **Venus figures**, with the occasional smiling baby, yet the sanctuary was not a healing centre; most of them come from outside the entrances and perhaps were bought as charms rather than for use as votive objects. The pins, brooches, rings and bracelets and the later Roman coins are unspectacular. Found scattered around the sanctuary, they look like losses rather than gifts to a deity; yet they are a reminder of the people who came here, in the same way the ceramics help us remember the offerings they made and the ritual feasting that took place. The **bone remains** show that pork then beef, were the most popular meats; they also indicate that after slaughter only the legs and heads were consumed on the spot, the remainder being given or sold to the populace (as it was in Rome) from stalls outside the sanctuary.

LUYNES, Indre-et-Loire
IGN 1822 O
GPS 30 T 0309550/5247667

Aqueduct.

10km W of Tours by D952. Turn N into village and take road for

seats near the arena and two precincts filled with rows of wooden benches.

The arena, 50.7m x 34.5m, is also grass covered and surrounded by a podium wall that survives in some places to 1.5–2.0m; in addition there are traces of a lower wall creating a drainage ditch to carry away rain. There were three entrances, two at the narrow ends and one by the road. Opposite the latter was a small chamber with a vaulted roof which is still in good condition. A broken bronze statuette of Mercury was found here, suggesting it was a tiny temple. Other possibilities include its use by gladiators or to secure wild animals, or maybe simply for storing material used in religious ceremonies.

Châtillon-Coligny Musée de l'Ancien Hôtel-Dieu
2 Faubourg du Puyrault
45230 Châtillon-Coligny

Hours: All year 2–5.30pm at weekends
        Easter–Oct. 2–5.30pm Tuesday–Friday

This sixteenth century mansion contains a small archaeological collection with a scattering of finds from **Montbouy**. These include a number of white pipeclay votive figures (Venuses, seated suckling goddesses and 'smiling' babies); the rarer wooden votive offerings are in Orléans. Metalwork ranges from nails to keys and shears. Of the six hoards found at Montbouy, three reached the museum; many coins had inevitably disappeared. Most interesting are the pictures and photographs recording the nineteenth century excavations. As elsewhere, J.-B. Jollois (see ORLÉANS) commissioner for Loiret ancient monuments in 1836, was the earliest to make accurate drawings of the sites exposed.

There is a display of La Tène I/II material from a small cemetery in the nearby hamlet of Cortrat, but more remarkable are the finds from Cortrat's 33 fourth century burials. The dead had been buried here fully dressed with offerings beside them. A number of the women wore massive bell-shaped *fibulae*, one on each shoulder, securing and decorating their tunics. They also wore necklaces of brightly coloured glass beads, coral and amber, with finger rings of gold and silver. Some of the male burials contained weapons: one had a Germanic throwing axe, a sword belt buckle and a crossbow brooch, the last two often signs of late Roman military rank. This could be a group of settler soldiers recruited in Pannonia where the *fibulae* were especially popular, perhaps a group of *laeti* settled in the district to defend the Empire. The *Notitia Dignitatum* mentions a *Praefectus Laetorum Teutoniorum Carnunta Senoniae Lugdunensis*, that is a commander of *laeti* based in Senonia (Lugdunensis IV) drawn from Germans in the Carnuntum area on the Pannonian Danube frontier.

NANTES, Loire-Atlantique
IGN 1223 E

Museum and sites.

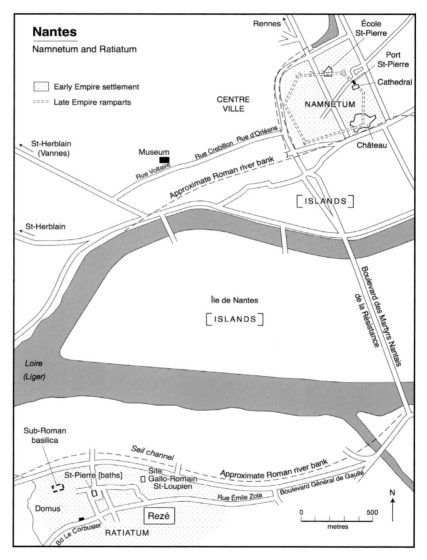

According to the second century Greek historian Polybius, Pytheas, on his epic voyage from Marseille around Spain through the Bay of Biscay and into the northern seas c.352BC, stopped at the trading centre of *Corbilo* on the river Liger (Loire). The most obvious site for *Corbilo* has always seemed to be Nantes, but no trace has been found of any fourth century BC settlement. This is not conclusive however: the lower Loire was a constantly changing environment and nowhere more so than at the head of the narrow estuary, 55km from the Atlantic. The relentless movement of currents and silt created new islands and new channels, undercut old banks and made fresh ones, yet the river and its valley were always a major route to and from the interior of Gaul.

When Augustus established the administrative structure for Gaul that was to last for three centuries, Strabo wrote 'The Liger discharges its waters between the Pictones and the Namnetes' (*Geography*, IV, 2.1). The Pictones were placed in Aquitania and the Namnetes in Lugdunensis, but the Ambiliati, an Armorican tribe, listed by Caesar (*BG*, III. 9) as supporters of the Veneti in the difficult 56BC campaign, are not mentioned by Strabo at all. It seems probable that by his time, the Pictones had been rewarded for their help in that campaign by the grant of Ambiliati territory south of the Loire. The Namnetes and Pictones chose to found Roman style port-towns facing each other across the Loire, though these were linked – to their mutual benefit – by a wooden bridge, they probably competed for the Atlantic and the river trade. Ptolemy, writing in the second century AD mentions *Ratiatum* (*Geography*, II, 7.5), today Rezé, and *Condevicnum* (II, 8.7), probably Nantes. There is uncertainty over this identification because no one else mentions *Condevicnum* and inscriptions found in the town only specify a '*vicus portuensis*'. Whether they refer to a part of the town, a perfectly acceptable use of the term *vicus*, or whether this means *Condevicnum* was somewhere else is still being debated.

The Namnetes' town was enclosed on the west and north by the final bend of the Erdre. During an active period of searching in the nineteenth century, traces of housing and small finds confirmed the town's existence, but little sign that it became much more than a riverside port backed by artisans' workshops and the occasional large house. By the end of the second century it seems that its maximum extent was barely 20ha. No public buildings are known apart from an inscription recording a temple to Mars Mullo. There is no mention of *civitas* administrators and a dedication by leading *vicus* inhabitants including the *nautae Ligeri* (Loire boatmen) may hint at where the real power lay: they dedicated a square, a portico and a 'tribunal' – perhaps really a theatre – to Augustus and Vulcan. If more excavations are permitted in the historic centre the picture may well change.

Nantes' late Roman development is perhaps surprising: the rampart enclosed 16ha, when most defended areas in northern Gaul involved major contractions from their high Empire peaks. Two factors possibly led to this: silting had made south bank *Ratiatum* more difficult to use and *Portus*

Namnetum was seen as a better strongpoint. A resident prefect and his troops organised regional defence against Saxon pirates, and a bishopric was established here in the later fourth century. By the beginning of the fifth century the town was known as *Civitas Namnetum* or simply *Namnetes*.

As Roman Gaul disintegrated in the fifth century, *Namnetes* maintained a semblance of vitality. Amphorae and early Christian sigillata continued to be imported from Aquitania and the Mediterranean whilst tin from north of the town was exported. But it faced Saxon pirates who used the coast and the Loire's many islands as bases; the emergence of a Breton identity from the mix of Roman Armorica with British immigrants: and, to their east, the growing power of the Franks. By 511, *Namnetes* was clearly under Merovingian control, its bishop attending the Church council in Orléans, under the auspices of Clovis. The first known cathedral on the St-Pierre site dates from the mid-sixth century.

Dramatic discoveries since the 1980s have exposed the unexpected importance of Gallo-Roman *Ratiatum*. The discovery of rich baths sites in the 1860s and 1890s and a *fanum* in 1915, demonstrated Roman occupation but not its type or extent. Jean-René Le Nezet, Stéphane Deschamps and Lionel Pirault have shown that at Rezé there was an urban centre of 40–50ha, at least twice the size of Roman Nantes. A further surprise was to find such clear evidence that this was a new foundation in the last years BC, not only was there evidence of a properly surveyed road grid, but there were also ditches defining building plots. When the southern limits of the grid were exposed in 1997, it became clear that the founders had ambitions to create an even bigger city as *insulae* here remained unused.

Widespread commercial districts have been revealed, including by the early second century an extensive and well-constructed quayside, warehouses, workshops, baths and toilets for the dockers and boatmen, shops, at least one public baths, and much varied habitation including grand peristyle houses. Today a large industrial zone covers the Seil channel, but palaeo-environmental research suggests that it was already experiencing silting problems in the Roman era; certainly urban decline had begun in the late second century, earlier than elsewhere, and continued through the third and fourth (perhaps with some citizens moving into *Namnetes*). Even so, in the fifth century a community was still functioning in the St-Pierre parish area, using pottery from Bordeaux and wealthy enough in the early sixth century to fund building a large *basilica* church.

The Nantes rampart

Virtually all the 1665m curtain wall, with horseshoe shaped towers and at least three gates, has been destroyed or remains hidden (the renovation of the château may mean some rampart exposure). Irregular thickness, differing construction techniques and non-standard facings imply a mixed team of builders, or a long time frame. No firm chronological evidence has been found and estimates have ranged from the 270s to 350s.

Port St-Pierre
Rue de l'Évêché on the northern side of the cathedral

Despite later medieval work, this single vaulted gate was shown in 1910–11 to be of Gallo-Roman origin with two towers protecting it.

École St-Pierre
Rue d'Aguesseau

In the schoolyard there is a section about 12m long and 5.1m high. The postern gates are later. Access is only possible with the school's permission.

Rezé

The extensive modern research carried out in this area, inspired particularly by Lionel Pirault, may result in more being presented to the public, particularly on the St-Loupien site, and perhaps the rare remains of a sixth century Christian church on the Champs-St-Martin site (shown on the Nantes plan as 'sub-Roman *basilica*').

Site Gallo-Romain St-Loupien
Rue St-Loupien

Trading quarter. Pillar panels are used to help visitors. Simple wood and earth habitations were replaced under Claudius (41–54) by the first storage buildings and shops. At the end of the first century these were rebuilt with new stone foundations and substantial timber and plaster walls. Finds suggest that this quarter was busiest during the second century but then saw marked decline, though low level activity continued through the third, fourth and fifth centuries. Rescue excavations in 2006 showed that the shops and workplaces continued westwards on the southern side of the road.

The public baths. In 1892 Léon Maître excavated two large rooms in the crypt of St-Loupien chapel. Since then the discovery of other walling and hypocausts have shown that here, on a low promontory near the Seil, was an extensive bath system that must have served both port and commercial workers. At the time of writing, only a glimpse through a low window indicates a small excavated area; group visits are possible.

Quayside. This was still being excavated 2011-12 and preservation is a possibility. The waterside quay was constructed with a thick oak timber base for a series of timber uprights with drystone infills between. A 20m section where ships were loaded, used the same construction method but in three steps, allowing heavy bags, barrels and amphorae to be lifted in stages. Slipways enabled small boats and carts to reach the water.

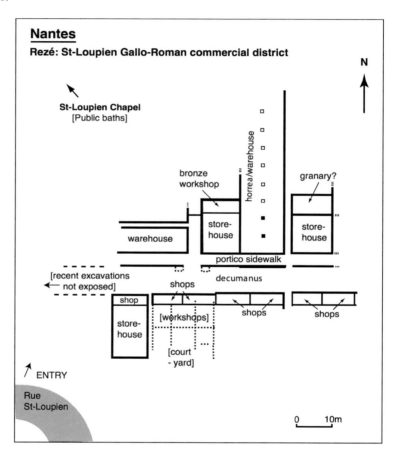

Domus site.
Boulevard Le Corbusier

In 1991, preceding the construction of new apartment blocks on the northern side of the boulevard, two peristyle *domus* houses were discovered. The block named *Domus* has been raised to enclose the preserved outline of the southern house. Stone and coloured gravels distinguish rooms, porticos and the internal courtyard. The modern *Domus* recalls Le Corbusier's 1950s designed flats across the road.

Musée Thomas Dobrée
18 rue Voltaire
44000 Nantes

Hours: 1.30–5.30pm Tuesday-Friday
2.30–5.30pm weekends

The following is based on visits before the closure of the museum for renovation. It reopens in 2015. The old museum demonstrated a real concern for meaning, relevant detail and visual imagination. Hopefully the new Musée Dobrée will be even better.

Iron Age
The sword display contains a fine first century BC **anthropomorphic sword-hilt** with a pommel in the form of a human bust. The more literal portrayal of the head hints at Roman influence, yet the pommel's 'arms' and handle guard 'legs' culminate in traditional Celtic ball design. Other metalwork has been imaginatively presented. A simple full-size black outline figure is dressed in **jewellery** showing how multiple bracelets and torcs were worn (the same technique is used to show Roman and Merovingian styles). A short video demonstrates a *fibula* being made by a modern craftsman, culminating in a photo of an Iron Age brooch, leading you back to the display case. A large map presents Breton **tribal coins**, encouraging you not only to admire the creative skills of Celtic coin engravers, but also to identify tribal variations. **Salt making** is enlivened by illustrations of workers and their furnaces by the foreshore and a site distribution map for the Atlantic coast and Breton peninsula indicates how archaeologists have classified variations in method according to the type of containers used in concentrating salt; it helps considerably in making sense of the real briquetage remains (see SALT, FISH AND ROMAN COOKING).

Gallo-Roman period
The twin city heritage is recognised in a large panel showing the Loire from the perspective of *Ratiatum*, a vision based on the results of recent excavations. Though little of this is reflected in the display cases, there is a set of bronzes thought to represent the *lararium* of a wealthy inhabitant found in the St-Pierre excavations in Rezé (1863). The dedication by the Namnetes' leading citizens Agedovir and Toutilla to Mars Mullo reinforces the gods leading position amongst eastern Armoricans as he was equally prominent with the Redones and Curiosolites. The continuance of the distinctly Gallic gods in this region is embodied most clearly in the crude earthenware 'horned one' or **Cernunnos**, portrayed here with a large penis and a dog at his feet. The dog attribute reinforces Cernunnos' animal power as a god of fertility. The **terracotta firedogs** are impressive and

rare, their massive animal busts suggesting they would have been used with ceremonial rather than domestic fires.

Nantes. Terracotta ram-headed firedogs. Cliché: Hervé Neveu-Dérotrie, Collection Musée Dobré, Conseil Générale de LoireAtlantique

In the cases covering the debris of daily life, the balsam bottles and a little candelabrum are attractive. However, the most important items displayed are both only fragments from the original finds. The **lead ingots**, of varying shape and size are late Roman, and no longer the standard rectangular blocks with imperial stamps. All come from Britain and were recovered (1983–6) from the Ploumanac'h shipwreck off the north Breton coast. They are the remnant of 371 ingots (22 tonnes) of such pure lead that the bulk were given to Grenoble to line the atomic research chambers used there! A much older cache is also represented by a fragment of the third century **Veillon hoard**. Its discovery in 1856 on the site of a coastal villa in the Vendée, led to a frenzy of treasure seeking and removal. Most of the gold and silver coins disappeared in days – an estimated 30,000 silver and at least 500 gold. Presented here are what reached the museum: silver spoons, rings and bracelets from one of the jars.

Sub-Roman world

That goldsmiths continued to produce high quality jewellery and coins is obvious from both the Merovingian and Visigoth material. The discovery of the Rezé early Christian church is recognised in a panel, but it is the pictorial **moulded bricks**, such as the Adam and Eve and the dog chasing a hare, that show the artistic freedom associated with the new faith.

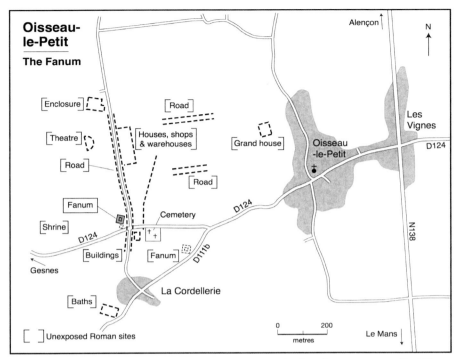

The excavations covered a wide area around the *fanum* as well. These demonstrated that the sanctuary filled an *insula* between paved north–south roads, with a narrower street on the southern side. There were other buildings close by including a shrine (*aedicula*). The *fanum* was abandoned in the third century and the site used as a workshop. This seems to have been part of a general movement by the dwindling fourth and fifth century population to an area on the eastern edge of the town focused around the church, which eventually evolved into the village of Oisseau-le-Petit.

ORLÉANS, Loiret
IGN 2219 ET

Major museum and rampart traces.

The prime reason for visiting Orléans is that here you can see a Roman sanctuary treasure, possibly the most remarkable and absorbing in all France. The town itself has only a few visible remains, but its history in Antiquity is better known than many, the result of an unusual number of written references and good archaeological research.

In the 20sBC, Strabo described the path of the Liger (Loire) from its upper reaches: 'the river after flowing past *Cenabum* -the emporium of the Carnutes at about the middle of the voyage- discharges its waters towards

255

the ocean.' (*Geography*, IV, 2.3). The Gallic settlement of *Cenabum* had developed at a natural transfer point. Where the river reached the furthest north, goods going up or down stream could be carried across the Beauce plain and from there reach the Paris basin or the Channel crossings. As Caesar made clear (*BG*, VII.11), a bridge had already been established at *Cenabum* replacing the fords and easing links with Aquitaine.

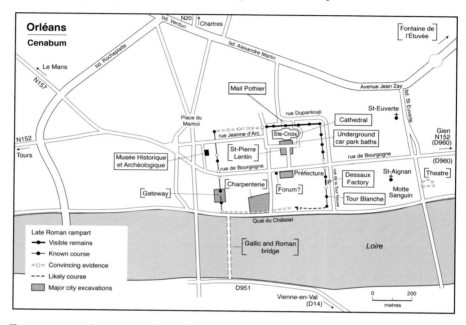

Carnutes territory stretched from the Sologne south of the Loire as far north as the banks of the Eure where it drained into the Seine. Caesar only mentions *Cenabum*, but the capital of the Gallo-Roman *civitas* was built at *Autricum* (Chartres) and this may well have been the tribe's major political centre before the conquest as well. The Beauce, a limestone plain between the two *oppida*, was productive: much was gently rolling countryside, already covered with cereals, rich in clover for sheep and with areas of deep oak forest. This was the largest tribal state in north-west France and symbolically important too: 'on a fixed day each year they [the Druids] assemble in a consecrated place in the territory of the Carnutes: that area is supposed to be the centre of the whole country of Gaul. People who have disputes to settle assemble there from all over the country.' (*BG*, VI.13).

Cenabum's trading possibilities had already made it important enough to be settled by Roman merchants before Caesar and his armies arrived in the Loire valley in 57BC; no doubt they made clear to him the strategic value of quartering troops amongst the Carnutes – permitting easy movement in any direction – and the availability of corn to feed them through the winter. Caesar overestimated the 'peace', or rather submission, that he had brought to Gaul by then and engaged in major propaganda and political exercises with his two expeditions to Britain during 56 and 55BC. When in the winter of 55–54 he spread out his legions in various encampments across north-eastern Gaul, his decision showed a concern that Gaul was not truly secured, though this policy exposed them to being picked off in isolation and helped encourage an atmosphere of rebellion.

The Carnutes, and their neighbours the Senones, took the first steps by killing their collaborator leaders, but the Belgic tribes in the north actually destroyed a Roman legion: Caesar's first counter-measures had to be against them. His success and rapid return led the Carnutes to back down. Caesar focused on the Senones, executing their leading rebel and wintering in their territory, again close to grain supplies from the Beauce and the Roman merchant suppliers of *Cenabum*. But the tensions of 54BC did not disappear. During the winter of 53BC, inter-tribal meetings were held hidden in the forests. The Carnutes then took the step that signalled a mass uprising. Their massacre of the Roman traders in *Cenabum*, including one of equestrian birth, led directly to Vercingetorix's inspirational actions – culminating in the final defeat of serious Gallic resistance in 52BC.

Before confronting Vercingetorix, Caesar began his punishment of the Carnutes by surprising *Cenabum* in a rapid movement and then sacking the settlement. It did not stop the tribe raising the largest single contingent from western Gaul (12,000 men) to join the force that failed to relieve Alesia and save Vercingetorix. Even after Alesia fell the tribe did not formally surrender: it took Roman occupation to bring this about, after the bitter winter of 52-1BC when people scattered, starved and died in the forests and fields around. The crushed Carnutes finally handed over Gutruatus, instigator of the *Cenabum* massacre, who was beheaded; all resistance was now over. Surprisingly, given Caesar's cold-blooded weighing up of the options, he claimed the execution was 'against his own natural inclination' (*BG*, VIII.38). Perhaps he foresaw the need to win over the tribe's aristocratic leaders to counter-balance the Druids' potential focus for Gallic resentment.

Interestingly, Tacitus notes the 21AD revolt began in the Loire valley amongst the Andecavi and Turones, not the Carnutes (*Annals*, III, 40ff). As the Carnutes forests had been the centre of Druidism, the subsequent grant of federate status to the tribe, mentioned by the Elder Pliny (NH, IV.107), could be seen as a reward and a move to ensure the local nobility valued the backing of Rome rather than separatist religious interests.

Cenabum: excavation history

Orléans was amongst the first French cities to translate antiquarian interests into archaeological research. Between 1820 and 1850 Jean-Baptiste Jollois and Charles François Vergnaud-Romagnési recorded numerous Roman sites. Though they were unable to get any remains preserved, they saved what finds they could. Their work stimulated the creation of the Société archéologique et historique de l'Orléanais in 1848 and their finds formed the core collection in the new museum founded seven years later. After this, despite Léon Dumuy's useful excavations during the 1890s, there was little progress until after the Second World War when the 1940 and 1944 bombardments destroyed many archives and finds in the museum. During the 1960s archaeology moved into the modern era with new insights and, eventually, preserved remains. The first professional rescue dig took place in 1969, concurrently Jacques Debal (see VIENNE-EN-VAL) revitalised the Orléanais society. Probably the most important excavations have been carried out by teams led by Yves de Kisch and Dominique Petit around the cathedral (1977–81) and those led by Thierry Massat in the Charpenterie district before its redevelopment (1997–8).

The Gallic town

The Charpenterie excavations revealed significant late Iron Age occupation, which, together with the spread of less substantial finds, indicated that the Gallic settlement had developed up the Loire north bank slope. By the conquest, there was a recognisable community spread over 10–15 ha. Traces of the Gallic rampart have not yet been noted and, despite evidence of ancient construction work in the river, the bridge Caesar used has not been firmly identified.

The Gallo-Roman town of the Early Empire

The town grew rapidly during the first century and maintained itself during the second. To the east, over a large zone north and south of St Euverte, roads and *insulae* were laid out in the first half of the century: the theatre was not, as it once seemed, outside the urban limits. To the west the town housing went beyond the Place du Martroi. Along the Loire, the Charpenterie site revealed that during the Augustan era the area was transformed with terracing, road building and the first deliberate quayside. This was replaced by a new quay, storerooms and large cellars in the AD50s and the district continued its dockland role into the late Roman period.

There has been debate about what this unusually large *vicus* looked like. Jacques Debal (1996) has argued that it was laid out as a new town according to Roman custom with a full-scale grid, but many of the town's professional archaeologists have argued that it only evolved a grid

stop Attila's 'machines of war'.

Rampart: Dessaux factory
Rue de la Tour Neuve

The Dessaux vinegar works lay between here and rue St Flou, north of the rue des Africains. Pulling down a lean-to section for a small car park exposed this multi-period construction. Summarised by Petit (1994) as 'a sort of cubist vision', certainly it is a mess of hideous 1900s factory brickwork, windows and sills, medieval church building (the arched doorway) and late Roman rampart. However, some of the late Roman work survives to 8m, not far short of the likely 10 metre level walkway.

Rampart: Tour Blanche
Rue St Flou, south of the rue des Africains

This tower was first rebuilt in medieval times and heavily restored in the 1880s; a false door has been added to give the impression of access to the rampart walkway. Genuine late Roman material is visible in the north-east foundations.

Baths: cathedral underground car park
Part of a second century *balneum* was found when excavating an area between St-Pierre Lentin and the Cathedral. A hypocaust room with painted plaster walls and a plunge pool have been preserved.

Musée Historique et Archéologique de l'Orléanais
Hôtel de Philippe Cabu
Square Abbé Desnoyers
Rue Ste Catherine
45000 Orléans

Hours: All year 2–6.30pm Sundays
July and August 9.30am–12.15pm, 1.30–5.45pm Tuesday–Saturday
May, June and Sept. 1.30–5.45pm Tuesday–Saturday
Oct. and April 1.30–5.45pm Wednesday

The Neuvy-en-Sullias treasure
In 1861, at Neuvy-en-Sullias 28km south-east of Orléans, seven sandpit workers cut into a hole lined and covered with tiles and filled with bronzes which they dug out and took to the mairie. Told about this treasure, Philippe Montellier, the Orléanais museum director, rushed to see it and negotiate its acquisition. His quick action ensured that not much was lost, though some of the smallest finds may not have reached, or quickly disappeared from, the unlocked room where they lay before Montellier arrived; a statuette from Neuvy certainly turned up later in a Paris sale. It

can only have belonged to a sanctuary.

A **magnificent horse** stands on a plinth over a metre high. The artist who made this captured the tension in the limbs and the martial pose. The use of a restrained decorative approach – excepting the many-curled mane – highlights the animal's balance; it is reminiscent of the four Roman horses at St Mark's in Venice. The four rings on the plinth allowed poles to be slotted through, enabling the horse to be carried in procession. The inscription records a god 'Rudiobus', a Gallic name implying red and warlike. Known only here, the name is probably a variant on the more widely found Rudianus who was undoubtedly a local Mars. The dedicants were the *curia* (council) of 'Cassicion', also unmentioned elsewhere but meaning the locality of horses. Two men, perhaps magistrates, with Roman cognomens but Gallic aristocratic forenames, ensured that the gift was carried out (FC, 'faciendum curaverunt').

Orleans. Stylised wild boar with striking bristle crest, strongly moulded snout and twisting tail. Neuvy-en-Sullias treasure. Orléans Musée Historique et archéologique de Orélanais

The **deer and boars** are equally impressive. The deer has a static, extended but harmonious body; it has prominent Celtic eyes, while the furry chest is an attempt at Romanising an animal with Iron Age antecedents. Two of the three boars are pure Gallic: massive with very stylised mouth features, one with a simple bristle crest; the other has lost his crest, though broken pieces of a decorative crest were found in the chamber. The aggression of boars was widely admired and models were carried as standards into battle. In contrast, the third boar is much more realistic, even down to the twisted tail. The **tiny bull** statuette is well proportioned and has a quiet charm; like the third boar it is first or second century AD.

Orléans. Grace and joy: 'la grande' female dancer. Neuvy-en-Sullias treasure.
Orléans Musée Historique et archéologique de Orélanais

Figurines that once adorned the sanctuary were also found in the chamber. The most astonishing are known as the **dancer statuettes**. Four of them are taller than the rest and remarkable in the ancient world: they do not follow classical norms nor are they markedly Gallic. When they were put on display in Paris in 1955, artists like Picasso and Miró and writers like Malraux and Breton were astounded: here were the very qualities they especially admired in so-called primitive art. Recent work compares them with Modigliani, but for me they have the spirit of Matisse.

The four tall dancers are naked with tiny feet, long, muscular thighs and extended torsos; the women have swollen midriffs, delicate faces and long hair, the men solid flat bodies and carefully differentiated heads. Though 'l'homme marchant' is the most awkward, all seem to have limbs and bodies joined in graceful, flowing movement: it is this, above all else, that characterises them. It is not surprising that modern metal analysis has shown that these bronzes all use the same alloy mixture: they must be the product of one artist with a completely personal vision.

The rest of the dancers are smaller (8–9cm high) but also express animation quite effectively with bent knees and extended arms, though their conventional proportions and faces lack subtlety. The alloys are different and so is the workshop. Nearly all these figurines would once have held divine symbols, yet whatever symbols these were, they simply denoted their role as sanctuary figurines.

The **brass trumpet** is an extremely rare object, known best from mosaic representations. Though mouthpieces have been found widely, only one other trumpet is known in the Empire: amazingly, it was also found at St-Just-sur-Drive in the Loire valley (now in Saumur Château museum). Made in sections of sheet metal pipe joined by moulded collars it culminated in a cone bell. Originally some 175cm long it could be dismantled for easy carrying. It was the trumpeter's skill in using the mouthpiece that produced the sound. The instrument would not have been able to produce a proper scale, but the timbre could be modulated, though the peal would always have been sharp and high: Roman writers commented on how piercing it could be. Naturally trumpets were used by the army, both in battle and ceremony. Trumpeters were present too in the amphitheatre, the circus and at religious ceremonies. This trumpet must once have heralded processions of divinities and leading citizens at the sanctuary.

Other bronzes include skillets used to contain offerings, a stubby version of Mars copied locally from a widely known example in Rome and the finely made **l'homme au sagum**, a man in a wide flowing tunic arm outstretched, once called an orator but now known to have held a stick in his hand. There is also an **Aesculapius**, identified by his pleated costume, a very rare example depicting this healing god and of such high classical quality that it is believed to be an eastern Mediterranean import.

Orléans. Aesculapius bronze statuette. Neuvy-en-Sullias treasure.
Orléans Musée Historique et archéologique de Orélanais

A simple statue of **Hercules as a child** (recognisable by his club), is considered to have been part of a table fitting that must have been given to the sanctuary.

Despite the renewal of research on the treasure, major questions remain and may never be answered. Why were they hidden? The mixed dating for the material, ranging from possibly pre-Roman boars to the Aesculapius and Hercules, which must be second century, points to the third or even fourth century for the treasure as a whole. Could the sanctuary be removing out-of-date displays – or (more likely) was it trying to save them from theft or destruction by bandits, barbarians or Christians? Just as interesting is where was the sanctuary they came from. Dismantled sanctuary reliefs and statuary have been found buried only 8kms away in VIENNE-EN-VAL, could there be any link? With so little to go on, few scholars will commit themselves.

The general collection

The display drawn from the town and the surrounding Orléanais is not large. It is depressing to think of how few of *Cenabum*'s inhabitants are known from either inscriptions or reliefs. 'Marcus, the son of Murillus' must represent them all. His tombstone was found near the Tour Blanche in 1833. He is depicted in characteristic Gallo-Roman pose: full length and full face, dressed in his tunic and *cucullus* or cape, clasping a tool of his trade (a mattock?) across his chest.

There are everyday objects of work and home like millstones, textile weights, a bucket, a grill and typical ram's head firedogs. For many in Roman Gaul, it was not necessary to have refined and realistic objects to embody the gods; crude representations were enough. On display are the easily broken pipeclay deities, a curious stone figurine from Chevilly of a thin bodied man with tiny arms, and three wooden votive figures, little more than outlines, from the healing sanctuary at MONTBOUY. Very similar offerings, found in far greater numbers at Sources de la Seine, are dramatically displayed in Dijon.

OUZOUER-SUR-TRÉZÉE, Loiret
IGN 2421 E
GPS 31T 0482722/5281605

Mosaics.

Ouzouer is 6km NE of Briare by the D47. Pont-Chevron château is 5km NW of Ouzouer by D45 and D122.

Smaller 'pseudo-emblema' mosaic

Once 6.38 x 4.36m but now without its north-west corner, the mosaic has a white surround and black frame. Multiple repeats of hexagons and six diamond lozenge shaped stars form a 'carpet' design, a type widely popular in western Europe. The masterful head in the centre ensures the mosaic's special status. Normally an emblema like this would be made at the mosaicist's shop and then inserted in an empty space by local craftsmen, but this one is unusual. The close integration of the coloured tesserae – tiny blocks – with the outer design reveals that this artist-craftsman had been paid to work on the spot. Framed by a grey cape, the head turns slightly and the eyes are raised and sensitive; the colours used are softly varied. It is like the Hellenistic 'baroque' portrayals of Alexander, but this figure is middle aged and his hair and beard are reminders of crashing waves, suggesting a sea-god. Over his right shoulder is a curious object. It is not a trident, so Neptune is ruled out; instead it is thought to be part of a Roman oar-rudder. He is generally considered to be Oceanus.

PITHIVIERS-LE-VIEIL, Loiret
IGN 2218 E
GPS 31U 0440906/5334691

Baths.

43km from Orléans by N152; 45km from Montargis by D950. At the junction 2km S of Pithiviers, take D928 N for 1km and then D927 W to Pithiviers-le-Vieil; signposted to 'site archéologique'. Turn left into village.

A steady stream of finds in the nineteenth and early twentieth centuries suggested that the village of Pithiviers-le-Vieil had an interesting past. Some were taken into the museum of neighbouring Pithiviers, most ended up in public and private collections much further away. It was D. Jalmain's aerial photographs taken in the hot summer of 1976 that revealed not just traces of Gallo-Roman settlement in this eastern quarter of the Carnutes *civitas*, but a town of c.50ha together with a sanctuary and an interesting set of baths.

The Roman Le Mans–Sens and Orléans–Reims roads crossed at Pithiviers. The *vicus* lay between them, 1.5km from both, on the edge of the Beauce plateau: the raison d'être must have been the sanctuary. Aerial photographs of the Grand Raye fields, confirmed by excavation (1983-6), showed this to have been a vast complex with at least eight *fanum* temples, laid out in three groups, with pairs of small *fana* set beside larger temples with forecourts. Multiple temples in western France, presumably each dedicated to a different god, are extremely rare (but see Le Vieil ÉVREUX), although dedications to a number of deities could be made at a single temple. This complex had a grid of good roads and many ancillary buildings that must have housed priests, guardians, shopkeepers, artisans and pilgrims. All are now re-buried beneath a housing estate.

The *vicus* spread out eastwards, below and beyond Pithiviers-le-Vieil village. Though occupation was extensive here too, no public buildings are known, though possibly the baths were for public use. Whilst the *fana* were abandoned in the fourth century the baths were not. A claim has been made for the presence of a late Roman troop of Goths based nearby at Gourvilliers: perhaps they succumbed to this luxury...

The baths

From the chemin des Petits Bois, take the rue des Lys into the Square des Thermes. Open access.

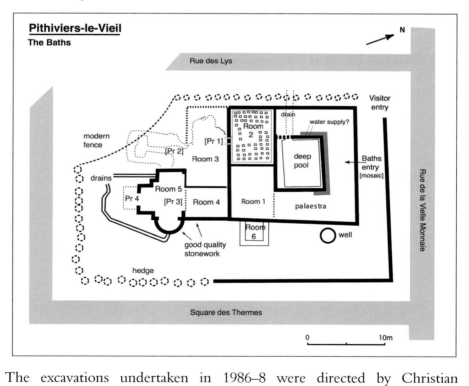

The excavations undertaken in 1986–8 were directed by Christian Cribellier from the Centre Régionale Service Archéologique. It was not an easy dig: the site had been effectively levelled and then ploughed for hundreds of years leaving it seriously damaged. The lack of finds made precise chronological sequencing difficult. Despite the problems, these baths demonstrate how variations within the overall baths formula were normal and how use changed over time.

The original baths

These were constructed at the end of the first century. Little remains of the surrounding wall, but the entrance was on the northern side. Bathers would first walk to **Room 1** on the left (no trace of its northern wall has survived). Here they would leave their clothes and perhaps wash in cold water: it was common to combine *apodyterium* and *frigidarium* at small baths. They would then go outside to the open air swimming pool, which was just large enough for a couple of swimming strokes. After their swim, the bathers must have done a few warming-up exercises in the *palaestra*, here little more than a yard. They would then have entered the hot room (**Room 2**) heated by a furnace (**Pr1**) on the southern side, revealed by the air passages in the southern wall. Nothing survives of the *suspensura* floor where the bathers once stood. They then returned to Room 1 for their final rubdown.

The expanded baths

Probably in the mid-second century, two new hot rooms were added at the southern end. **Room 3**, destroyed on its western side, was a *caldarium*, built where **Pr1** had stood. A new larger furnace (**Pr2**) was built, allowing for water to be boiled on top of its two or three chambers. Hot air still passed into the old hot room but inevitably at a lower heat; it became a *tepidarium*. **Room 4** was a second *caldarium*, or perhaps a dry heat *laconicum*, this one heated by another new furnace (**Pr3**), revealed by traces of burning.

The fully developed baths

The last changes were made at the end of the third or beginning of the fourth century with the addition of **Room 5**. This was a new hot room where **Pr3** had stood and involved constructing a new furnace (**Pr4**) on the southern side. The room had two or three apses – the western end was so damaged it is difficult to tell what might have been here. They are thought to have contained hot plunge baths, supplied with water from a boiler over **Pr4**. The original hot **Room 2** now became a *frigidarium*. A well-preserved channel carried away waste from **Room 3**, but water supply evidence is absent. There were a number of wells near the baths, but consumption must have been high; the nearest spring was at Segray, but evidence for an aqueduct is lacking.

Other changes were made. The swimming pool was filled in, a new external wall was built extending the *palaestra* and a small room (**Room 6**) was added to this outer wall; all are undated. The baths seem to have been abandoned sometime after mid fourth century, though limited usage could have continued during the early Merovingian period. For Alain Bouet, author of a major survey of Gallo-Roman baths, all the final variations were made at one time to create a double baths system: a western system with two rooms for women and a three room eastern system for men. The filled in pool would have been essential to allow women access into their *frigidarium*; **Room 6** was constructed for a small pool. Either alternative seems possible.

Pithiviers-le-Vieil Museum
Ask at the mairie, rue de la Mairie.

This is little more than a site storeroom, often closed. If it is open, note the rare bobbin shaped *tubuli* for heating hot room walls from Room 3 in the baths.

Musée d'Art et d'Histoire de Pithiviers
17 rue de la Couronne

Hours: 10am–noon; 2–6pm daily (Saturday closes at 5pm)

The museum contains an exceptional red marble man's head supposedly found at Pithiviers-le-Vieil in the nineteenth century, but doubts about its discovery here have been expressed. There are also ceramics from Sceaux-en-Gâtinais.

STE-GEMMES-LE-ROBERT, Mayenne
IGN 1517 E
GPS 30 U 0695713/5343623

Fort.

From Jublains 13km SE by D7, E by D517 to Ste-Gemmes and then 2.5km by D37, signposted Le Rubricaire 'camp romain' on the W side of the road. 100m by footpath rising behind the house to the site.

Perched on Le Rubricaire promontory below Mont Rochard, looking out over the Laval basin to the south-west, was a Roman fort. The ruins consist of two rampart sides, 2m thick the longer being c.40m, with a projecting square corner tower between them and an inner right angled wall; even now some sections survive over 2.5m high. They suggest a late Roman design called a *quadriburgium*: a rectangular fort with four towers at the angles and barracks around an inner courtyard to accommodate a small garrison. The ruins of a tiny external bath complex stand 60m down the slope.

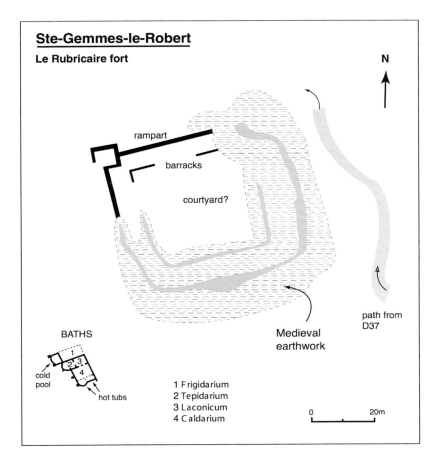

Ste-Gemmes-le-Robert

Le Rubricaire fort

rampart

barracks

courtyard?

N

path from D37

Medieval earthwork

BATHS

cold pool

hot tubs

1 Frigidarium
2 Tepidarium
3 Laconicum
4 Caldarium

0   20m

The earliest recorded digs were in 1834 and the first serious survey by the Abbé Angot in 1903; professional excavations finally came in the 1970s led by René Rebuffet and Joëlle Napoli. Despite these efforts surprisingly little is known. Crucially missing is any dating evidence. The site could be third or fourth century: context would suggest it could be part of the steps taken by Aurelian and Probus to recover Gaul in the 270s, or perhaps the fort formed part of Carausius' separatist empire when he was trying to defend his British and northern Gallic provinces from Maximian in the late 280s. Most probable is that it was contemporary with the JUBLAINS fortress rampart, itself convincingly linked to measures undertaken by Maximian to strengthen the imperial grip on Gaul in the 280s–290s. If so, it would have been built to oversee the transfer of army supplies. However, its location is.puzzling. It is not on the Roman Jublains–Le Mans road: it does overlook it in the valley below, but from c.3km away when, more usually, a fort would control a road from much closer. On a fine day, there is a magnificent panoramic view, but in these broken uplands cloud and rain can reduce visibility to a few hundred metres. It could of course be later in date and may even have provided a base for a troop dealing with the *Bagaudae*.

A further twist is that the ramparts here, like those at Jublains, may never have been finished. Most of the defences are formed by medieval earth banking, with the south-east prong creating the base for a castle. Yet what if the castle builders simply used the visible stone ramparts (an estimated 8m high at the time) and instead of the rest of the *quadriburgium* being buried underneath banking, as has generally been assumed, there is nothing more than incomplete foundations?

SCEAUX-DU-GÂTINAIS, Loiret
IGN 2418 O
GPS 31 T 0471862/5329177

Sanctuary and museum.

20km NW of Montargis by D94, D38 and D841; 38km SE of Pithiviers by D950, D165 and D31. From Sceaux take D120 Château-Landon road, E 2km to La Rivière. Signposted Aquis Segetae, 300m N by the chemin de la Rouelle. Parking area.

The local name for the site is Le Préau, a patois word meaning 'a place for stones'; in reality, it has meant rather more. Over the years peasants ploughed the land, their children followed picking up coins and statuettes; there was always a local collector or dealer willing to pay. The tradition has gone on. In 1966, a farmer found a cache hidden in a tile-covered pit, remarkably like that from Neuvy-en-Sullias [see ORLÉANS], with numerous bronze divinities and a trumpet mouthpiece, all now in private collections. Fortunately the large-scale excavation of 1966–77 organised by the Montargis Groupe Histoire et Archéologique ensured that their finds were displayed in Montargis museum and that the remains of the sanctuary they worked on were protected.

In 1836, Jean-Baptiste Jollois (see ORLÉANS) was the first to recognise that the site was a town with remains spread over a wide area. In the 1860s, the Abbé Cosson, who gained funding from Napoleon III by asserting – incorrectly– that a town here was mentioned in Caesar's writings, made numerous sondages, identified a 25km aqueduct coming from the south-west, and made useful site plans. Michel Roncin led the modern Montargis team for 10 years, and since the 1980s the regional archaeological service has undertaken further work.

Aquis Segetae was firmly identified when a marble dedication naming Segeta was discovered in 1972, so confirming the stop named in the Peutinger Table on the major east-west Roman road linking *Cenabum* (Orléans) and *Agedincum* (Sens). The road itself is still recalled by the traditional name 'Chemin de Caesar' (Marked on Michelin and IGN maps: a section to the east of Sceaux village can still be driven along).

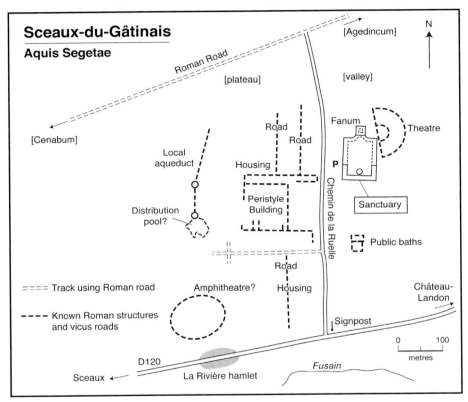

The setting is a low plateau cut by a shallow dry valley overlooking the Fusain to the south. The sanctuary and its ancillary buildings lay in the valley covering c9ha. At its centre was a mineral spring feeding a pool surrounded by a large courtyard linked to a *fanum*. To the south was a bath system, presumably supplied by the aqueduct though nearby evidence has not yet been found. To the north-east, built into the hillside, was a large theatre (104m in diameter), traces of which have been identified, though nothing is today exposed. The town covered 12ha of plateau and aerial photographs make clear that it had a grid layout, partially preserved by farm tracks; an unexcavated oval disturbance could be an amphitheatre, though it would be unusual for a place this size to have had two performance centres.

This important *vicus* and sanctuary of the Senones tribe, near the Carnutes border would have attracted inhabitants from the Gâtinais district, passing travellers and pilgrims seeking the healing properties of *Segeta*'s spring water. Although late La Tène material has been found at the site, the sanctuary does not seem to have been important before the later first century when major monumental construction work began. Both the sanctuary and the town experienced rapid growth during the early second century. Recent excavators consider decline set in early, during the Severan dynasty. In the second half of the third century, there is widespread evidence for fire and destruction and the lack of late third century finds suggests that the town was possibly abandoned. However signs of life returned in the early fourth century. Coin and other offerings show that the spring's powers were still respected, but the surrounding buildings were becoming ruins and by the end of the century the water supply network no longer functioned. Upstream, Merovingian cemeteries indicate a new settlement was emerging by a ford across the Fusain, this was not only a crossroads position, but also enabled resources in the marshland to the south to be exploited more intensively.

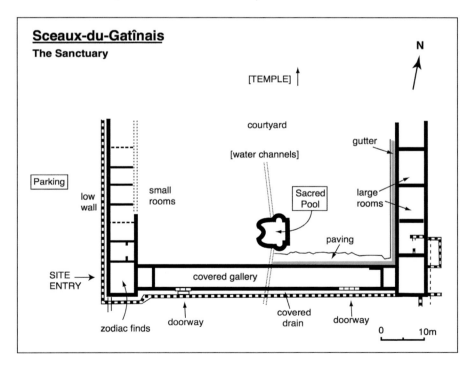

276

The Sceaux collection dominates the archaeological display. Samples of the **votive material** include a typical range of pipeclay: standing Venuses, seated mother-goddesses suckling babies, smiling infants; out-of-the-ordinary Neolithic axes; and representations of sickness, like the miniature arms and legs, eye plaques and bronze penis-set triangles. Most important of all is the finely inscribed marble **votive disk to Segeta**. The dedication to the goddess indicates that though it was Marius Priscinus who made the vow – a pity we do not know in what way he thought the goddess had helped him – it was his daughter Maria Sacra who donated the plaque.

There are a few bronze figurines, a fine bronze vase from the room where the possible zodiac fragments were found and a **coin hoard**, found in 1977 by a metal detectorist, well presented in a clear plastic mounting allowing the visitor to see both obverse and reverse faces. These are third century *antoniniani* marked with the radiate crown and little silver content. Long distance trade is suggested by the *amphorae*, the usual sigillata (largely from Lezoux in central Gaul) and *terra rubra* from the Paris region. The Argonne pottery demonstrates the continued activity at the site in the fourth century. A **headless Epona** riding a headless horse side-saddle could embody fertility or simply the interests of horsedealers.

Modern Sceaux grew to replace the Gallo-Roman *Segeta* in the early Middle Ages. Typically for the period, it is material from two cemeteries on the outskirts of Sceaux that has survived. The earliest **Merovingian grave goods**, from the fifth and sixth century, come from the 370 burials found at La Mérie. Some males are represented by *francisca* (throwing axes), *saxes* (knives), and *scramasaxes* (single bladed short swords); large inlaid belt buckles are more frequent but few are of high quality. The later seventh and eighth century burial material from Le Grand Bezout is characterised by smaller belt buckles and some enamel gold and garnet jewellery.

THÉSÉE-POUILLÉ, Loir-et-Cher
IGN 2023 E

Major Roman building, small site and museum.

9km E of Montrichard by D176 or 9km north-west of St-Aignan taking D17.

Prosper Mérimée, in his role as Inspector-General of Historical Monuments, did not hesitate when he saw the considerable remains at Les Maselles on the edge of Thésée and classed the site as protected (1841): they were, and are, truly impressive. Since then, chance finds and systematic survey work have shown that Les Maselles formed part of a 25ha Gallo-Roman settlement which spreads below modern Thésée and across the river towards Pouillé. Tracing the evolution of its name and location demonstrates that this was *Tasciaca*, a stop in the Peutinger Table.

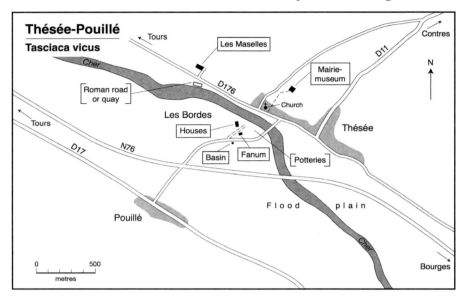

The community would have depended on its Cher valley situation with traffic using both the river and the east–west road between Bourges and Tours. A ford would have enabled north–south movement across the river. The *vicus* was also a production centre. Georges Gaume's 1960s excavations revealed numerous pottery workshops on the south bank; 19 are now known in Les Bordes fields, and one was fortuitously discovered in a resident's garden in Thésée itself. Their products have been found in a 70km radius around *Tasciaca*. A small *fanum* in Les Bordes was exposed during the 1970s.

Les Maselles
GPS 31 T 0371220/5243236

Signposted on the northern side of D176, 0.75km west of Thésée church by the main road. Parking in V172 side road. Much of the site can be seen even without access.

Hours: July–August 10am–12.30pm 2–6pm daily
June and Sept 2–6pm daily

nearby basin and well, indicate that the god here was associated with healing; typical bronze and lead strips marked with eyes and oculist's tools point to a common Gallic problem, sight disorders, and the hope that the god and his human assistant could help. On an inscription found here, 'Virticombo', a grateful survivor, thanks the god and the Emperor for helping him to survive a capsize on the river or a flood.

Housing

Beyond the red gate, traces of Roman strip houses are visible. No more than three or four courses survive, but there are also fragments of concrete flooring and roof tiles. They were probably the homes of the potters who operated the numerous second century furnaces north-west of here nearer the riverbank. A nearby reconstructed furnace is gradually disintegrating.

Musée Archéologique de Thésée-la-Romaine

Parc du Vaulx-St-Georges
41140 Thésée

The museum is in the palatial mairie, a 300m walk through a park.

Hours: July and August 10am–12.30pm, 2–6pm closed Tuesdays
Easter–June 2–6pm weekends and holidays only

A pleasant museum that makes the most of its material, displaying photographs of the 1960s–1980s excavations, a model of the Pouillé site, reconstructed rooms including a kitchen with real handmills and diagrams to illustrate ceramic manufacturing techniques; examples of local ceramics are laid out to illustrate the different types produced. Amongst the small finds are an intaglio ring, a *fibula* of a rabbit held by a hunting bird and an oculist's instruments. As well as the unusual **Virticombo inscription**, there is an attractive tufa **statuette of a man in a Gallic cloak**; he holds pipes in one hand and a crook or staff in the other. He could be a pilgrim or a shepherd.

TOURS, Indre et Loire

IGN 1822 E

Rampart and museums.

Caesar's account does not suggest that the Turones tribe figured as leaders in the Gallic wars and little is known about them before the conquest, though they issued their own coinage. Nor has convincing evidence yet been found to suggest Tours or *Caesarodunum* was a major Turones *oppidum*, though possibly there had been a sanctuary here. The site may have been chosen by the Roman authorities if a legion had used it during the conquest: the easiest route to the central Loire coming from Lyon was via Bourges and the Cher valley, only 2km to the south, giving the fairly stable triangle of land beside the Loire a strategic significance and so making it an appropriate site for a city. The existence of a Roman bridge here was confirmed in 2006 when timber piles were found in the Loire.

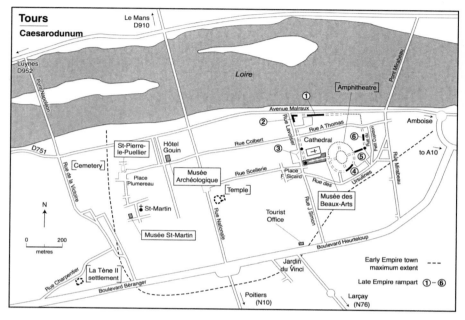

Early Roman Tours

Of the town's public buildings the *forum* and *basilica* remain to be identified. An aqueduct (no visible remains) brought water from Fontenay by the Cher valley, some 25km away and two public baths are known, but the most convincing evidence for Roman Tours' *civitas* capital status is the amphitheatre, whose southern half is still clearly shown by the curving rue des Ursulines. Unfortunately, only the *cavea* foundations have survived, hidden in the cellars of eastern Tours. Henri Gallinié's 1978-82 excavation revealed the Flavian masonry and metal workshops established to build what was one of the largest amphitheatres in Gaul, bigger than that in Lyon: confidence in the future was clearly high at this point.

Recent archaeological work has demonstrated *Caesarodunum* did not evolve into a major centre during the first centuries of Roman imperial rule. In particular, Gallinié's excavations from the 1970s onwards have shown that whilst a grid covering some 80ha was laid out – the rue Colbert and rue Scellerie are *decumani* – the city never grew to fill it. Although archaeologists have identified an early burst of building under Augustus and another phase of construction in the later first century, no truly 'noble' domestic housing nor a well-developed centre has been found. Roads were gravel surfaced and few streets were porticoed. Mosaics, inscriptions, sculpture and fine reliefs are all noticeably scarce.

A shallow branch of the Loire running south of the town must have caused problems with periodic flooding. This was only dealt with when it was filled in during the second century, too late to stop urban contraction which is marked by enlarged gardens and renewed agricultural usage. Maybe the Loire was not the economic engine that some have assumed. Commercial development seems to have been limited, though it could be that the banks of the Loire are further south than they were in the Roman era and that Gallo-Roman wharves and warehouses have either been destroyed or have not been found.

Late Roman Tours

Many *civitas* capitals in the north experienced a series of shocks from the third century onwards producing such a dramatic shrinkage in urban occupation that by the fifth and sixth centuries there is little more than a rampart and the memory of city life. Tours is different. Pockets of occupation were spread widely, though increasingly focused on two areas. The first around and within a *castrum*, initially believed to have been the converted amphitheatre then extended by the construction of a rampart enclosing about 8ha. The second in an area due west 800-1000m away, near what had been the Angers road (now the D751) cemetery.

This resilience was recognised in the last major administrative restructuring of the Empire when *Civitas Turonorum* or *'Turoni'* was made the capital of Lugdunensis III (according to the *Notitia Dignitatum*), probably in the 370s. But another contemporary event, the appointment of Martin as bishop of Tours (371), probably did more to transform Tours than anything else. There had been an unbroken episcopate in Tours since 337 and there was already a Christian community who chose and enthusiastically welcomed their new bishop. Unusually Martin had a contemporary biographer, Sulpicius Severus, a totally committed admirer, but even if his *Vita* was typical of the genre it brings out very clearly what made Martin exceptional.

Martin of Tours

Martin was an outsider. He came from Pannonia, the Balkan province which in the third and fourth centuries was famous for its military men of all ranks; indeed in the later fourth century the Emperors Valentian I (364-75), Gratian (367-83) and Valentian II (375-92) all came from there. His father had been a tribune and Martin, raised at a base near Milan, followed in his footsteps. Severus explains, in a story typical of many saints' *Vitae*, how Martin became a militant Christian. He was sent to Amiens where, meeting a poor shivering beggar at the city gates and struck with pity, he cut his cloak in two, giving half to the man. Soon afterwards he had a vision of Jesus wearing the half cloak; he then refused to continue in service and sought out Hilarius, the famous mid-fourth century bishop of Poitiers, to deepen his understanding of the Faith. Subsequently he took up the life of a hermit both in Italy and again near Poitiers, where he combined a simple asceticism with preaching around central and western Gaul. It was his reputation as a great holy man that attracted the people of Tours.

Martin always saw himself as a soldier in the service of God's army, one of the first to provide this model for how to be a Christian. He preached passionately in the city and countryside, combating the many devils he saw governing the misguided; he instigated the destruction of pagan temples and Jupiter columns; he travelled everywhere on foot, caring little for his appearance; he began the process of establishing rural parishes; he healed the sick; he confronted the great, not to influence them through his sophisticated understanding of the complex world, as most Gallic bishops attempted to do, but challenged Emperors, prefects and governors with his convictions, once even waiting for an Emperor to stand for him – *he* spoke with God's approval. He created a hermitage for himself across the Loire at Marmoutier to which he went for recuperation, attracting devoted followers. Some compared him with the prophet Elijah: many Gallic bishops saw him as an illiterate rabble-rouser.

By the time he died in 397, Martin was widely known, both directly and through Severus' *Vita*. His fame continued to grow. Whereas in Brittany and the British Isles Martin's hermit-preacher style came to epitomise the saintly holy man, in Gaul, his wilder behaviour was forgotten instead he was remembered as the firm defender of his community. As imperial power collapsed in the fifth century, bishops had the self-confidence to assert themselves as the pre-eminent powers locally. Under threat from Saxon pirates along the Loire, Breton and British kings to the north-west, regional Roman rulers like Syagrius and his son Aegidius to the north-east, and finally from the struggle between Merovingian Franks and Visigoths for dominance, provincial imperial government disappeared. But at Tours, the line of bishops was maintained without break through the fifth and sixth centuries, able to assert their status as metropolitan bishops above all others in the north-western diocese.

Gregory of Tours, bishop here 573–94, could see *Turonus* as a thriving city, with a large number of churches both in the *castrum*, where he had his

The corner of rue des Ursulines and rue du Cupidon gives access to this garden where an 80m section reaches a height of 8–9m, though there is no original walkway. Still impressive despite having been seriously ransacked, repaired with plain stonework and cut into by windows and a cellar. At the western end, a few bricks indicate the original semi-circular arch above the postern with its modern triple brick lintel. Excavation has revealed the massive foundation blocks rising seven courses in some places. Rather more upper facing *petit appareil* and brick survives on the eastern side. There are foundations to a tower in the middle and the circular south-east corner tower with its patched blockage rising almost as high as the rampart.

6 Eastern face
Reached via the passage beside no.5 rue du Capidon, the rampart here is preserved as a rear wall behind the flats' car parking area.

St-Pierre-le-Puellier site
Place Plumereau
37000 Tours

An arch, beside an Irish pub and close to a tourist information office, surrounded by sixteenth century timber and brick houses, leads to surviving fragments from Gallinié's 1969–74 excavations. Sadly, the few courses of recognisable Gallo-Roman walling make little sense now. A panel helps.

Gallinié identified the entrance to a public building of the first half century AD and residences from the same period which were modified in the second century with some mosaic flooring. These were abandoned in the late second century. The site was re-occupied by workshops during the fourth century and then by a Roman road which was to become rue de la Paix. They formed part of the *vicus Christianorum*.

Musée Archéologique de Touraine
Hôtel Goüin
25, rue du Commerce
37000 Tours

Hours: 10am–1pm, 2–6pm. closed Tuesdays

The museum is not big and needs updating; material comes from all over Touraine, little is new. An Etruscan bronze vase and *amphorae* point to Iron Age imports but are presented without any explanation of whether imports were found in significant numbers, what they say about Gallic Iron Age society or how they got here.

Most interesting as examples of Gallo-Roman 'folk art' are **the rams' headed firedogs** found in second and third century contexts (see also NANTES). At the other extreme there is the high quality but body only **dolphin mosaic**, found by Gallinié in St Pierre-le-Puellier. There are a few attractive bronzes: a small deer and a couple, the man lying down with a seated woman beside him (unlabelled). There is a milestone commemorating Claudius Tacitus, 275–6, re-used to make a sarcophagus, and a copy of the most significant inscription found in Tours, recording the CIVITAS TURONORUM LIBERA, indicating that the *civitas* was proud of its 'free' status, however meaningless this was (original in Musée des Beaux Arts). The early medieval period material is also limited: there are some typical Merovingian belt buckles and less common, **early Christian architectural earthenware**. A small stele of a figure praying is supposedly a portrayal of St Martin himself.

Musée St-Martin

Chapelle Saint-Jean
3 rue Rapin

Hours: Mid-March–mid-Nov. 9.30am–12.30pm, 2–5.30pm Wednesday-Sunday

A series of panels in three languages including English, outline Martin's life and after-life with surprisingly little hyperbole, but also without much dynamism. The panels use photos of major sites and buildings, illustrations drawn from medieval texts, and, most attractively, quotations from both Severus' Vita and other historical writings. There are a few near-contemporary objects.

Musée des Beaux-Arts

18 place François-Sicard

Hours: access to Roman material only by approaching Tours Office de Tourisme for a group visit. Tel (00 33) 2 47 61 14 22

The basement contains part of the rampart foundations, and the inscriptions naming the *Civitas Turonodunum* are still here. Other objects include a dedication to Hadrian and damaged tombstones, amongst them an early medieval horseman called Aigulfus from Langeais. Gallo-Roman art is poorly represented by a crudely sculptured male head with hair standing on end and startled eyes. Architectural fragments include entablature, pilasters and reliefs, largely drawn from the rampart.

An **inscription**, written twice on the plinth, records a dedication to Jupiter for the health of the imperial family and that of the '*Curia* Ludn' – here meaning a group or district within the *civitas* - put up and paid for by Perpetus, son of Rullus, and Maternus son of the Gallic named Toutorix. The formula is remarkably like that on the Neuvy-en-Sullias horse plinth [see ORLÉANS]. It also names a *curia* and the dedicators are equally drawn from local nobles proud of their Gallic names.

The plinth or base is decorated with four divinities: Jupiter striking down a giant, Mars with lance and shield, Vulcan and Venus. The quality is mediocre. The most interesting is Vulcan: he holds a spear in one hand that he has made, and in the other tongs, whilst resting his arm on a ship's prow; Vulcan was the patron divinity of the Loire shippers.

The two **altars**, both clearly made by much better craftsmen, also display reliefs drawn from the Roman pantheon. One altar was decorated by an artist steeped in classical technique, recognisable by the **excellent Apollo**, left arm raised to hold his upright lyre on a snake-entwined tripod. The faceless Minerva, broad-chested Hercules and Goddess of Well-Being (her left hand rests on a cornucopia) are equally finely carved. The other altar is again classical, but less elegantly crafted. It shows Vulcan, a warrior woman (Virtus?), Mars, gracefully posed here, and another Goddess of Well-Being, this time with a long cornucopia on an altar.

The scene of a **horseman** riding down a pitiful monster is a reminder that the Gauls did not simply add on a mythology and divine pantheon from another culture; the imagery of the rider, Jupiter and Emperor, symbolising the defeat of imperial enemies, was an independent development of Roman Gaul. The **headless creature** sitting on its haunches is a reminder of the pre-Roman world where human as well as animal sacrifice could occur. He wears a Gallic torc round his neck and there are two tiny human feet on his chest: other similar sculptures show the man he was devouring. Any one Gallo-Roman sanctuary could embrace many things.

YZEURES-SUR-CREUSE, Indre et Loire
IGN 1926 O
GPS 31 T 0337503/5183594

Museum.

67km S of Tours, the museum is in the centre of this small village, 10km by D104 from Preuilly-sur-Creuse and 6km by D725/750 from La Roche-Posay.

Musée Minerve
Place François Mitterand
37290 Yzeures-sur-Creuse

Hours: July– August 9am–5pm
    Sept.–June: ask for access at the mairie (Place de Mado Robin)

In 1894, it was decided to demolish the dilapidated medieval parish church at Yzeures. The following year, whilst the ground was being cleared, the foundations of a Merovingian church were revealed, but it was obvious that much of the stonework was in fact Roman. The Société archéologique de Touraine was slow off the mark and Father Camille de la Croix, a well-known archaeologist from Poitiers – actually nearer to Yzeures than Tours – was able to step in and supervise the extraction of 80 large blocks. He made plans neither of the Merovingian church nor of the find spots, but recognised that the blocks were drawn from separate structures including a temple and altars. For many years they were simply stacked under a lean-to shed, until 1970 when Jean-Pierre Adam, the Centre national de la recherche scientifique specialist in ancient architecture, was asked to conduct a new study with Fabienne Jambon and prepare the material for display in a small dedicated museum.

Amongst the 80 blocks, the most important are an inscription and those decorated with figured reliefs. The three-block inscription shows that it came from a temple dedicated to the Emperors (the *numina* or divine spirits of the *Augusti*) and the goddess Minerva. Some of the architectural fragments could come from that building.

On the basis of size, the figured reliefs divide into three groups. The largest are all **figures of major Roman gods**: Jupiter, naked except for a windblown cloak, carrying a thunderbolt in his raised right hand; Mars, the best preserved; Vulcan, barely recognisable but dressed in a short tunic and carrying his tongs; and Apollo, of whom only the lower figure survives but whose left hand holds a lyre. These are clearly four sides of one structure.

The second group features **gods or demi-gods from classical mythology**. Perseus and Hercules deal with notably similar problems: rescuing maidens tied to coastal rocks guarded by monsters. Perseus saves Andromeda whilst Hercules frees Hesione; both go on to kill the monsters. The other two myths also form a pair, both involve gods crushing the snake-limbed giants grovelling below them. Mars is barely recognisable in his scene, but the Minerva relief, despite the absence of the upper block, is much better. The goddess, recognisable by her long dress and shield, dominates the twisting bodies of two giants hopelessly raising their arms against her power.

The last group formed an **octagon of reliefs**, though only three survive. Whilst Neptune is very poor and the Diascuri or twins not much better, Leda and the Swan were carved with some grace.

Yzeures-sur-Creuse. Jean-Pierre Adam's reconstruction as a votive 'column'

Adam noted that the relief work was the lightest on the first group and deepest on the third and that these types of multi-faced portrayals of gods and myths were a characteristic part of Jupiter columns, dedicated to glorifying the Emperors in the guise of the chief god crushing his foes, who are symbolised generally by agonised snake-tailed figures. He therefore saw the three sets as decreasing drums, set on a plinth and once crowned with a statue of Jupiter, which has unfortunately never been found. His reconstruction drawing is reproduced here. Though he accepted the actual form of his votive 'column' is more like a mausoleum, he pointed out its similarities with the *Nautae* monument (in the Musée de Cluny, Paris), which is equally multi-faced and multi-levelled, and actually has an inscription dedicated to Jupiter. His reconstruction may well be right, though he recognised that the reliefs in the third group are not simply deeper, but also inferior in quality. He noted too that the divine iconography draws purely on classical sources without any reference to Gallic gods, yet Jupiter columns were limited to Gaul and the Rhineland and included non-classical references. He explains this by identifying the reliefs as Severan, when the eastern Mediterranean was particularly influential, and most scholars would agree. Yet doubts have resurfaced. Minerva features strongly in the second group and it was her temple. She too was closely identified with the Imperial Cult and the introduction of a supposed Jupiter statue may be unnecessary: perhaps they were distinct altars from within a sanctuary dedicated to Minerva.

OTHER SITES IN THE LOIRE VALLEY

AMBOISE Indre-et-Loire
IGN 1922 E
GPS T 0349000/52522880

The promontory formed by the Loire and Amasse valleys, on which the château stands at the apex, was made into a defended *oppidum* site by a massive north–south rampart and vallum (ditch), enclosing 52ha. Excavations have shown that there was occupation from the Neolithic onwards and finds suggest that by the late La Tène this was extensive: coin moulds were found here indicating that the site could even have been the Turones tribal capital. Occupation continued in the Roman period through the first and second centuries. Excavation in the 1980s revealed housing, workshops producing pottery and metalwork and a large *fanum*. The Châtelliers site is most easily approached via the D751, rue du Clos de Belle Roche, rue de Bel air and right turn into rue Augustin Thierry for 200m to a preserved section cut through the *vallum*. Panels explain its development from the Hallstatt to Augustan era.

ARTHON-EN-RETZ Loire-Atlantique
IGN 1123 OT
GPS 30 T 0581180/5220490

37km W of Nantes and 11km E of Pornic by D751.

Though Gallo-Roman traces have been found at Arthon spread over 1ha, little is known about them. An extensive bath system, including two marble paved swimming pools, was identified around Arthon church presbytery. However, the only visible remains are those of a 3.5km aqueduct that once supplied the baths. From Arthon 3km north by the D67 to the junction and turn east for Chéméré. The crossroads c.700m along, marks where the aqueduct came south from a spring. To the north towards La Poitevinière, on the right beside the road there is c100m of Roman walling that supported the channel; south towards Arthon, the track follows the line of lost arcading and underground sections. The lack of any brickwork hints at a first century date.

BÛ Eure-et-Loir
IGN2114O

15km NE of Dreux by N12.

Ask at the mairie for directions. Hidden in woodland 2km north-east of Bû, at the Bois du Four à Chaux clearing (100m from the main track) there are traces of a sanctuary. Finds of Gallic material revealed that the *fanum* temple here was preceded by a La Tène sacred site. Constructed in the early first century, the *fanum* was replaced by a slightly larger structure in the second century, built with flint stonework in a chalk mortar. Finds (kept in Dreux museum) including votive eye plates and oculists equipment, suggest the sanctuary was dedicated to healing; it fell into decline in the third century with a short revival in the fourth.

CHARTRES Eure-et-Loir
IGN 2116 O

Autricum was the *civitas* capital of the Carnutes tribe during the Roman era and was one of the largest cities in the region extending over 200ha including suburban development. The major find here in the nineteenth century was an amphitheatre and a suspected *forum*. In recent years, extensive excavations have revealed an aqueduct, traces of monumental building, rich town houses, workshops, road system and burials; unfortunately most of them have been rescue digs and currently there are no visible remains. Even the **Musée des Beaux-Arts'** old archaeological collection is not on display (written application to see it is rarely approved). The **Maison d'Archéologie** is run by one of the largest municipal archaeological services in France; it holds small temporary exhibitions displaying a few of their finds but there is no permanent display. Chartres and its visitors deserve more.

CHÂTILLON-SUR-COLMONT Mayenne
IGN 1517 O
GPS 30 U 0667675/5356207

22km W from Jublains by the D5 via Mayenne.

A **Roman milestone** stands inside the parish church, 2.4m high and made of granite. It claims to have been ordered by Lucius Domitius Aurelianus in 273. In reality Tetricus still ruled Gaul at this date as the last Gallic Emperor, so it may have been raised later to imply local loyalty to Aurelian. It originally stood on the Roman road to Avranches about 1.75km north from here. It is marked on the bottom as 'L[eugae] VIIII' or nine leagues, about the distance from Jublains to which it must refer. Three-quarters of the milestones found north of Lyon use leagues rather than the 1000-pace Roman mile. The league is thought to be a Gallic measurement around 1½ times as long as a Roman mile or 2200–2400m.

Châtillon-sur-Colmont. Roman milestone

FRÉTEVAL Loir-et-Cher
IGN 2019 O
GPS 31 T 0364251/5306381

15km NE of Vendôme by N10 and 2km W of Fréteval by the N157. On a slope below the N10, NE of junction.

The **Tour Grisset** is an isolated tower 8.6m high, first identified by Gervais Launay in the 1860s as the *cella* of a *fanum*. The thick walls were made using flint set in a clay mortar, rather than small blocks and are decorated with triple course bricks on the corners. Inside there are two niches, but nothing has been found to identify the gods worshipped here. The 7m high ceiling is vaulted entirely in brick. Excavations by Claude Leymarios in 1964–5 revealed a sanctuary enclosure wall and a bath complex which was spread out over the damp land below. Pottery finds in the baths suggested it was in use during the second and early third centuries, implying a similar period for the *cella*. Finds made during the N10 road widening (1990s) show that there was Iron Age occupation in the vicinity.

MARCILLÉ-LA-VILLE Mayenne
IGN 1517 E
GPS 30 U 0686079/5353466

7.5km NW of Jublains.

East of the village on the D113, **four Iron Age stelae** stand on the southern side of the Petit Croix roundabout. Their abbreviated height and smooth finish indicate their early Iron Age origins. Such stones are widespread in Brittany, but they are rare further east and have been used to support Caesar's claim that the Diablintes tribe had Armorican links. Stele like these often record burials. Their different sizes, two large and two small, could even evoke a mother, father and children, but sadly it is possible that they may simply have been gathered together to clear a field and even deliberately re-erected to suggest a family group.

GLOSSARY

Amphora/amphorae: A large two-handled storage jar. The wide variations in shape and size were first catologued and numbered by Dressel.

annona: The rations supplied to the army. Primarily grain, it became a regular tax in kind during the late Empire.

apodyterium: The changing room of a bath building, sometimes large enough for preliminary exercises.

appareil: (in masonry) *Grand appareil* consists of large rectangular blocks; *petit appareil* refers to small rectangular blocks, 10–15cm long, often used as a facing for a rubble core.

archaeomagnetic dating: A method based on the realignment of magnetic particles according to the Earth's magnetic field at the time, when heated above 650° C. Cross-referencing with other dating methods allows regional series to be developed. It has been useful with ancient bricks, kilns and hearths.

attribute: Roman deities had particular associations drawn from myth or religious practice that help identify them in paintings, reliefs or statuary. Examples include Mercury's wand, Jupiter's thunderbolt and Minerva's helmet.

bagaudae: Bandits were known throughout the ancient world but these Gallic outsiders formed significantly larger groups who challenged the imperial order and were mentioned in sources from the late third to the mid-fifth century.

ballista: An artillery weapon based on catapult torsion.

basilica: One of the main public buildings in the *forum* used by magistrates to dispense justice and as a political or commercial meeting place. Its oblong structure, often with an apse at one or both ends, inspired early church design.

caldarium: The hot, wet heat, room in a bath system.

cardo (maximus): The main road running north–south in a Roman town.

castrum and castellum: Large and small forts; in France they generally refer to late Roman strongpoints.

castellum divisorium: The water distribution tank at the end of an aqueduct.

cavea: The seating area of a theatre or amphitheatre.

cella: The cult room inside a temple.

chi-rho: A monogram of the first two letters in Greek of Christ's name.

civitas: A self-governing community answerable to imperial authority, based on a city with its surrounding supporting countryside. Gallic tribes were recognised and organised as *civitates*, despite varying traditions and levels of urbanisation.

clients: Beyond the immediate household of family, slaves and freed men and women, were clients. These were the master/patron's dependants drawn from tenants, business associates and socially inferior political allies; they showed their status by regular visits to the *domus*.

cob: A building method used to construct walls using lumps of clay, straw and gravel.

decumanus (maximus): The main road running east-west through a town.

decurio: A member of the *ordo* or municipal council. The position was held for life.

dendrochronology: A dating method based on examining annual growth shown by tree rings. Climatic variation in a locality will affect ring size and, using overlapping samples, sequences can be built up to give absolute dates for timber.

domus: A rich town house with Roman features.

duumvir: A municipal magistrate and chief local administrator.

dux: A late Roman military commander of frontier forces in one or more provinces.

entablature: The collective term for the superstructure carried by columns, including the architrave, frieze and cornice.

Epona: The Gallo-Roman goddess usually appears mounted side saddle on a mare and was associated with fertility, healing and looking after the dead. Adopted widely in the Roman world, appealing particularly to those with links to horses.

exedra: A curved or rectangular recess in a wall or colonnade.

fanum/fana: Romano-Celtic temple(s), typically of square design with a *cella* and surrounding portico.

fibula/fibulae: The Roman term for a brooch. Their basic role was to pin clothes together, but there were many decorative forms. They ranged from the simple bow to a plate in the form of an animal. Decorative crossbow *fibulae* were a sign of high status in the fourth and fifth centuries, particularly military.

forum: A central open space surrounded by public buildings.

frigidarium: The cold water room in a bath system.

Gaul: The land between Spain and Germany, known as 'Gallia' to Roman writers. Caesar recognized three broad groups so called it the 'Three Gauls' and Augustus divided the territory into Aquitania, Lugdunenis and Belgica.

hypocaust: A heating system where the floor was supported by small columns to allow hot air to circulate below. The air was warmed by an external furnace and escaped via box flues (*tubuli*) in the walls.

Imperial cult: the worship of the Emperors' spiritual being (*genius* or *numen*), an attribute of the gods. At first Emperors were seen to be deified at death, but it soon became normal to worship the living emperor as a god as well as his predecessors.

in situ: Used by archaeologists to describe (a) artefacts found in their place of original use, or (b) artefacts where they were discovered.

insula/insulae: Normally urban rectangular street block(s).

itineraries: Diagrammatic maps marking roads and stops (e.g. *mansiones* or post-inns as well as towns). The Antonine Itinerary was probably second or third century and the Peutinger Table a third or fourth century compilation. The fourth century Bordeaux Itinerary showed pilgrim routes.

Jupiter column: A lone column surmounted by a horseman riding down a monster; its base would be decorated with reliefs of gods. The horseman is usually interpreted as Jupiter, the supreme god of the Roman state, but with a dual interpretation as the Emperor crushing enemies. Occasionally a column might simply be topped with a Jupiter figure alone.

laconicum: A dry hot chamber, often circular, in a bath system.

laeti: Barbarians given land on condition that they provide men to fight for the Empire. They were supervised and commanded by a Roman prefect.

lares (familiares): The household guardian spirits or gods with a shrine in the house. There were also *lares* of crossroads or even cities.

limitanei: Late Roman frontier troops.

liturgies: Public offices or duties performed by the wealthy at their own expense. It enhanced their status, but became increasingly onerous and in the late Empire many sought to avoid them

maenianum: A tier of seats in a theatre or amphitheatre. Access was limited by hierarchy: the top tier was for the lowest ranks.

mansio: A post-inn where those carrying imperial letters could stay and have their horses changed.

Mercury: A god in Gaul depicted with Mercury's Roman attributes including his wand or *caduceus*, his winged hat and a purse, embodying prosperity and success. He often appears with a consort Rosmerta; as a divine couple they provide well-being at home and at work.

Merovingian: Family name of Frankish kings from c450 onwards claiming descent from 'Merovech', probably a mythical ancestor. Also used to describe the late fifth to eighth century period.

murus gallicus: A method of constructing ramparts used in the late Iron Age, based on a mix of logs, rubble/earth and facing stones. Precise designs varied.

noble: Collective term for the Roman elite. Often used with 'rooms' to distinguish those that are large and well decorated, but where there is not enough evidence to distinguish precise usage.

Notitia Dignitatum: A document listing late Roman military commands, thought to reflect the position in the late fourth and early fifth centuries.

nymphaeum: A decorative shrine associated with water nymphs.

oppidum/oppida: General Latin term for settlement(s). Used by archaeologists to define large non-Roman settlements with a range of urban features. Also more loosely used to describe hillforts.

opus: Latin term for work, used in descriptions of walls and floors. *Opus mixtum:* walls where bands of stone alternate with brick courses in the facing; *opus vittatum:* walls faced entirely in stone; *opus testaceum:* masonry faced with bricks. There are many more.

pagus: A lesser tribe or clan associated with a defined territory, generally rural. Their people were *pagani*.

palaestra: Exercise courtyard often linked with public baths.

patera: The saucer shaped bowl used for religious offerings.

peribolus: The enclosing wall of a temple precinct.

peristyle: An open courtyard or garden surrounded by porticos. In Gaul, peristyles were a major feature in many *domus* or villas, often overlooked by 'noble' rooms.

Peutinger: See itineraries.

pipeclay: A white earthenware terracotta used to make small figurines. It was imported from the major production centres in the Allier region and also copied locally.

podium: A high platform on which a Roman temple was built. It could also be a wall separating the audience from danger in an amphitheatre or just the elite from the rest.

postern: A small doorway in a fortification.

praefurnium: The furnace to heat a hypocaust, generally in a small room next to the *caldarium*.

prefect (*praefectus*): A title used for imperial officials of widely differing status and powers.

procurator: A middle ranking official in the Emperor's civil administration often responsible for provincial financial matters, estate management or commercial activities.

remploi: The French term for re-used stone material often decorative architectural pieces or statuary.

sherd: A broken fragment of pottery.

(terra) sigillata: The most widely found fine ware in the Empire. A glossy red to pink pottery called samian ware in Britain. First made in Italy and called Arretine, then manufactured in Gaul on a large scale starting in Lyon and La Graufesenque, later Lezoux and then the Rhineland.

sondages: Test-holes investigating a restricted area on a site. Usually sampling to establish answers to specific questions.

souterrain: An underground stone-built chamber often found in Iron Age settlements in Brittany and in other parts of the Atlantic zone. They probably had many uses.

stele: Upright stone slabs, generally seen as tombstones, sometimes inscribed.

stylobate: The course of masonry on which a series of columns were set.

Sucellus: 'The Good Striker' is a mature god with rich, curling hair and beard, in Gallic tunic and cloak, carrying a mallet or hammer; this perhaps marked the renewal of life and nature. A people's god, he supports the harvest.

suspensura: The floor 'suspended' on top of the pillars in a room with a hypocaust.

tablinum: In the first and second centuries it specified the reception room where a *'salutatio'* or greeting of clients/dependants took place; later it became the household office where archives were kept.

tepidarium: The warm room in a bath system.

terminus post quem: 'The end after which'. Used by archaeologists to indicate something, for example a coin, found in a stratigraphy so indicating that succeeding strata must belong to a later date.

theatre/amphitheatre: In a Roman theatre the audience sat in a semi-circle facing a stage; in an amphitheatre the audience sat all round an oval arena where the shows took place. In Gaul, there were various mixtures of the two.

torc/torque: An open ended neck-ring, sometimes twisted, made of gold or bronze. Particularly popular during the late Iron Age Celtic world.

tractus Armorica: Linked in this way, *tractus* means district or region.

triclinium: The formal dining room in a Roman house.

tufa: A creamy coloured calcite sedimentary rock. When hard enough an easy stone to work. Found along the Loire valley.

Tuscan: The Romans used four major architectural styles: Corinthian, Doric, Ionic and Tuscan most easily recognised from their columns. Tuscan is a simplified version of the Doric with plain unfluted columns and capitals.

vicus: The smallest recognised unit of self-government in the western Empire. *Vici* could be urban districts within a city, but this was rare in the provinces where the *vici* were villages and small towns, each with their own magistrates.

villa: A large house or mansion in the country. Sometimes the farming and living areas are distinguished as *rustica* and *urbana*. It is hard to classify villa and *domus* in a suburban context.

vomitorium: A spectator's entrance into the *cavea*. In larger theatres and amphitheatres it was a covered passage.

votive: Where a person dedicates something to a god. This can be a vow or an offering.

SELECT BIBLIOGRAPHY

The material listed here is simply a selection of consulted works. Many of the books can be obtained from good bookshops or via the web; other texts, especially the academic journals, are largely restricted to specialist libraries. Museum guides are often limited in scope and are not included.

ORIGINAL SOURCES

Most are available either as Penguin Classics or in the Loeb Classical Library series.

Ammianus Marcellinus, *History*

Anon. *Lives of the Caesars /Scriptiones Historia Augusta* (*SHA*)

Apicius (Ap) *Recipes*

Julius Caesar, *Gallic wars/De Bello Gallico* (*BG*)

Gregory of Tours, *History of the Franks*

Pomponius Mela, *Book of Places*

Pliny the Elder, *Natural History* (*NH*)

Pliny the Younger, *Letters*

Procopius, *The Histories*

Ptolemy, *Geography*

Sidonius Apollinaris, *Poems and Letters*

Strabo, *The Geography*

Tacitus, *Annals, Histories, Agricola, Germany*

Zosimus, *New History*

Corpus Inscriptionum Latinarum (CIL XIII contains most of the inscriptions from Gaul)

GENERAL

Bedon, R. (2001) *Atlas des villes, bourgs, villages de France au passé romain,* Paris: Picard

Brunaux, J. L. (1988) *The Celtic Gauls: Gods, Rites and Sanctuaries*, London: Seaby

Cambridge Ancient History 2nd edition. See particularly Volume 12 (2005) *The Crisis of Empire 235–337*, Cambridge: CUP

Collis, J. (1984) *The European Iron Age*, London: Batsford

Coulon, G. (2007) *Les Voies romaines en Gaule*, Paris: Errance

Cunliffe, B. (2001) *Facing the Ocean,* Oxford: OUP

Drinkwater, J. F. (1983) *Roman Gaul,* London: Croom Helm

Esperandieu, É. (1907–81) *Recueil général des bas-reliefs, statues et bustes de la Gaule romaine,* Paris: Imprimerie Nationale

Ferdière, A. (2011) *La Gaule Lyonnaise*, Paris: Picard

Geary, P. J. (1988) *Before France and Germany*, Oxford: OUP

Green, M. (1986) *The Gods of the Celts,* Gloucester: Alan Sutton

Green, M. J. (ed) (1995) *The Celtic World*, London: Routledge

Grenier, A. (1931–60) *Manuel d'archéologie gallo-romaine*, vols V–VII, Paris: Picard

Henderson, J. C. (2007) *The Atlantic Iron Age*, London: Routledge

Izarra, F. de (1993) *Hommes et fleuves en Gaule romaine*, Paris: Errance

James, E. (1988) *The Franks*, Oxford: Blackwell

Jullian, C. (1920–6) *Histoire de la Gaule* (8 vols), Paris: Hachette

King, A. (1990) *Roman Gaul and Germany*, London: British Museum

Knight, J. K. (1999) *The End of Antiquity*, Stroud: Tempus

Le Bohec, Y. (2008) *La province romaine de Gaule Lyonnaise*, Dijon: Editions Faton

Maligorne, Y. (2006) *L'Architecture romaine dans l'ouest de la Gaule*, Rennes: PUR

Mathisen, R. W. (1993) *Roman aristocrats in barbarian Gaul*, Austin: University of Texas

Péchoux, L. (2010) *Les sanctuaires de périphérie urbaine en Gaule romaine*, Montagnac: Monique Mergoil

Swift, E. (2000) *The End of the Western Empire: an archaeological investigation*, Stroud: Tempus

Topographie Chrétienne des Cités de la Gaule des origines au milieu du VIII siècle,
   Vols V, VIII and IX (1987–96) Paris: De Boccard

Trevor Hodge, A. (1992) *Roman Aqueducts and Water Supply*, London:
   Duckworth

Van Andringa, W. (2002) *La religion en Gaule romaine*, Paris: Errance

Various. (1997) 'Les Francs ou la genèse des nations' *Dossiers d'Archéologie*

Woolf, G. (1998) *Becoming Roman: the origins of provincial civilisation in Gaul*,
   Cambridge: CUP

Journals
The national magazines *L'Archéologue* (Paris), *Archéologia* (Dijon) and *Les Dossiers d'Archéologie* (Dijon) are monthly or bimonthlies, available in good newsagents and excellent for keeping up-to-date. French academic journals covering western France include the national *Gallia*, the *Revue Archéologique de l'Ouest*, the *Revue Archéologique du Centre* and *Aremorica*; there are in addition many departmental and local journals. The Service Regional de l'Archéologie (SRA) in each Direction Régionale des Affaires Culturelles (DRAC) produce an annual *Bilan Scientifique* (free), though they have difficulty in keeping these up-to-date; many museums produce material but few have published catalogues of their Gallo-Roman collections. Two English language journals cover the whole Roman world including Gaul the *Journal of Roman Archaeology* and *Journal of Roman Studies*.

TOPIC BIBLIOGRAPHIES

Salt, Fish and Roman Cooking

Curtis, R. I. (2001) *Ancient Food Technology*, Leiden: E J Brill

Daire, M.-Y. (2003) *Le Sel des Gaulois*, Paris: Errance

Grocock, C. and Grainger, S. (2006) *Apicius*, Totnes: Prospect Books

Sanquer, R. and Gaillou, P. (1972) '*Garum*, sel et salaisons en Armorique romaine' *Gallia*, 30: 199–223

Wilson, A. (2006) 'Fishy business: Roman exploitation of marine resources.' *JRA*, 19, Fasc.2: 525–537

The Defence of Western Roman Gaul

Guilleux, J. (2000) *L'enceinte romaine du Mans*, St-Jean-d'Angély:
   Bordessoules

Johnson, S. (1983) *Late Roman Fortifications*, London: Batsford

Reddé, M. (dir) (1996) *L'armée romaine en Gaule*, Paris: Errance

Reddé, M. et al. (2006) *L'Architecture de la Gaule Romaine 1: les fortifications militaires*, Bordeaux: MSH-Ausonius

Southern, P. and Dixon, K. (1996) *The Late Roman Army*, London: Batsford

REGIONAL BIBLIOGRAPHIES

BRITTANY

General

Gaillou, P. (2005 new edition) *L'Armorique romaine*, Brest: Armeline

Gaillou, P. and Jones, M. (1991) *The Bretons*, Oxford: OUP

Giot, P. R., Guignon, P. and Merdrignac, B. (2003) *The British Settlement of Brittany*, Stroud: Tempus

Mortimer Wheeler, R. E. and Richardson, K. M. (1957) *Hill-forts of Northern France*, Oxford: Society of Antiquaries

Pape, L. (1995) *La Bretagne Romaine*, Rennes: Ouest-France

Various, (2011) 'Dossier Bretagne', *Archéologia*, 493: 48–61

Some sites:

Bardel, J.-P. (1997) *Les Thermes Gallo-Romains de Plestin-les-Grèves*, St-Brieuc: Conseil Général Côte d'Armor

Bardel J.-P. (2007) 'L'établissement antique de Plomarc'h Pella à Douarnenez', *Aremorica*, 1: 101–116

Cunliffe, B. and Gaillou, P. (2004–7) *Les fouilles du Yaudet en Ploulec'h, Côtes d'Armor*, Vols 1, 2 and 3, Oxford: School of Archaeology

Gaillou, P., et al. (1987) *Aux Origines de Carhaix*, Ville de Carhaix

Kérebel, H. (2001) *Corseul (Côtes d'Armor), un quartier de la ville antique*, Paris: DAF 88 La Maison des Sciences de l'Homme

Langouët, L. (1996) *La Cité d'Alet*, St-Malo: Ce.R.A.A.

Maligorne, Y., Eveillard, J.-Y. and Chauris, L. (2003) 'Extraction et utilisation des granites en Armorique Romaine', *Gallia*, 59: 133–143

Provost, A. (2000) 'Sanctuaire de Haut Bécherel', *Archéologia*, 364: 30–31

Provost, A. (2000) 'L'Aqueduc romain de Carhaix', *Archéologia*, 364: 32–3

Provost, A. (2007) 'La "villa" maritime de Mané Véchen à Plouhinec' *Aremorica* 1: 85–100

Royer, R. (1981) 'Un monument gallo-romain en Armorique: la chapelle de Langon', *Archéologia*, 157: 16–21

The Channel Islands

Rule, M. and Monaghan, J. (1993) *A Gallo-Roman Trading Vessel from Guernsey*, St Peter Port: Guernsey Museums and Galleries

Sebire, H. (2005) *The archaeology and early history of the Channel Islands*, Stroud: Tempus

NORMANDY

General

Deniaux, E., et al. (2002) *La Normandie avant les Normands*, Rennes: Ouest-France

Kazanski, M. (1997) 'Francs et autres barbares dans le royaume mérovingienne' *L'Archéologue*, 29: 16–19

Marin, J.-Y., et al. (1990) 'L'évangélisation de la Normandie' *Dossiers Historie et Archéologie*, 144: 2–77

Various. (2009) 'Normandie: celte et romaine' *L'Archéologue*, 102: 12–35

Some sites

Aupert, P. (dir) (1997) *Les Thermes d'Évreux*, Documents de L'Ouest (RAO)

Cliquet, D., Eudier, P. and Étienne, A., et al. (1996) *Le Vieil-Évreux: un vaste site Gallo-Romain*, Conseil Général de l'Eure

Delaval, E and Hincker, V. (2003) 'Vieux/*Aregenua*: de la ville au village' *L'Archéologue*, 66: 21–22

Delestre, X. (1996) 'Rouen: des origines à la fin de L'Antiquité' *Archéologia*, 322: 50–57

Exposition Musée de la Ville de Lisieux. (1994) *Lisieux Avant l'An Mil: essai de reconstitution*, Alençon

Follain, É. (2004) 'Fontaines gallo-romaines en Haute Normandie', *Dossiers d'Archéologie*, 295: 50–59

Follain, É. and Lepert, T. (2005) 'Manche: les thermes d'*Alauna*', *Archéologia*, 421: 42–51

Guyard, L. and Bertaudière, S., et al. (2007) 'Les thermes de la ville sanctuaire du Vieil Évreux', *Dossiers d'Archéologie*, 323: 52–65

Musée Municipal de Lillebonne. (2001) *Lillebonne au temps des Gallo-Romains*, Lillebonne

Remy-Watté, M. (1990) *Le Camp du Canada de Fécamp*, Fécamp: Musées municipaux

Vipard, P. (2002) *La Cité d'Aregenua (Vieux, Calvados): chef-lieu des Viducasses*, Paris: Exé Productions

THE LOIRE VALLEY

General

Bellet, M.-É., Cribellier, C., Ferdière, A. and Krausz, S. (1999) *Agglomérations secondaires antiques en Région Centre*, Tours: FERACF/ARCHEA

Bedon, R. and Malissard, A. (eds.) (2001) *La Loire et Les Fleuves, Caesaradunum XXXIII–XXIV*, Limoges: Pulim

Buchsenschutz, O. and Fichtl, S. (2008) 'Les Celts et la Loire' *Dossiers d'Archéologie*, 326: 2–95

Dubois, J. (2003) *Archéologie Aérienne: Patrimoine Touraine* St-Cyre-sur-Loire: Alan Sutton

Provost, M. (1993) *Le Val de Loire dans l'Antiquité*, Gallia Suppl. 52, Paris: CNRS

Various. (2000) 'Dossier – les Pays de la Loire' *L'Archéologue*, 48: 13–33

Some sites

Anon. (2002) *Le Site Archéologique de Thésée-Pouillé*, Thésée: Les Amis du Musée

Buron, G. (1990) 'De l'origine des marais salants guérandais' *Bulletin de la Soc. Archéologique et Historique de Loire-Atlantique*, 126: 9–62, Nantes

Brouquier-Reddé, V. and Gruel, K. (2004) 'Le Sanctuaire de *Mars Mullo* chez les Aulerques Cénomans (Allonnes, Sarthe) Vs. av. J.-C. – IVs. apr. J.-C.' *Gallia* 61: 291–396

Debal, J. (1979) 'Divinités Gallo-Romaines de Vienne-en-Val', *Archéologia*, 127: 6–19

Debal, J. (1996) *Cenabum Aurelianis Orléans*, Lyon: Presses Universitaires de Lyon

Marot, E. and Marlet, O. (2006) 'Les Mystères de Sabazios à Cinq-Mars-la-Pile' *L'Archéologue*, 83: 48–49

Monteil, M. and Mouchard, J. (20012–13) 'Un port sur la Loire: Rezé' *L'Archéologue*, 123: 44–45

Musée des Beaux-Arts d'Orléans, (2007) *Le Cheval et la Danseuse: à la redécouverte du trésor de Neuvy-en-Sullias* (catal. Expo.), Paris: Somogy

Naveau, J., et al. (1997) *Recherches sur Jublains et sur la cité des Diablintes*, Rennes: Documents archéologiques de l'Ouest (RAO)

Naveau, J. (2002) 'Un Patrimoine Gallo-Romain à Découvrir: les Thermes d'Entrammes', *Arts, Recherches et Créations*, 72: 49–56

Petit, D., et al. (1994) 'L'Enceinte du Bas-Empire [Orléans]', *Revue Archéologique du Loiret*, 19 and 20: 19–130

Provost, M. (1985) 'Le sanctuaire des eaux de Gennes', *Bulletin de la Societé Nationale des Antiquaires de France*, 92–105

Wood, J. (1983) 'Le *castrum* de Tours: études architecturale du rempart du Bas-Empire', *Recherche sur Tours*, 2: 11–60

INDEX

BOLD used for sites listed as separate entries in text